Privatization and
the Welfare State

STUDIES FROM THE PROJECT ON THE FEDERAL SOCIAL ROLE

FORREST CHISMAN AND ALAN PIFER, SERIES DIRECTORS

The Politics of Social Policy in the United States
Edited by Margaret Weir, Ann Shola Orloff, and Theda Skocpol

Democracy and the Welfare State
Edited by Amy Gutmann

Social Security: Beyond the Rheoric of Crisis
Edited by Theodore R. Marmor and Jerry L. Mashaw

Privatization and the Welfare State
Edited by Sheila B. Kamerman and Alfred J. Kahn

Privatization and the Welfare State

EDITED BY

SHEILA B. KAMERMAN

ALFRED J. KAHN

PRINCETON UNIVERSITY PRESS

This book has been composed in Linotron Sabon

Clothbound editions of Princeton University Press books
are printed on acid-free paper, and binding materials are
chosen for strength and durability. Paperbacks, although satisfactory
for personal collections, are not usually suitable for library rebinding

Printed in the United States of America by Princeton University Press,
Princeton, New Jersey

Designed by Laury A. Egan

Library of Congress Cataloging-in-Publication Data

Privatization and the welfare state / edited by Sheila B. Kamerman and Alfred J. Kahn.
p. cm.—(Studies from the Project on the Federal Social Role)
Includes index.
ISBN 0–691–07811–4 (alk. paper)—ISBN 0–691–02307–7 (pbk.)
1. Human services—United States. 2. Privatization—United States. 3. Welfare state.
I. Kamerman, Sheila B. II. Kahn, Alfred J., 1919–   . III. Series.
HV95.P736 1989   361'.973—dc19   88–39316

CONTENTS

Foreword   vii

Acknowledgments   xi

Introduction: Privatization in Context   3

PART I. DEFINING PRIVATIZATION

1. The Meaning of Privatization
PAUL STARR   15

2. The Social Structure of Institutions: Neither Public nor Private
MARTIN REIN   49

3. Welfare: The Public / Private Mix
RICHARD ROSE   73

4. Privatizing the Delivery of Social Welfare Services: An Idea to Be Taken Seriously
MARC BENDICK, JR.   97

5. Making Sense of Privatization: What Can We Learn from Economic and Political Analysis?
EVELYN Z. BRODKIN AND DENNIS YOUNG   121

PART II. CASE STUDIES

6. Social Welfare and Privatization: The British Experience
MICHAEL O'HIGGINS   157

7. Governmental Responsibility and Privatization: Examples from Four Social Services
ARNOLD GURIN   179

8. The Local Initiatives Support Corporation: A Private Initiative for a Public Problem
MITCHELL SVIRIDOFF   207

9. Child Care and Privatization under Reagan
    SHEILA B. KAMERMAN AND ALFRED J. KAHN   235

Conclusion: Continuing the Discussion and Taking a Stand   261
Notes on Contributors   271
Index   273

FOREWORD

This book is one of several volumes based on activities sponsored by the Project on the Federal Social Role. The Project was a nonprofit, nonpartisan enterprise established in 1983 to stimulate innovative thinking about the future directions of federal social policy.

Americans are doubtless more preoccupied than any other people with questions about the fundamental purposes and directions of their national government. In part this concern reflects a healthy political culture. We are always searching for better ideas about government and always disagreeing about which ideas are best. In part, too, our concern reflects a longstanding ambivalence about the value of national institutions. We still honor the tradition of Thomas Jefferson, which presumes against an active federal role, in an era when programs and policies emanating from Washington permeate every aspect of our lives.

But while Americans never seem to tire of arguing about the proper role of national government, systematic thinking on this subject has been neglected in recent years. Scholars have produced a great deal of excellent research about specific policies and programs. But there has been too little careful study of what effect those measures, considered as a whole, have on the American people.

This neglect of the larger issues of public policy is deeply troubling. The federal social role is more than the sum of its parts. The various policies and programs that constitute it interact with each other in a great many ways. Collectively they have a far greater impact on our future as a nation than the study of particular issues can reveal.

More importantly, the specific measures of government are all parts of a broader commitment by the American people to employ their common resources toward achieving common goals. Only a strong sense of what those goals are and what overall directions of policy are required to achieve them can ensure that so large and diverse an enterprise as the federal government serves the general welfare.

The problems that arise when basic issues of purpose and direction are neglected have been vividly demonstrated in recent years. For half a century Americans supported an almost continual expansion of the federal social role. But the growth of federal activism slowed in the late 1970s and early 1980s, and there were dire predictions that national government had exhausted its possibilities as an instrument for social betterment. A period of reassessment followed. For over a decade, virtually every aspect of the social role was closely scruntinized by politicians, scholars, and the press.

As an exercise in public educaion, this reassessment was undoubtedly a success. But as an exercise in policy development it was a dissappointment. No clear directions for the future emerged. The federal role was neither greatly augmented nor diminished; nor was it set on any new course. The nation remained locked in political stalemate.

Although periods of national stock-taking are often healthy, prolonged stalemate is a luxury that the United States cannot afford. While national policy has been standing still, major forces of change have been at work in our social and economic life. Transformations in the nature of our economy, evolving personal lifestyles, societal aging and worsening conditions for many of the poor are the largest and most visible developments. We are no longer the nation that we were a few decades ago, and because government pervades so many aspects of our lives, we need new measures to suit our new circumstances.

The recent reassessment of public policy failed to come to grips with the forces of social and economic change in large part because it proceeded in a piecemeal fashion. Debate was confined primarily to the merits and demerits of policies and programs already in place. As a result, the nation artificially constrained its options. We failed to examine carefully enough the need for major new initiatives by the federal government and ways to make them work.

In this static and backward-looking environment, destructive myths and misunderstandings found fertile ground—most notably the myth that there are severe limits to what activist government can achieve. This idea takes various forms, and in most of those forms it is seriously misleading. If our national history teaches us anything, it is that each generation is capable of accomplishing far more through the use of government than previous generations would have dreamed possible. History also teaches that we *must* accomplish more: that effective government is a never-ending process of responding to needs and opportunities. This requires breaking with the ideas and patterns of the past. As often as not, the social role has evolved through large measures that defied past skepticism and cut across the categories of previous thought.

But to move boldly into the future, as it must, the nation needs to raise its sights above the terms of the current debate. The American people need to understand the full dimensions of the federal social role, how it evolved and the ways in which it operates. Based on that understanding, they need to consider what they want to do with this enormously complex and valuable machine—how it should be used to meet the challenges of today and of the decades to come.

The Project on the Federal Social Role was established to shed light on basic questions of purpose and direction. Its activities were designed to raise issues that transcend the usual domains of public policy analysis and to enhance public understanding of national government. Our report to the general public (*Government for the People*, 1988) and each of the specialized volumes that have resulted from the Project's work advance these goals in a different way. Individually and collectively, they grapple with many of the larger concerns that have been neglected during the recent period of reassessment. And they exemplify the type of informed debate that must become a larger part of our public life if the United States is to move beyond political stalemate and toward a stronger sense of common purpose.

Washington, D.C.   Forrest Chisman
                                                                          Alan Pifer

ACKNOWLEDGMENTS

We are in the debt of Alan Pifer and Forrest Chisman, who conceived of and gave creative leadership to the Project on the Federal Social Role—of which this undertaking was part. While providing material support, they left responsible leadership to us. A large debt is also owed to some thirty non-authors who discussed these issues over an eighteen-month period and enriched both the individual papers and the editors' summations. Finally, we note with gratitude and admiration the substantial contribution of editorial consultant Felicity Skidmore. Readers of a significant number of public policy books owe much to her technical skills and substantive expertise.

SBK

AJK

Privatization and
the Welfare State

Privatization in Context

Regardless of how one defines "privatization," neither the activity nor the hopes engendered under this rubric are new. Observe New York City in the 1840s:

> If government was such an obvious and obnoxious failure, critics reasoned, then the best way to reform it was to reduce its responsibilities and powers as much as possible. If street cleaning seemed to be a costly mess, let the streets be cleaned by businessmen acting under contract with the city rather than by the government itself. If public markets and docks cost more than the revenues they produced for the city, then dissolve the markets and sell off the docks. Such steps would both simplify administration and reduce the costs of government. The Corporation, too, should disentangle itself from its role as the city's largest property owner. Faced with mounting debts, the Common Council in 1844 decided to sell off all unnecessary and unproductive property, especially in land, in order to provide for the redemption of the city debt, a step which would also place more property in private hands and so increase the tax tolls. Retrench, reduce costs, simplify government, let businessmen do what politicians so obviously could not do—these were rallying cries for reform which suited not only the interests of taxpayers but the rising faith in the virtues of private enterprise as well. (Spann, 1981, p. 50)

Strong opposition stood in the way of full implementation of the proposed reforms. Nor were many of the objectives realized:

> Even when enacted, such measures fell short of reformers' promises. The contract system, tried on an off-again, on-again basis, failed significantly to reduce either cleaning costs or the level of dirt in the city streets. The sale of city property also was far from satisfactory. To achieve a modest reduction in its indebtedness, the city auctioned off lands in the 1840s at bargain prices. Most of the properties, located in the area between 39th and 42nd Streets and Fifth Avenue and Broadway, skyrocketed in value during the prosperous 1850s, lead-

ing one critic to complain that the Corporation had virtually given away lands whose later value was more than sufficient "to wipe out at once the entire debt of the city." (Spann, 1981, p. 51)

Arnold Gurin (Chapter VIII) reminds us of the active discussion of the appropriate roles of public and private sectors during the Progressive Era, at the turn of the century, as well as in the 1930s and during the War on Poverty. But even though the manifestations are historically familiar, privatization clearly has become a word for our times, associated with recent discussions of the "future of the welfare state" or of the social policies of the Reagan and Thatcher governments. It is heard in debates and advanced in policies in France, Sweden, Germany, New Zealand, and Israel, among other countries of diverse political balances. Headlines from the *New York Times* and the *Wall Street Journal* from the 1980s to the present suggest the terrain:

"More Cities Paying Industry to Provide Public Services"
"U.S. Pressing Plan to Contract Work: Idea Is Private Enterprise Can Do Much Better and Cheaper"
"City Is Seeking to Turn Park Operation Over to Private Organizations"
"Nonprofit Groups Said to Face Big Cuts in U.S. Aid"
"More Nonprofit Groups Make Imaginative, Aggressive Sales"
"As HMOs Increasingly Become a Business, Many of Them Convert to Profit-Making Status"
"Thatcher's Lessons on Privatization" (". . . Margaret Thatcher's government will sell the state-owned British Gas Company within two years . . .")
"Long-time U.S. Workers Feel the Edge of Cost Cuts" (civilian workers demoted or reassigned as a private contractor takes over the custodial services at a Marine Corps logistics base)
"New Studies are Planned on Trend Toward Privately Owned Jails"
"Private Courts with Binding Rulings Draw Interest and Some Challenges"
"Making War the Private Way" (The U.S. Council for World Freedom raises money for "contra" rebels in Nicaragua with "the blessings of the government.")
"Have You Heard the One About Selling the Debts?"
"Reagan Appoints Privatization Unit: Panel Will Propose Ways for Washington to Turn Over Functions to Business"

Little that is done by government or by the nonprofit sector escapes mention somewhere in connection with "privatization" actions, proposals, and analyses: social security, medical care, nursing homes, child care, housing, counseling and rehabilitation, the National Institutes of Health, transportation, power, parks, airport terminals, loans, and so forth.

Administration policy in the Iran-contra affair was attacked as "the ulti-mate turnover of government to private enterprise" (*New York Times* editorial, Nov. 22, 1987).

At the very beginning of the Reagan Administration there was a much-publicized Private-Sector Initiative, offered in part as a justification for funding cutbacks in the social services. Numerous other volunteer efforts were officially promoted throughout both Reagan terms, and a new panel, charged with promoting turnover of government functions to busi-ness was to report as the Administration reached its final year. In that context, privatization proposals were made in many quarters, covering everything from Social Security alternatives to the contracting out of many public services at local, state, or federal levels. As much as devolu-tion and defunding, calls for privatization became a hallmark of the 1980s.

This book seeks to clarify privatization as concept and as phenomenon and to assess its potential contributions or dangers to public policy and to the public policy debate. In commissioning papers, we did not begin with conclusions or certainty of outcome. Indeed, although much here is clarified, the separate authors are still far from unanimous.

For we did not simply invite preparation of papers and edit them for publication. The volume is the product of a process in which authors, editors, and others in a forty-member seminar met over an eighteen-month period, exploring and debating. Participants came from academic, social service, and business organizations, all established leaders; but their positions on privatization covered a considerable range. They had joined a "rolling" debate. Each paper was circulated and discussed before another was presented. In between, there were roundtable sessions and overviews. Previously published work, new articles, press clippings were grist for the mill. Later papers were written in relation to earlier ones. Authors edited and rewrote at the end, by which time they were part of an ongoing conversation.

Here we present all of the specially commissioned work, but in a se-quence based on the editors' final understanding, not in the order written. Thus although Marc Bendick (Chapter 4) introduced the "load-shed-ding" concept to describe current objectives in privatization, it is now used in earlier chapters. Martin Rein (Chapter 2) urged the imagery of "blurring" and it became an important concept in the group's area of shared conclusions.

Definitions and Scope

At the core of the privatization discussion is the notion that the non-governmental sectors should take on more of what are currently governmental functions. Advocates want to roll back state activities, some in a major way. Anti-privatization analysts worry about the implications of a reduced role for public programs. The pro-privatization arguments, as will be seen, are sometimes made in the name of efficiency, effectiveness, economy, and choice. At other times the case on one side or the other is in the value area or ideological: fairness, view of government, pluralism, choice, accountability.

No nine chapters could possibly cover all viewpoints but (although we did not know at the outset what to expect) one has here a good represen-tation, except from the extreme right and the libertarians who would on principle decrease as much government as possible. With few exceptions our authors assume that a modern mixed economy in a democratic soci-ety is bound also to have "a mixed economy of social welfare." With important exceptions, however, their prevailing mood is to worry that the current strong overlay of ideology renders privatization an instrument that can be drawn upon in the political process to do considerable dam-age to United States social welfare programs.

Although we never proclaimed precise limits on our scope, we have concentrated largely on privatization in what is variously described as the social services, social programs, the social sector, or the human services. We here pay little attention to agriculture, manufacturing, or business services. Unlike the French and the British, for example, who had nation-alized more utilities and businesses and have recently moved to privatize, the United States, according to Paul Starr (Chapter 1) has a public sphere in the production of goods and services too small to support the argument that we need to be freed of it.

Much of the White House privatization advocacy has been with regard to social programs. In any case, the issues of social policy do attract most of our authors' attention. Indeed, the majority were invited as people con-cerned with or expert in social programs.

The group finds it useful to distinguish privatization in the production and delivery of services and benefits from privatization in financing. As will be noted, several authors find such distinction essential to the devel-opment of a point of view. Michael O'Higgins (Chapter 6) also identifies regulation as another domain that is affected. Here he reflects the British discussion. Several other authors discuss regulation in a secondary con-text, and Sheila Kamerman and Alfred Kahn highlight it.

They do, however, introduce other specifications that some see as es-sential. To several, the question of whether a private group is a nonprofit or a for-profit organization is very important. To Richard Rose (Chapter 3) and to some of our discussion participants, the key distinctions to be made are among household, government, and the market. They hold that organizations in the market identified as "for profit" and "not for profit" prove not to be as different in the real world as in claims made for them.

On the ideological level, the privatization discussion includes family, church, kin network, and neighborhood as contrasted with the governmental and the formal. Our authors recognize the difference between informal and formal institutions and the problems of interrelating the two realms—but the debate about financing and production refers to formal societal provision. There are no proposals from either side to undermine primary groups. Our authors regard as legitimate the issue of whether privatization of finance and delivery are helpful in offering support and context for wholesome primary group life.

The insights and the judgments are best appreciated in their specifics and detail, and in the context of the authors' overall and quite distinctive approaches.

Major Arguments Made by the Authors

The essays in Part I of this book take an essentially theoretical perspective—seeking to make sense of the term privatization and of the various meanings it has been given.

Paul Starr (Chapter 1) leads off the discussion by clarifying in considerable detail the meaning of privatization on three levels: as idea, as theory or rhetoric, and as political practice. It becomes clear that there are many meanings of public and private. Temporal, contextual, and structural aspects are critical. It is easier to describe privatization as a direction of change than as a specific origin or destination. For many reasons, boundaries are blurred. Starr's analysis leads him to conclude that it is not possible to develop a general theory about the performance of public versus private institutions apart from a theory of politics. Indeed, he finds many specific proposals that can be described as privatization that have merit; but his final verdict is that "privatization needs to be understood as a fundamental reordering of claims in a society." It derives from "the countermovement against the growth of government in the West," promotes contempt for public services, particularly those upon which the poor depend. Concerned about these and other political consequences, Starr concludes: "I am opposed to privatization."

Martin Rein (Chapter 2) argues that "dualist" theories do not hold up in the face of institutional realities. He pursues the blurring of the public/private boundaries in extensive detail, using examples from the U.S. and abroad in the social services and income security. He predicts that, if anything, the blurring will steadily increase. And he adds "that the future of the welfare state will be the invention of institutions that are not private and not public . . . If we are to understand social reality, we must look at all the institutions that provide social protection and not only the institutions of the state."

Richard Rose (Chapter 3) examines this proposition further by analyzing the public/private mix from the perspective of a society's total welfare. He defines the public contribution as goods and services produced by public agencies (whether federal, state, or local) and the private contribution as coming from the market sector (profit and nonprofit) and the household. He sees welfare—whatever its source—as "profoundly social, depending on the social action in the household, in the market, and with state institutions." He points out that the "welfare mix, as well as total welfare in society, is continuously subject to change." He sees current economic strains as raising questions about the capacity of the public and nonpublic sectors to finance a continued expansion of monetized welfare. And he concludes that "in a mixed society, the guiding principle for budget choices of public policymakers should be to look after those who are at least able to meet their welfare needs through the market (for example, the unemployed) or through the household (for example, single-parent families).

Marc Bendick (Chapter 4) changes the focus from the blurred nature of the public/private distinction to a discussion of the way concepts of privatization can be used to expand, rather than contract, social welfare in the United States. As he points out, "America has always been a reluctant welfare state . . . The [privatization] idea needs to be treated seriously, not because of who currently holds power in Washington, but because of the perennial fascination it has held for American thought and action." The ethic emphasizes the voluntary sector and chooses business over government whether or not the facts warrant it. There is in any case widespread dissatisfaction at present with the public sector. To Bendick, a crucial criterion for judging privatization initiatives is the degree to which governmental funding continues to support nongovernmental service delivery. He sees two major possible shifts: "government load-shedding" encompasses arrangements under which financing and delivery are divorced from government; "empowerment of mediating institutions" encompasses arrangements under which government retains some or all funding responsibility while delegating production and/or delivery. Bendick's strategy for expanding social welfare through privatization calls for co-opting the political momentum for privatization by suggesting that empowerment versions of privatization substitute for load-shedding versions.

Evelyn Brodkin and Dennis Young (Chapter 5) search the economics and political science literature for guidance on the "key features of the conceptual landscape relevant to privatization and . . . the possibilities and hazards in following current paths of analysis." From the "collage of [economic] failure theories" they see "an economy that may be best described in ecology-like terms. Various arrangements . . . may be seen as niches into which different goods and services fit . . . in the most efficient way." They conclude that the strength of economic theory lies primarily in its precise focus on efficiency and the depth of the deductions permitted by simplified assumptions. They note, however, that such theory is typically static and cannot take account of environmental or organizational pressures for change. Nor can it account for the "likely possibility that privatization may be adopted or opposed" for reasons unrelated to efficiency. Applying the political lens as well makes it possible to discern that embedded in debates about the "best way" to organize policy delivery structures is an ongoing political battle over the scope and substance of the welfare state.

The group of essays in Part II of the book are empirical. They variously use the case-study approach to shed light on the relationship between privatization and efficiency, on the one hand, and equity, on the other.

Michael O'Higgins (Chapter 6) uses the insight that the location of the public/private balance boundary and the determination of the public/private balance is a strategic decision, to examine the British experience under Margaret Thatcher's conservative governments. He identifies three potential forms of privatization—transferring production to the private sector, exacting a private but regulated responsibility, and stimulating service consumers to greater use and reliance on private provision.

Recent British experience with each of these routes to privatization—at the time of his analysis—leads O'Higgins to conclude that the impact of strategic shifts in the public/private balance of service provision is not determinate, but varies with the context in which such shifts are implemented. His examples show that privatization can not only improve social provision but even potentially foster increases in income equality. "If much privatization is unequalizing in practice, this is the result not of any qualities inherent in privatization provision structures, but of the political and social values that generate the pressure for privatization."

Arnold Gurin (Chapter 7) traces the history of the development of public social services and the shifting views of private versus public provision that accompany that development. He shows that the attitudes toward the social role of government have been both ambivalent and unstable over time, and as a result, social services have developed in a patchwork fashion rather than as a comprehensive and integrated system. He offers four case histories—community mental health services, long-term care, youth employment and training, and child welfare—and concludes that both government responsibility and private involvement are present in all of them in varying degrees. He singles out as the critical issue "the capacity of government to perform well its roles in policy planning, financing, monitoring, and regulating." He says it is difficult to build such a capacity in an atmosophere that denigrates government. And he ends with a warning: "The reality is that the place of government in the social services will continue to be dominant. The greater danger is that it will play its part with a diminishing capacity to do it well."

Mitchell Sviridoff (Chapter 8) chooses a single instance of privatization to demonstrate that foundations, individuals, corporations, and community organizations can work together effectively to alleviate social problems. His chosen area is the problem of urban blight and the relatively unsuccessful efforts of government programs over the years to alleviate it. His case study is of the Local Initiatives Support Corporation (LISC), a predominately privately financed intermediary designed to seek out promising community development corporations and stimulate investment resources to help them achieve higher levels of self-sufficiency. LISC's seed money came from the Ford Foundation. Since its founding in 1980 it has generated more than $100 million, 90 percent of which is not government money, which it has invested in more than 500 community-initiated urban development projects. Sviridoff does not claim that LISC-like ventures can solve the whole problem, but he does believe that there are already valuable and solid accomplishments and that "when the climate changes and the pendulum swings again toward a more expansive federal policy" the activities strengthened by this type of effort "will already have laid the groundwork for a revival of the inner-city neighborhood."

Sheila Kamerman and Alfred Kahn (Chapter 9) examine child care and privatization under President Reagan. They trace the recent history of more subsidization of demand (primarily by tax subsidies) combined with reduced public funding of supply and examine the implications of these trends for availability of services, equity, quality of care, and efficiency. Considerably hampered by reduced national data collection and public monitoring of day care provision since 1980, they nonetheless are able to shed light on all these dimensions.

The overall supply of child-care services has probably increased, although this may be due as much to demographic pressure as to the privatization initiatives. The quality of care available to low-income families appears to have declined. Per-child costs of publicly subsidized care have been reduced. But staff/child ratios have probably also declined, group sizes have increased, and the for-profit day care chains that are the main beneficiaries of privatization acknowledge that their programs either serve a predominately affluent, problem-free group of youngsters—or move into areas where low standards enable them to profit with low-quality, low-fee services.

The concluding essay in the book reviews all the arguments, weighs the various recommendations, and takes a stand. The reader will want to assess this conclusion only after considering the previous nine essays, noting their several understandings of privatization, their interpretation of the debate as both ideological and empirical, and their general consensus that, preferences apart, the reality remains a "mixed economy" of welfare.

I

DEFINING PRIVATIZATION

1

The Meaning of Privatization

PAUL STARR

Privatization is a fuzzy concept that evokes sharp political reactions. It covers a great range of ideas and policies, varying from the eminently reasonable to the wildly impractical. Yet however varied and at times unclear in its meaning, privatization has unambiguous political origins and objectives. It emerges from the countermovement against the growth of government in the West and represents the most serious conservative effort of our time to formulate a positive alternative. Privatization proposals do not aim merely to return services to their original location in the private sphere. Some proposals seek to create new kinds of market relations and promise results comparable or superior to conventional public programs. Hence it is a mistake to define and dismiss the movement as simply a replay of traditional opposition to state intervention and expenditure. The current wave of privatization initiatives open up a new chapter in the conflict over the public/private balance.

This paper attempts to clarify the meaning of privatization as an idea, as theory and rhetoric, and as a political practice. In the process I hope to explain why I generally oppose privatization, even though I favor some specific proposals that privatization covers. But apart from this political judgment, I take privatization seriously as a policy movement and as a process that shows every sign of reconstituting major institutional domains of contemporary society.

Work on this paper was supported by a grant from the Pew Charitable Trust for the study of "Public Sector Reform and Privatization." An earlier version was completed at the Institute for Advanced Study in Princeton, N.J., and delivered at a conference there on "The Public Sector and Its Problems." I wish also to express my general debt to Stephen Holmes, Jeffrey Weintraub, the members of the Yale Legal Theory Workshop, and others to whom I am indebted for ideas and suggestions. This article also appears in a slightly different version in the *Yale Law and Policy Review* 6 (Spring 1988), 6–41.

Privatization as an Idea

In the ideological world we inhabit, contesting interests and parties use "public" and "private" not only to describe but also to celebrate and condemn. Any serious inquiry into the meaning of privatization must begin, therefore, by unloading the complex freight that the public/private distinction carries. In this section I analyze, first, the general uses of the public/private distinction and, second, the recent political application of the concept of privatization.

THE PUBLIC / PRIVATE DISTINCTION AND THE CONCEPT OF PRIVATIZATION

The terms *public* and *private* are fundamental to the language of our law, politics, and social life, but they are the source of continual frustration. Many things seem to be public and private at the same time in varying degrees or in different ways. As a result, we quarrel endlessly about whether some act or institution is really one or the other. We qualify the categories: this group is quasi-public, that one is semi-private. In desperation, some theorists announce that the distinction is outdated or so ideologically loaded that it ought to be discarded, or that it is a distinction without a difference (Klare, 1982; Kennedy, 1982; Freeman and Mensch, 1988). Yet the terms can hardly be banished, nor ought they be (Starr, 1988a). To speak intelligently about modern societies and politics without using the words "public" and "private" would be as great an achievement as writing a novel without the word "the." However, neither is necessarily the sort of achievement that other theorists or novelists would care to imitate.

The frustration with these ubiquitous categories partly arises because public and private are paired to describe a number of related oppositions in our thought. At the core of many uses are the two ideas that public is to private as *open* is to *closed* and as the *whole* is to the *part*. In the first sense, of public being open, we speak of a public place, a public conference, public behavior, making something public, or publishing an article. The private counterparts, from homes to diaries, are private in that access is restricted and visibility reduced. The concepts of publicity and privacy stand in opposition to each other along this dimension of accessibility. Public is to private as the transparent is to the opaque, as the announced is to the concealed. Similarly, a man's public life is to his private life as the outer is to the inner realm.

On the other hand, when we speak of public opinion, public health, or the public interest, we mean the opinion, health, or interest of the whole of the people as opposed to that of a part, whether a class or an individual. Public in this sense often means "common," not necessarily governmental. The public-spirited or public-minded citizen is one concerned about the community as a whole. But in the modern world the concepts of governmental and public have become so closely linked that in some contexts they are interchangeable. The state acts for the whole of a society in international relations and makes rules binding on the whole internally. Public thus often means official. In this sense a "public act" is one that carries official status, even if it is secret and therefore not public in the sense of being openly visible. Indeed, "private" originally signified, according to the Oxford English Dictionary, "not holding public office or official position." As Albert Hirschman (1982) points out, this is a meaning that survives in the army "private," that is, the "ordinary soldier without any rank or position." Now, of course, private is contrasted with public to characterize what lies beyond the state's boundaries, such as the market or the family.

These different contrasts between public and private lead to some apparent conflicts in defining what lies on each side of the boundary. One such conflict concerns the location of the market. To an economist, the marketplace is the quintessentially private. But to a sociologist or anthropologist concerned with culture, the marketplace is the quintessentially public—a sphere open to utter strangers who nonetheless are able to understand the same rules and gestures needed in what may be a highly ritualized process of exchange. While economists use the public/private distinction interchangeably with the contrast between state and market, analysts of culture—particularly those concerned with the roles and relations of men and women—take the public sphere to include the market as well as politics and contrast them both with the private domain of the family. In this sense, the public/private distinction is sometimes taken to mark out the contested boundaries of the male and female worlds—a usage that takes us back to the notion of the private as being more closed, more shielded from contact and view, than the open encounters of public life (Elshtain, 1981; Rosaldo, 1974; Imray and Middleton, 1983).

From these varying uses of the categories come several contrasting conceptions of the public sphere. The public sphere may be conceived as the open and visible—the sphere of public life, public theater, the public marketplace, public sociability. It may also be conceived as that which applies to the whole people or, as we say, the general public or the public at large, in which case the public may consist of an aggregate or a mass who have no direct contact or social relation—the very opposite of a sphere of sociability. Or the public sphere may be conceived specifically as the domain circumscribed by the state, although exactly where to draw the state's boundaries may be difficult indeed.

The general meanings of privatization, then, correspond to withdrawals from any of these variously conceived public spheres. Historians and sociologists write about the withdrawal of affective interest and involvement from the sphere of public sociability. For example, in their work on the development of the modern family, Michael Young and Peter Willmott (1973), argue that as the modern household became equipped with larger homes, private cars, televisions, and other resources, more time and capital came to be invested in the private interior of the family and less in public taverns, squares, and streets. Similarly, Richard Sennett (1977) suggests that since the eighteenth century modern society has seen a decline of public culture and sociability, a deadening of public life and public space, a privatization of emotion. Such arguments shade into a second meaning of privatization: a shift of individual involvements from the whole to the part—that is, from public action to private concerns— the kind of privatization that Hirschman (1982, pp. 121–130) describes as one swing in a public/private cycle of individual action. In this sort of public-to-private transition, the swing is not from sociability to intimacy but from civic concern to the pursuit of self-interest.

Privatization can also signify another kind of withdrawal from the whole to the part: an appropriation by an individual or a particular group of some good formerly available to the entire public community. Like the withdrawal of involvement, privatization in the sense of private appropriation may well alter the distribution of welfare.

From these meanings it is but a short step to the sense of privatization as a withdrawal from the state, not of individual involvements, but of assets, functions, indeed entire institutions. Public policy is concerned with privatization at this level. But the two forms, the privatization of individual involvements and the privatization of social functions and assets, are certainly related, at least by ideological kinship. A confidence that pursuit of private gain serves the larger social order leads to approval for both self-interested behavior and private enterprise.

Thus far I have been talking about privatization as if both spheres, public and private, were already constituted. But in a longer perspective, their constitution and separation represent complementary processes. Much historical experience corresponds to Simmel's paradoxical dictum that "what is public becomes ever more public, and what is private becomes ever more private" (Simmel, 1950, p. 337). This is true specifically of the histories of the state and the family. The difference between patrimonial domination and modern bureaucracies, as Weber describes the two, is precisely that in the patrimonial state public and private roles were mixed and in the modern state are more clearly distinguished (Weber, 1968). The modern state distinguishes offices and persons. The office is public, and its files, rules, and finances are distinct from the personal possessions and character of individuals. As public administration and finance were separated from the household and personal wealth of the ruler, the modern state became, in effect, more public; the person and family of the ruler, more private (Braun, 1975; Webber and Wildavsky, 1986, pp. 148–151). That the domestic sphere has generally become more private is one of the classic themes of modern sociology and the history of the family (Ariès, 1962).

The rise of the liberal state specifically entailed a sharpening of the public/private distinction: on the one hand, the privatizing of religious and moral belief and practice and of economic activity formerly regulated by the state; on the other, a commitment to public law and public political discussion. Classical liberalism is often represented as a purely privatizing ideology, but liberals were committed to suppressing markets in votes, offices, and tax collection, not to mention human beings. Strengthening the public character of the state is a continuity in liberal thought from its classical to contemporary phases. Moreover, as Stephen Holmes (1984) argues, the liberal effort to privatize otherwise rancorous religious differences promoted a civilized public order. In this way, some kinds of privatization are not the enemy of the public realm but its necessary support.

In liberal democratic thought, public and private are central terms in the language of claims making. In particular, they provide a deeply resonant vocabulary for the making of claims against the state. These are of two kinds. First, the concept of a public government implies an elaborate structure of rules limiting the exercise of state power. Those who wield power are to be held publicly accountable—that is, answerable to the citizens—for their performance. Government decisions and deliberations must be public in the sense of being publicly reported and open to general participation. In short, the citizens of a liberal state are understood to have a right to expect their government to be public not only in its ends but also in its processes. Second, when the members of a liberal society think of their homes, businesses, churches, and myriad other forms of association as lying in a private sphere, they are claiming limits to the power of that democratic state. The limits are not absolute—private property rights, for example, are not an insuperable barrier to public control or regulation—but when crossing from public to private the presumptions shift away from the state and any state intervention must meet more stringent tests of the public interest.

Public and private in liberal thought have become pervasive dualities—or, perhaps better said, polarities—associated with the state in one direction, the individual in the other. Intermediate entities such as corporations have typically been divided between the two categories. Until the nineteenth century in the United States, there was no clear legal distinction between public and private corporations. Initially, cities were not sharply distinguished in the law from business enterprises. But in the mid-

1800s cities became classified as agencies of the state, whereas business corporations came to be treated as individuals. As public agencies, cities were allowed only such powers as states delegated to them; as fictive individuals, private corporations came to enjoy rights protected by the Constitution (Frug, 1980). This bifurcation between powers and rights lies at the foundation of the contemporary legal distinction between the public and private sectors.

Behind the legal categories, of course, the boundaries are blurred. On the one hand, private interests reach into the conduct of the state and its agencies; on the other, the state reaches across the public/private boundary to regulate private contracts and the conduct of private corporations and other associations. Through tax preferences and credit guarantees, the state shapes private economy and society. But the degree of penetration varies, and the public/private system of classification is used to express these variations. So, for example, among private corporations, we distinguish those that are privately held from those that are publicly traded and subject to the regulations of the Securities and Exchange Commission. The latter are often called public corporations, by which we actually mean *public private* corporations. Among those public private corporations are some subject to more extensive regulation, such as the utilities, which are especially *public, public private* corporations. And since the utilities, in turn, have some lines of business defined as public and others as private, the public/private boundary runs within them as well as around them.

It is as if, on finding two boxes labeled public and private, we were to open the private box and find two more boxes labeled public and private, which we would do again—and again—opening ever smaller boxes until we reached the individuals far inside, whom we then split into respective offices and persons.[1] Moreover, if the boxes have been assembled by reasonably competent lawyers, they may be extremely intricate and some will have misleading labels. But this complexity and the legal manipulation of the categories do not invalidate their usefulness or underlying meaning. To speak of a public corporation in the private sector ought really to be no more confusing than saying that North Carolina is in the South. Public and private give us relative locations.

A further source of frustration with the public/private distinction is that the terms do not have consistent meanings from one institutional sphere to another. In the United States, the difference between public and private schools is not the same as the difference between public and private broadcasting. An American public school is public, not only in that it is state-owned and financed, but also because it is open to all children

---

[1] I owe this metaphor to Gerald Frug.

of eligible age in its area. Private schools can reject applicants, but public school systems are denied that option. Public is to private not only as state is to nonstate but as open is to closed. In television broadcasting, however, the viewing public has open access to commercial as well as public channels. The difference lies in financing and programing. The public channels receive government support and do not choose programing to maximize audience ratings, though in fact even public broadcasting now competes for private corporate sponsorship and some public stations are legally organized as private nonprofit corporations. To make matters still more complicated, the differences between public and private institutions do not follow parallel lines in other countries. To take broadcasting again, public television or radio in the United States is more dependent on private financing, less subject to control by political authorities, and less the symbolic voice of the state than the state-owned networks of other Western nations, not to mention the Soviet bloc and Third World.

To say public or private, therefore, is not sufficient to specify a form of organization or even its relation to the state. Consequently, it is extremely risky to generalize about public versus private organizations—and, therefore, about the merits of privatization as public policy—beyond a particular institutional or national context. No general theory about the performance of public versus private organization is likely to succeed if it fails to distinguish among political systems and the structural variety of public and private institutions. Privatization describes a direction of change, but it does not denote a specific origin or destination. Its meaning depends on the point of departure—the public/private balance previously struck in a particular domain. And it is a critical question whether moving from public to private in the sense of state to nonstate entails a movement in the other senses: from open to closed (in access to information) or from the whole to the part (particularly in the distribution of benefits).

THE POLITICAL MEANING OF PRIVATIZATION

The term privatization did not gain wide circulation in politics until the late 1970s and early 1980s. With the rise of conservative governments in Great Britain and the United States, privatization came primarily to mean two things: (1) any shift of activities or functions from the state to the private sector; and (2) more specifically, any shift from public to private of the *production* of goods and services.[2] Besides directly producing services, governments establish the legal framework of societies and regulate

[2] On the ambiguities of classifying public and private organizations, see Musolf and Seidman (1980); on the ambiguous character of public authorities in the United States, see Walsh (1980).

social and economic life, and they finance services that are privately produced and consumed. The first, broader definition of privatization includes all reductions in the regulatory and spending activity of the state.
The second, more specific definition of privatization excludes deregulation and spending cuts except when they result in a shift from public to
private in the production of goods and services. This more focused definition is the one that I shall use here. It leaves open the possibility that
privatization may not actually result in less government spending and regulation—indeed, may unexpectedly increase them.

Several further points about this definition need clarification. First, the
public sector here includes agencies administered as part of the state and
organizations owned by it, such as state enterprises and independent public authorities like the British Broadcasting Corporation (BBC) or the Port
Authority of New York and New Jersey. In the private sector I include
not only commercial firms but also informal and domestic activities, voluntary associations, cooperatives, and private nonprofit corporations.[3]

Second, in the definition I am using, privatization refers to shifts from
the public to the private sector, not shifts within sectors. Thus the conversion of a state agency into an autonomous public authority or state-
owned enterprise is not privatization, though it may well put the enterprise on a commercial footing.[4] This was the objective, for example, of
the conversion of the United States Post Office into a public corporation,
the United States Postal Service, in 1971. Similarly, the conversion of a
private nonprofit organization into a profit-making firm is also not privatization, though it, too, may orient the firm toward the market. Both
of these intrasectoral changes might be described as commercialization;
in the case of public agencies, commercialization is sometimes a preliminary stage to privatization.

Third, shifts from publicly to privately produced services may result
not only from a deliberate government action, such as a sale of assets,
but also from the choices of individuals or firms that a government is
unwilling or unable to satisfy or control. In many countries, private demand for education, health care, or retirement income has outstripped
public provision. As a result private schooling, medical care, and pensions

---

[3] Savas defines privatization as "the act of reducing the role of government, or increasing
the role of the private sector, in an activity or in the ownership of assets" (Savas, 1987, p.
3). I see nothing wrong with this broad definition, as long as one realizes that some actions
may reduce one role of government but increase another. For example, selling government-
owned utilities may result in a new system of public utility regulation (as it has in Great
Britain). Setting up a voucher plan for education and housing may produce more public
regulation of private schools. In other words, policies conceived of as privatization may
have unintended consequences for other dimensions of state intervention.

[4] William Glade (1986) uses the term "simulated privatization" to refer to the effort to
put a public enterprise on a commercial footing.

have grown to relatively larger proportions. This is *demand-driven privatization*. When privatization is a demand-driven process, it does not require an absolute reduction in publicly produced services. Stagnation or slow growth in the public sector may be the cause. In some socialist societies the growth of an "underground" economy represents a form of privatization that is not a planned development (though it may well result from development planning). In other words, as a process, privatization encompasses more institutional changes than those brought about by self-conscious privatization policies. It seems useful, then, to distinguish instances of privatization according to whether they are predominately *policy-* or *demand-driven*.

Fourth, if one shifts attention from the sphere of production to the sphere of consumption, one may alternatively define privatization as the substitution of private goods for public goods. A public good, in the economist's sense, has two distinguishing properties: One person's consumption does not preclude another's and to exclude anyone from consumption is costly, if not impossible. The prototypical example is fresh air. A public good need not be governmentally produced. A broadcast television program is a public good even if it is provided by a commercially owned station; but videotape is not, nor is programing on subscription cable services. Any shift toward these forms of nonbroadcast television represents a privatization of consumption, even if the local cable service is municipally owned (Starr, forthcoming).

Depending on whether one is talking about the locus of production or the forms of consumption, privatization can mean rather different things. In regard to production, "privatization of health care" might mean a transfer of medical facilities from public to private ownership; regarding consumption, it might refer to a shift in expenditures from public health (that is, environmental protection, vaccinations, and the like) to individual medical care. Similarly, "privatization of transportation" might refer to the conversion of an urban bus system from public to commercial ownership, or it might mean a shift in ridership from buses to private automobiles, regardless of whether the bus company is municipal or commercial. Strictly speaking, public transit is not a public good, since exclusion is possible and only one person can sit in a seat; however, because buses and trains are open to the public at large, common carriers are a distinctively public form of consumption compared to private cars. More generally, the historical process described by Young and Willmott (1973)—the concentration of consumption activities in the home—represented a shift toward more privatized forms of consumption. This shift has been the source of much criticism of contemporary society, as in John Kenneth Galbraith's famous contrast of private affluence and public squalor in *The Affluent Society* (1958). In my work, whenever referring specifically to a shift from public goods to private goods, or from common carriers to private carriers, I use the phrase "privatization of consumption." Otherwise, I take privatization to mean a shift from public to private in the locus of the production of services.

Four types of government policies can bring about such a shift:

1. the cessation of public programs and disengagement of government from specific kinds of responsibilities ("implicit privatization") or, at a less drastic level, the restriction of publicly produced services in volume, availability, or quality, leading to a shift by consumers toward privately produced and purchased substitutes (also called "privatization by attrition");

2. the transfer to private ownership of public assets, including sales of public land, infrastructure, and enterprises;

3. the financing of private services—for example, through contracting out or vouchers—instead of direct government service production; and

4. the deregulation of entry by private firms into activities that were previously treated as a public monopoly.

These forms of privatization vary in the extent to which they move ownership, finance, and accountability out of the public sector. The spectrum of alternatives runs from total privatization (as in government disengagement from some policy domain) to partial privatization (as in contracting out or vouchers). As I conceive the term, privatization may include policies anywhere along this spectrum; however, the implications of privatization vary with its degree. In the cases of partial privatization, the government may continue to finance but not to operate services, or it may continue to own but not to manage assets. Privatization may, therefore, dilute government control and accountability without eliminating them. Where governments pay for privately produced services, they must continue to collect taxes. Privatization in this sense (number 3 above) diminishes the operational but not the fiscal or functional sphere of government action. By putting the delivery of services into the hands of a third party, governments may divert claims and complaints to private organizations, but they also risk seeing those third parties become powerful claimants themselves. Whether this sort of partial privatization achieves any reduction in government spending or deficits must necessarily be a practical, empirical question.

Even asset sales sometimes involve only the transfer of a partial interest. Often governments sell some voting stock in an enterprise but refuse to surrender governmental control. In these instances, privatization may amount to little more than a revenue-raising measure, as there may be no change in management, management behavior, or the relation of the enterprise to state authorities. Though it may seem odd, the product of privatization is not always a private firm; privatization also yields hybrid enterprises with varying balances of influence.

The different techniques used to privatize assets affect what emerges from privatization. Among the methods used are sales to private bidders; sales by public stock offering; conversion to employee ownership; and transfer of title to the firm's current managers. In the case of unprofitable businesses, far from charging a price, governments sometimes guarantee the new owners future public contracts, tax benefits, or the monopoly on a franchise. These variations in privatization policy complicate simple-minded predictions of the effects of privatization on economic efficiency.

Just as there are various methods for the divestiture of assets, so, too, various methods are available for shifting from publicly produced services to publicly financed private provision. Governments face a basic choice as to whether state agencies or private parties will do the purchasing. If the state purchases services, it may enter into contracts or grants. If, on the other hand, the government allows private parties to purchase services, it may distribute vouchers, offer tax credits or other tax preferences, indemnify beneficiaries directly for some proportion of their costs, or pay providers chosen by beneficiaries. (The latter shades into contracting if the transactions become routine.) To introduce yet a further complication, the private parties whose costs the government defrays in whole or in part may be individuals (the consumers of the services) or employers. Privatization policy might, for example, call for the use of tax preferences to induce a shift from publicly provided retirement benefits to benefits provided by employers or to benefits provided through individual retirement accounts (Ferrara, 1985; Goodman, 1985; O'Higgins, 1986; Starr, 1988b). When governments give up producing services, they can "empower" many different parties.

Privatization should not be automatically equated with increased competition. Two related processes, privatization and liberalization, need to be carefully distinguished. By liberalization one generally means a reduction of government control; in this context, it refers to the opening up of an industry to competitive pressures. Entry deregulation of public monopolies is a form of privatization that is also liberalizing. It is entirely possible, however, to privatize without liberalizing. When the Thatcher government sold shares of British Telecom and British Gas, it substituted private monopolies for public ones and introduced new regulatory agencies to perform some of the functions previously undertaken through public ownership. The option of putting liberalization first—that is, encouraging greater competition—was expressly rejected, perhaps for fear that it would reduce the share price of the companies (Kay, Mayer, and Thompson, 1987; Brittan, 1985). It is also possible, conversely, to liberalize without privatizing—that is, to introduce competition into the public sector without transferring ownership. For example, governments may allocate funds to schools according to student enrollments where families are free to choose among competing public schools; or they may require public enterprises or operating agencies to compete for capital or contracts from higher-level authorities. Indeed, it is even possible to pursue nationalization and liberalization at the same time, as the French socialists demonstrated in the 1980s when they first nationalized banks and then liberalized financial markets.

Finally, as there are different routes out of the public sector, so there is a range of destinations in the private sector to which privatization may lead. The alternative possibilities may be classified according to the two dimensions of organizational complexity and proprietary status:

1. the personal, domestic, or informal sector, thought to exemplify the virtues of self-reliance, mutual aid, and sensitivity to individual preferences;

2. the voluntary nonprofit or "independent" sector, consisting of formal, complex organizations, thought to display the same virtues as the informal sector, plus the advantages of professional leadership and management;

3. the small-business sector, acclaimed for entrepreneurship and revered as a fountain of new jobs; and

4. the large-scale corporate sector, where hopes for improved performance rest not only on the profit motive but also on professional management and economies of scale.

The first two of these destinations, the informal and nonprofit sectors, remind us that privatization does not necessarily mean a reliance on commercial markets. Indeed, instead of one destination and one map, the advocates of privatization have several, distinctly different conceptions of where they are going. I turn now to the theories that provide the movement with its logic, intellectual coherence—and rhetoric.

Privatization as Theory and Rhetoric

The normative theories justifying privatization as a direction for public policy draw their inspiration from several different visions of a good society. By far the most influential is the vision grounded in laissez-faire individualism and free-market economics that promises greater efficiency, a smaller government, and more individual choice if only we expand the domain of property rights and market forces. A second vision, rooted in a more socially minded conservative tradition, promises a return of power to communities from a greater reliance in social provision on families, churches, and other largely nonprofit institutions. Privatization here means a devolution from the state to ostensibly nonpolitical and noncommercial forms of human association. Yet a third perspective sees privatization as a political strategy for diverting demands away from the state and thereby reducing government "overload." This last view, identified particularly with recent neoconservative thought, does not necessarily conflict with the other two—indeed, some advocates of privatization draw on all three—but each suggests a different framework for analysis and policy. Even among the economic models of privatization, there are some subtle but important differences between two approaches—the radical view of privatization as a reassignment of property rights and the more moderate, conventional view of privatization as an instrument for fine-tuning a three-sector economy.

ECONOMIC MODEL 1: PRIVATIZATION AS
A REASSIGNMENT OF PROPERTY RIGHTS

Private ownership and competitive markets are normally thought to go hand in hand, but the two issues of ownership and market structure are often separate. For the economist devoted to both, the question then arises as to which object of affection is more beloved: private ownership or competition? Here a difference of opinion appears among economists that corresponds to a preference for either privatization or liberalization. Those who believe that efficient performance depends on private ownership per se favor privatization, even in cases generally regarded as natural monopolies. Conversely, those who see competition as the critical spur to efficiency are more skeptical about the benefits of privatizing monopolies and often put emphasis on other policies, such as deregulation. In the case of a government telecommunications monopoly, for example, those who stress ownership may be willing to privatize the monopoly intact, whereas those who stress competition may prefer to break it up before sale or even keep it in public ownership while allowing private firms to compete with it on equal terms.

Thus the perspective that unequivocally points to privatization as desirable policy holds that property ownership is the fulcrum of political economy. Curiously, the two unlikely bedfellows sharing this appreciation of ownership are Marxism and Chicago School economics, which draw from it opposite but equally strong conclusions about the overriding importance of getting ownership into the right sector. From the Chicago tradition come two closely related clusters of work: the theory of property rights and the theory of public choice. Both attempt to enlarge the conventional economic paradigm by treating the classical firm and modern package of property rights as only one of various possible institutional forms. In this enlarged model, public institutions merely represent an alternative property rights configuration, which on theoretical grounds the Chicago School predicts will regularly perform less efficiently than private enterprise.

As developed by economists such as Armen Alchian, Ronald Coase, and Harold Demsetz, the theory of property rights explains differences in organizational behavior solely on the basis of the individual incentives created by the structure of property rights (Alchian, 1965; Demsetz, 1967; Furubotn and Pejovich, 1972, 1974; de Alessi, 1987). Property rights, in this view, specify the social and economic relations that people must observe in their use of scarce resources, including not only the benefits that owners are allowed to enjoy but also the harms to others that they are allowed to cause. A right of ownership actually comprises several rights, chiefly the rights to use an asset, to change it in form, substance, or location, and to transfer all or some of these rights. Insofar as the state restricts these rights, they become "attenuated." Thus the key issues for the theory are, first, to whom are property rights assigned, and, second, how, if at all, are they attenuated?

Like other branches of microeconomics, the property rights school conceives of human action as purely individualistic. The more individuals stand to gain from tending to their property, the better it will be tended. Conversely, the more attenuated and diluted their property rights, the less motivated individuals will be to use property under their control efficiently. Private ownership concentrates rights and rewards; public ownership dilutes them. The property rights school does not recognize any fundamental change in the working of private enterprise as a result of the separation of ownership and management in the modern corporation. To be sure, shareholders in large corporations cannot monitor management as closely as the owner of the classical firm could oversee his enterprise. However, in this view, the market generates the needed spur to prevent corporate management from dissipating value through excessive salaries or slack attention. If returns from the enterprise are low, shareholders will sell their stock and the price will be depressed. In the extreme case, the firm may be acquired by outsiders and the managers may lose their jobs. These crucial deterrents to inefficient management are missing from the public sector. Since "shareholders" (citizens) have no transferable property rights in public enterprise, they cannot sell stock as a signal of dissatisfaction with performance; even moving to another jurisdiction is costly. Moreover, there is no "market for corporate control": public enterprises cannot be taken over by bidders who believe that they can make more efficient use of the assets. Hence, according to the theory, there is no check to the dissipation of value by the management of public enterprises.

It is worth taking note of the premises and implications of the property rights approach. First, the theory says that when comparing the performance of different organizations, ownership effects dominate any other sources of variation. The theory gives no importance whatsoever to organizational characteristics such as size, centralization, hierarchy, or leadership. Nor does it recognize any variation in performance that might stem from task characteristics, such as poor information or ambiguity about goals. The theory does not even recognize the effects of economic incentives unrelated to property rights, such as those originating in various types of contracts. The theory does not point to any contingencies in generalizing about public/private differences; it does not identify any particular conditions or characteristics that might cause public institutions to perform well. The disease the theory diagnoses in the public sector is genetic and incurable.

Second, the theory takes the market as the standard for judging value and finds public institutions deficient because they fail to measure up to that standard (for example, their "shareholders" cannot sell stock). Survival in the market, of course, depends on the capacity of organizations to produce a residual reward for the owners—that is, a profit. This is not the standard that public institutions generally need to meet. The property rights approach says that society would be better off if, instead of meeting approval in the political process, public organizations or their assets were privately owned and had to meet the test of profitability.

Third, the property rights theory assumes that the market for corporate control is highly efficient and that the chief reason corporations are acquired is their management's poor performance. In the United States today, however, some corporations are acquired because they have built up large pools of cash, while other corporations avoid being acquired because their managers take preventive, but inefficient, measures, such as piling up debt. Frequently, behemoths with large cash flow but low returns on equity and other indicators of poor performance have taken over firms with much better records. Virtue is not always rewarded in the market for corporate control; nonetheless, according to the property rights view, market discipline forces managers of private firms to be more efficient than public managers. The theory gives no weight at all to the monitoring capacities of the state, the public at large, and the various institutions of a liberal democracy, such as the press, that routinely scrutinize the performance of public institutions. The reasons for this dim view of public monitoring are spelled out in the theory of public choice.

"Public choice," ill-named because the only choices it recognizes are essentially private, is both a branch of microeconomics and an ideologically laden view of democratic politics. Analysts of the school apply the logic of microeconomics to politics and generally find that whereas self-interest leads to benign results in the marketplace, it produces nothing but pathology in political decisions (Borcherding, 1977; Niskanen,

1971). These pathological patterns represent different kinds of "free-riding" and "rent-seeking" by voters, bureaucrats, politicians, and recipients of public funds. Coalitions of voters seeking special advantages from the state join together to get favorable legislation. Rather than being particularly needy, these groups are likely to be those whose big stake in a benefit arouses them to more effective action than is taken by the taxpayers at large over whom the costs are spread. In general, individuals with "concentrated" interests in increased expenditure take a "free ride" on those with "diffuse" interests in lower taxes. Similarly, the managers of the "bureaucratic firms" are said to maximize budgets, thereby obtaining greater power, larger salaries, and other perquisites. Budget maximization results in higher government spending overall, inefficient allocation among government agencies, and inefficient production within them. In addition, when government agencies give out grants, the potential grantees expend resources in lobbying up to the value of the grants—an instance of the more general "political dissipation of value" resulting from the general scramble for political favors and jobs.

Thus, like the theory of property rights, the public choice perspective indicts public ownership and management across the board. The exponents of these views have elaborated and documented their position with studies of the public management of land, forests, water, and other natural resources and comparative analyses of public and private enterprises in a variety of industries, including airlines (Davies, 1971), fire protection (Ahlbrandt, 1973), and solid waste disposal (Bennett and Johnson, 1979). The property rights view of natural resource management exemplifies application of the theory. Public ownership, in this view, inexorably leads to what Garrett Hardin (1968) has called "the tragedy of the commons." Acting out of rational self-interest, individuals abuse and ultimately destroy the commons but take good care of their own private property. Thus publicly managed grazing land and forests purportedly suffer from worse management than privately owned land and forests. Moreover, the public agencies responsible for resource management, such as the Forest Service, dissipate value through self-aggrandizing expansionary policies. Consequently, privatizing the public domain would better ensure its conservation and efficient use (Hanke and Dowdle, 1987). One plan for "privatizing the environment" calls for the sale to private investors of federal lands, including national parks, or their transfer to private associations such as the Audubon Society (Smith, 1982); the same author even recommends solving the problem of endangered species by creating new property rights in wildlife (Smith, 1981).

In short, starting with an individualistic model of human behavior, the public choice school makes a series of empirical claims: (1) that democratic polities have inherent tendencies toward government growth and excessive budgets; (2) that expenditure growth is due to self-interested coalitions of voters, politicians, and bureaucrats; and (3) that public enterprises necessarily perform less efficiently than private enterprises.

A thorough analysis of the claims of the public choice school would be a book in itself, but the general lines of criticism may be at least briefly suggested. First, while the theory presents voters as narrowly self-interested, considerable evidence suggests that even on economic issues voters identify their interests with the overall performance of the economy, rather than simply voting in line with their private experience (Orren, 1987; Kelman, 1987). Voters, in other words, are capable of recognizing a collective interest apart from their own. Indeed, the whole point of "government by discussion" is to discover and express common interests not easily voiced or achieved in the private sphere; the public choice approach simply does not comprehend this preference-shaping function of political democracy. It also neglects the restraints built into the architecture of liberalism. While the theory says that government is systematically biased toward dissipating value and increasing expenditure, it disregards the checks and balances among branches of government and within them. (Scrutiny of spending programs by Congress and the Office of Management and Budget is an example.) According to the theory, spending programs get approved because they have concentrated benefits and diffused costs; however, the same arguments apply to tax reductions for specific interests (that is, tax expenditures). Thus "fiscal illusions" should be symmetrical on the spending and tax sides of the budgetary process and cannot explain long-term tendencies toward higher tax levels. The Leviathan theorists, as Richard Musgrave calls them, also overstate the historical trend toward higher government expenditure; the evidence does not show an accelerating increase as a proportion of national income (Musgrave, 1981).

The empirical evidence comparing efficiency in public and private organizations is also more complex than the property rights and public choice schools acknowledge. To take the example of resource management again, Carlisle Ford Runge (1984) points out that the evidence suggests federally owned rangeland is in better condition than nonfederal rangeland. In one of the few relevant studies of forestland, a survey in Minnesota indicates that extremely few private purchasers of tax-forfeited public forests did anything whatsoever to maintain them (Ellefson, Palm and Lothner, 1982). The "tragedy of the commons" argument confuses resources in common ownership with resources in public ownership; it fails to give any credit to the democratic process or to professional management in raising the time horizons of voters, politicians, and bureaucrats to a level higher than that prevailing in the marketplace. Many observers have noted the propensity of American managers for concentrating on short-term profits; the property rights school, by contrast, bravely asserts that private firms have sufficient incentives to preserve wildlife and wilderness for future generations.

The rhetoric of the public choice school is a kind of hard-nosed realism. The theory dismisses as naive civic ideals such as public service; it denies the capacity of voters or politicians to act on the basis of a national interest wider than their own private aggrandizement. Rather like Marxism, it claims to face up to the self-interested basis of democratic politics and presents all claims of higher purpose as smoke and deception. And also like Marxism, it presents itself as a scientific advance over earlier romantic and idealized views of the state. But rather than being an advance of science over intuition, the appeal of the public choice school is precisely to those who are intuitively certain that whatever government does, the private sector can do better. Together, the property rights and public choice schools show only that, if you start by assuming a purely individualistic model of human behavior and treat politics as if it were a pale imitation of the market, democracy will, indeed, make no sense.

ECONOMIC MODEL 2: PRIVATIZATION AS A RELOCATION OF ECONOMIC FUNCTIONS

Compared to the right-wing schools that condemn the public sector as irredeemably inefficient, policy analysts trained in conventional microeconomics tend to have a more qualified, though still highly critical, view of public institutions. Rather than attribute the performance of public organizations to the incentives created by public ownership per se, mainstream policy analysts generally think of designing the right incentives within the framework of public organization. Of course, the overwhelming consensus is that private ownership is more efficient in providing private goods in competitive markets; hence it is rare to find any respectable opinion in favor of government ownership of factories producing high-performance sports cars. Mainstream views do vary, however, about the proper role of public institutions in producing public goods and managing natural monopolies. Viewing competition as the critical issue, the neoclassically trained are inclined to favor privatization insofar as it represents a move toward competition under conditions when markets should be expected to work efficiently. In recent years, however, the requirements for efficient markets have come to be understood more liberally, while the reputation of public enterprise has markedly declined. Hence, the prevailing consensus in economics and policy analysis has become more sympathetic to privatization than it was two or three decades ago.

While the property rights view is parsimonious and unambiguous in analyzing the basis of public/private differences, the more conventional approach is a patchwork of theories about the conditions under which the market, the state, and the nonprofit sector fail to perform efficiently. In this tradition, the theory of market failure was the historical point of departure. According to the received neoclassical wisdom, imperfect information, externalities, increasing returns to scale, and (in some versions) inequalities of wealth prevent the market from achieving optimal performance; it is then a short—though not a necessary—step to say that where the market fails, some form of public ownership or regulation is justified. (The theory says nothing about the choice between regulation and ownership.) However, two recent developments have suggested more caution about public intervention. First, markets do not have to be perfectly competitive; they only need to be contestable—and the requirements for contestability are more easily met (Baumol, Panzar, and Willig, 1982). Second, public choice theory has successfully raised the challenge that where markets fail, so, too, may government; indeed, the theory suggests government will only be worse. Attempting to state the argument symmetrically, Charles Wolf, Jr. (1979) has spelled out a series of conditions for "nonmarket failure."

These twin theories of market and nonmarket failure have, in turn, suggested a role for the nonprofit sector; for if states and markets have peculiar weaknesses, perhaps philanthropy can be explained as an attempt to fill the void (Douglas 1983). But, rather than define the voluntary sector as residual, Lester Salamon (1986) has argued that in the United States nonprofits are a "preferred" mechanism for delivering public services and that government programs arise to meet the problems of "voluntary failure"! The upshot is a theoretical amalgam that defines the limits of the three sectors and suggests in what form different kinds of activities are most efficiently organized. From this perspective, privatization becomes a way to move activity from a less efficient to a more efficient form—a tool of economic adjustment rather than radical reconstruction (Brodkin and Young, in this volume).

The expanded theory of sector failure is a kind of ecological approach to institutional choice. The various sectors provide alternative environments, and the problem then is to decide whether a particular set of tasks is best carried out in one or more locations. However, the theory does not exhaustively assign all activities. No sector gets high marks for performing tasks for which there is poor information. The theory is also ahistorical; it makes no allowance for sunk investments in organizational capacity. Relocating an industry in a different sector is not, after all, a costless exercise. However, the most serious defect of this approach is that, like all the economic models, it is principally concerned with efficiency and has little to say about the effects of organizational design on other values.

To subject an organization to market forces is to push it to maximize the returns to residual claims holders; perhaps it will generate those returns more efficiently, but as George Yarrow (1986) has observed, some activities have been turned over to the public sector precisely to be protected from such pressure. The economic models cannot say whether or not that is a sensible choice.

PRIVATIZATION AS COMMUNITY DEVELOPMENT

A different set of arguments, not chiefly concerned with efficiency, comes from a more sociological theory of privatization that emphasizes the strengthening of communities. In the most noteworthy exposition of this position, Peter Berger and Richard Neuhaus (1977) propose that government "empower" voluntary associations, community organizations, churches, self-help groups, and other less formal "mediating" institutions that lie between individuals and society's "alienating megastructures." In their view, the modern liberal state has undermined these "value-generating," "value-maintaining," "people-sized institutions" by establishing service bureaucracies that take over their functions. Berger and Neuhaus are not opposed to social welfare provision, but they urge that, whenever possible, public policy rely on mediating institutions for the delivery of publicly financed services.

The view of privatization as community empowerment stands in sharp contrast to the conception of privatization as an extension of property rights. Berger and Neuhaus emphatically reject a narrowly individualistic view of human motivation. Indeed, they criticize liberalism precisely for defending individual rights over the rights of social groups to assert their own values; for example, they defend the capacity of neighborhoods to sustain "democratically determined values in the public sphere" by exhibiting religious symbols in public places (Berger and Neuhaus, 1977, p. 11). They also suggest that attacks on the ideals of voluntary service "aid the expansion of the kind of capitalist mentality that would put a dollar sign on everything on the grounds that only that which has a price tag has worth" (ibid., pp. 36–37). Their concern is not to expand the domain of the profit motive but rather to strengthen local, small-scale forms of social provision. This is privatization with a human face, and it bears some resemblance to left-wing interest in community organizations and cooperatives (Donnison, 1984).

Though I find the community empowerment view more attractive than the property rights perspective, the Berger and Neuhaus claim that the liberal state undermines mediating institutions ignores the historical partnership between the two. The history of social provision in the United States does not, in fact, betray a disregard for the virtues of voluntary institutions. Salamon (1986) points out that the twentieth-century expansion of social spending in the United States has been largely a growth of what he calls "third-party" government (the third parties including local government as well as private nonprofit agencies). Many nonprofit community organizations have depended for their survival on government subsidies. Moreover, today there is often a division of labor between the public and voluntary sectors. A still greater reliance on the nonprofit sector might pose serious problems for the voluntary institutions themselves. To be sure, privatization is taking place in many social services, but the growth is chiefly of new for-profit organizations that are far from the local "people-sized" institutions envisioned by Berger and Neuhaus. Some of them, like the national chains of nursing homes, are every bit as alienating as other corporate "megastructures." It is probably an illusion to think that a big shift toward private social services would lead to a proliferation of community organizations, if only because the private institutions would need much more capital than they traditionally have had available. And if not supplied by the state, the capital must be supplied by the capital markets. In health care, the demands of capital formation are one of the principal pressures producing a shift from nonprofit to commercial organization, often national in scale. Community empowerment might be a good idea, but if it is to come at all, it will come from more government intervention, not privatization.

PRIVATIZATION AS A REDUCTION OF GOVERNMENT OVERLOAD

A final theory justifying privatization holds that privatization is desirable because it will likely deflect and reduce demands on the state. In the 1970s, some critics suggested that the Western democracies were suffering from an "overload" of pressure, responsible for excessive spending and poor economic performance (Huntington, Crozier, and Watanuki, 1975). In that framework, privatization represents one of several policies encouraging a counterrevolution of declining expectations. In a similar vein, Stuart Butler of the Heritage Foundation has argued that privatization can cure budget deficits by breaking up the kind of public spending coalitions described by public choice theory. Privatizing government enterprises and public services, in this view, will redirect aspirations into the market and encourage a more entrepreneurial consciousness (Butler, 1985).

This political theory of privatization has several different, overlapping elements. First, the privatization of enterprises is a privatization of employment relations. The advocates of privatization hope to divert employees' wage claims from the public treasury, with its vast capacity for taxing and borrowing, to private employers, who presumably will have more spine in resisting wage demands. Moreover, the proponents hope for a trickle-down of entrepreneurship from the newly privatized managers to the workers; for that very reason, privatizers often are perfectly willing to sell to the workers at an advantageous price whole enterprises or at least some portion of the shares. In addition, by shifting to private contractors even in a few selected areas, governments might signal a harder line on wage concessions and thereby weaken public employee unions.

Second, these advocates of privatization hope also for a privatization of beneficiaries' claims. Instead of seeing beneficiaries march outside of government offices when things go wrong, the privatizers want them to direct their ire to private service providers—or better yet, simply to switch to other providers. In other words, privatization could mean a wholesale shift, in Hirschman's terms, from "voice" to "exit" as the usual and preferred tactic of coping with dissatisfaction (Hirschman, 1970).

Third, the privatization of public assets and enterprises is also a privatization of wealth. Advocates such as Margaret Thatcher want privatization to increase the proportion of the population who own shares of stock and therefore take a more positive view of profit making. "People's capitalism" is an old idea, but using privatization of public assets to bring it about is new. Moreover, by privatizing other assets such as public housing and Social Security trust funds, privatizers hope to turn public claimants into property owners and engender in them a deeper identification with capitalism. They expect the worker who receives a retirement income from a private pension or individual retirement account to have a more conservative view of the world than that of the worker who depends on rent subsidies and a government check every month.

This political theory of privatization, like the economic and sociological theories, contains empirical predictions as well as normative judgments. The predictions concern the probable effects of privatization on political consciousness and action; the normative judgments concern the desirability of weakening the political foundations of public provision. Empirically, it seems unlikely that contracting out, vouchers, and other arrangements for paying private providers will reduce pressure on government spending; the contractors are as likely as public employees to lobby for larger budgets (Starr, 1987). However, some other forms of privatization may, indeed, change the underlying political values, understandings, and capacities for action in a society. Turning public tenants into private homeowners, public employees into private employees, and social security beneficiaries into investors in private retirement accounts could very well change their frame of social and political thought. These prospects raise rather different issues from the usual efficiency-minded discussions of privatization; they demand that we consider the meaning of privatization not only as a theory but also as a political practice.

Privatization as a Political Practice

I said earlier that the structural variety of public and private organizations, political systems, and national contexts makes it difficult to generalize about public/private differences and the effects of privatization. The task of generalization is still more complex because the forms of privatization vary so greatly. Now I want to spell out some of the contextual factors and critical choices that shape what privatization means in practice and that help to explain why political practice often conflicts with theory.

The Political Contexts and Uses of Privatization

The meaning of privatization depends in practice on a nation's position in the world economy. In the wealthier countries it is easy to treat privatization purely as a question of domestic policy. But where the likely buyers are foreign, as in the Third World, privatization of state-owned enterprises often means denationalization—a transfer of control to *foreign* investors or managers. Since state ownership often originally came about in an act of national self-assertion, privatization appears to be a retreat in the face of international pressure. In that sense, national memory colors the meaning of privatization. Even in the United States, privatization would be understood rather differently if public assets up for sale or contracts up for bid were likely to be taken over by the Russians or the Japanese. The more dependent a nation on foreign investment, the greater the likelihood that privatization will raise the prospect of diminished sovereignty and excite the passions of nationalism. Where privatization raises such issues, it is often blocked, or citizens and domestic firms are reserved exclusive rights to publicly offered assets, shares, or contracts. In many Western countries, state ownership owed more in the first place to nationalist than to socialist sentiment; hence it is scarcely surprising that nationalism is liable to derail or distort privatization plans.

Throughout the world, the privatization of enterprises with strategic military or economic significance raises especially sensitive questions of sovereignty and security. In most oil-producing countries, for example, no government is likely to try to privatize the state oil companies because of the likely domestic political reaction. Even in Britain the prospective sale of a helicopter company to an American firm caused a political stir. Despite its commitment to free markets, the Reagan Administration intervened in 1987 to prevent the sale to a Japanese corporation of a private American semiconductor company with important defense contracts. On the other hand, the Reagan Administration has sought to privatize some of NASA's satellite launching partly in the hope of strengthening the private American space industry in its competition with the Europeans. Yet this case only reinforces the general point: the conflict between privatization and national interests depends on the relative power of states in the world system—the weaker the state, the more likely the conflict. Economically strong nations, knowing that they can privatize without jeopardizing their sovereignty, lecture the weak on the perils of state enterprise and restrictions on investment.

Like national interests, the more parochial concerns of politically dominant racial and ethnic groups may also confound privatization plans. In many countries, ethnic minorities, such as Indians in East Africa, make up disproportionate numbers of the potential domestic buyers of public assets. When a country's bureaucratic and entrepreneurial classes differ in ethnic composition, privatization may be understood as a transfer of wealth and power from one group to another and be politically resisted for that reason. Even if privatization is adopted, the field of potential buyers may be so restricted that potential gains from more efficient management evaporate.

The larger point in these examples of "distorting" influences on privatization is that private sectors are not only characterized by private ownership in the abstract. The potential private owners of public assets and contractors for public services represent specific interests and groups. Privatization is unlikely to be carried out with indifference to those social facts.

In general, the political uses of privatization are bound to compromise the avowed efficiency objectives. Governments that are in a hurry to sell state-owned enterprises may make concessions to current managers, whose cooperation is instrumental in divestiture. Privatization then becomes an occasion for managerial enrichment and entrenchment. It is striking that in Great Britain, France, and other countries that have privatized state-owned enterprises, privatization usually brings about little or no change in top management. Moreover, governments commonly offer assets and enterprises up for sale to political allies. Some of these properties, such as broadcasting stations, are not simply economic but political assets. The political incumbents gain obvious advantages by placing them in the hands of a political ally. The same patterns have long been evident in the contracting of public services; indeed, contracting is the locus classicus of the political payoff. Even public offerings are not immune from political use. When governments underprice shares—as the evidence indicates has been the overwhelming pattern in Britain (Mayer and Meadowcroft, 1987)—they may be seeking to ensure not only that privatization is successfully realized, but also that happy shareholders have the opportunity to repay the government at the next election. Indeed, rather perversely, one could turn the whole force of public choice analysis on privatization itself: The logic of concentrated benefits and diffuse costs makes it altogether likely that the diffuse efficiency gains of privatization will be sacrificed in the effort to satisfy the big stakeholders—incumbent politicians and bureaucrats and their allies and supporters.

Politically inspired privatization is all the more likely because privatization attracts support not only from economists with a disinterested belief in liberalized markets but also from a privatization lobby consisting of investment banking firms, government contractors, and other corporations whose businesses stand to benefit if the public sector cedes ground. Rather than being an escape from interest-group influence and the politicization of resource use, privatization is typically a prime example.

I do not want to suggest, however, that the view of politics as pure self-interest captures all that is going on, even in the case of privatization. Privatization is a worldwide policy movement carried along by a combination of objective forces, imitative processes, and international financial sponsorship. Many countries whose public sectors expanded sharply in recent decades now find themselves confronted by rising debt and strong resistance to higher taxes. Privatizing state-owned firms promises to bring some fiscal relief, particularly where the treasury has been heavily subsidizing unprofitable enterprises. Privatization may help both to cut expenditures and boost revenues, and by converting debt to equity states may improve the overall financial structure of their economies and reduce pressure for even less palatable austerity measures. Privatization is not the only possible response, but as in other institution-shaping movements, like the postwar proliferation of public enterprises, organizational forms spread by imitation. Institutional models are disseminated through a variety of political networks and the direct influence of international lending organizations. Privatization is now one of the policies that the International Monetary Fund promotes in negotiating loans with developing countries.

Of course, proponents of privatization see the process more as learning than as imitation or imposition. In their view, the poor performance of public enterprise and, more generally, overexpanded public sectors has simply taught that privatization makes sense. But experience is never so transparent. Even where state enterprises are generally agreed to be highly inefficient, it is not necessarily clear that privatization will be a remedy. Moreover, the performance of some state-owned enterprises—

for example, in Malaysia and France—has been excellent, and it is simply not true that as public sectors grow, rates of economic growth fall (Saunders, 1986; Kuttner, 1984). To be sure, the record of central government planning is dismal, but that experience cannot simply be extrapolated to all publicly owned organizations, particularly in states with more decentralized structures and more autonomous forms of public sector management.

The property rights approach predicts politically imposed inefficiency on the basis of public ownership alone, but the empirical variety of public sectors and state-owned enterprises in the world suggests instead that performance may be contingent on political culture, the structure of the state, and government policy toward public enterprises. In some countries public management is well-established, highly professional, and prestigious, whereas in others the political party in power expects to give its own people jobs at every level. The mode of public sector control depends also on the structure of political-administrative relationships. It is a mistake in this context to view the state as a unitary actor. Public sectors often comprise a vast sprawl of organizations in public ownership, many of them, like public universities in the United States, only loosely connected to the centers of political decision making. A great array of institutional devices, such as independent governing boards with self-perpetuating membership and earmarked financing, can serve to insulate public organizations from political intervention. In their legal status, public organizations variously include agencies under direct political authority, independent authorities incorporated under public law, state-owned enterprises incorporated under private law, and private companies in which the government has some ownership. Of course, the legal differences may or may not matter; autonomy is never guaranteed purely by formal structure. Finally, as a matter of policy, governments may or may not require particular public enterprises to be run on a commercial, business-like basis. Privatization may have little impact on the efficiency of organizations already operated on a commercial basis, and the effect of privatizing more "politicized" organizations depends on their previous political uses, some of which may be eminently defensible.

Political culture and preexisting administrative capacities are not unreasonable bases for choices about state versus private ownership. Where the state is the only domestic institution capable of sustaining the confidence of foreign creditors or administering large undertakings and where it has demonstrated management competence, the case for state enterprise may be correspondingly strong. On the other hand, in some regimes the penchant for political intervention produces endemic overstaffing, poor location of plants, extravagant wage concessions, and prices far out of line with market levels. Like alcoholics unable to cut down except by quitting altogether, these governments may be unable to avoid disrupting public enterprises, except by privatizing them altogether. Moreover, in much of the world, state enterprise gives the dominant elites too powerful a grip over civil society. For example, the Argentine military is said to use its huge network of industrial enterprises as an instrument of patronage and power. In such cases, privatization may well be justified as a means of releasing society from bureaucratic domination.

Whether the advanced capitalist societies suffer from too strong a bureaucratic grip is, of course, exactly where the right and left disagree. In this respect, the United States, which never nationalized industry in the first place, stands in a position fundamentally different from the Western European countries with extensive public enterprise sectors. The sphere of public ownership in the United States has been so limited that I find implausible the view that Americans suffer from an oppressive government role in the production of goods and services. Moreover, the relations between the public sector and political leadership are drastically different in the United States from those prevailing in Latin America, the Soviet bloc, and even many Western European countries. If political meddling is the chief problem in public sector organizations, the United States has an effective alternative to privatization in the establishment of public corporations (often called public authorities here). Their insulation from political control, the independence of the judiciary, and the decentralization of power in the federal system prevent public authorities from being easily bent by political caprice.

Indeed, the problems of the American public sector seem to be of the opposite kind. So deeply entrenched are the barriers to unitary control that legitimate interests in coordinated management are thwarted. American public institutions at all levels of government suffer from rampant credentialism and proceduralism that hamper the ability of managers to hire and fire, reward, and motivate their subordinates. Ironically, many of these rigidities result from previous reforms, passed in the name of curbing corruption. For a variety of reasons, public organizations also do not respond quickly to change, such as the emergence of new technologies and consumer demands. The long lead times required by the appropriations process often prevent agencies from adapting quickly. Privatization is one route out of the procedural thicket, but we might achieve some of the same ends by making public administration more flexible and giving public managers greater authority.

To be sure, government cannot be run "just like a business" in part because its more elaborate procedures are meant to produce something else besides the specific services that the private sector provides. Reviews by advisory committees and congressional hearings, designed to increase accountability or to give a fair hearing to complaints by clients, contractors, or employees, cannot be dismissed simply as a source of inefficiency. Democratic government cannot narrowly concern itself with getting the job done, which is one reason why it should not concern itself with all the jobs that need doing. Privatization is a legitimate tool for sharpening the focus of government on those activities most important to the general welfare, but it is never simply efficiency that is at stake in such decisions.

PRIVATIZATION AS A REORDERING OF CLAIMS

Privatization needs to be understood as a fundamental reordering of claims in a society. As I indicated earlier, in the liberal world the terms "public" and "private" sum up a whole structure of rules and expectations about the proper conduct and limits of the state. To say some activity is public is to invoke claims of public purpose, public accountability, and public disclosure. To say something is private is to claim protection from state officials and other citizens. The theory of property rights sees privatization as a reassignment of claims to the control and use of assets, but it misses the special claims of the public sphere in a democratic society—claims for greater disclosure of information, which should improve the social capacity to make choices, and for rights of participation and discussion, which permit the discovery and formation of preferences that are more consistent with long-term societal interests. As a general movement of institutional design, privatization undermines the foundation of claims for public purpose and public service.

This reordering of claims holds distributive implications. It shifts power to those who can more readily exercise power in the market. It may also shift income and wealth, depending on the specific form that policy takes. A shift from direct services to vouchers is one thing; government disengagement from social provision is quite another. Privatization does not logically require a reduction of public benefits to the poor. It is hypothetically possible to conceive of a privatization program with highly progressive effects on income distribution. Imagine, for example, a program involving the sale of heavily subsidized, poorly managed public enterprises; the conversion of a publicly budgeted health service, covering only a minority of employed workers, into a voucher system covering the whole population; and the empowerment of local nonprofit, grassroots organizations with funds stripped from elite-dominated central bureaucracies. Taken together, these steps would redistribute benefits to previously excluded or short-changed groups.

In practice, however, a progressive effect on income distribution seems highly improbable. The same political forces that support privatization generally also support cutbacks in public spending for social welfare; the same arguments about incentives and efficiency used in favor of privatizing public services are also cited by those who want to terminate public financing for the services altogether. In addition, private service providers often maximize profits, not by producing services more efficiently, but by seeking out the least costly clients or by employing lower-wage workers, often on a part-time basis. Since wages tend to be more equal in the public sector, privatization is likely to skew income in the direction of greater inequality. Furthermore, while unions have lost ground in the private sector, they have generally made advances in organizing public employees. Privatization tends to undermine those gains—an effect not overlooked by advocates of privatization.

In the extreme case, privatization is an instrument of class politics. Where privatization is used to break up public employee unions and reduce the provision of services, it effectively represents a means of reordering class relations. Privatization in Chile in the mid-1970s had this character. A vast shift in wealth took place with the privatization not only of industry but of the financial assets of the social security system, which ended up concentrated in the hands of a few private financial groups (Foxley, 1983). At the other extreme, privatization is a relatively modest tool of public management. In many cases of contracting, the private firms receiving contracts are as unionized as the public sector and there is no change in wage levels. If a city privatizes its buses, but the drivers continue to be represented by the same union, service costs are unlikely to change (Bailey, 1987). But this is scarcely what privatization advocates are looking for. While privatization hypothetically does not mean wage reductions, the intentions behind the policy raise strong and entirely reasonable suspicions that it will.

Privatization is not only a policy; it is also a signal about the competence and desirability of pubic provision. It reinforces the view that government cannot be expected to perform well. If, to many Americans, private means better, it is partly because of long-existing restrictions on the scope and quality of public provision. We commonly limit public services to a functional minimum and thereby guarantee that people will consider the private alternative a step up. This niggardliness shows itself in ways large and small. In the 1960s one congressman who was indignant over the costs of a public housing program succeeded in persuading his colleagues specifically to forbid flower boxes as an unnecessary extravagance.[5] The restricted quality of public provision is a self-reinforcing feature. Because the poor are the principal beneficiaries of many programs, the middle-class public opposes expenditures to produce as high a quality of service as they must pay for privately; and because the quality is held down, the poor as well as the middle class develop a contempt for the

---

[5] I owe this story to Lester Thurow.

public sector and an eagerness to escape it. The movement toward privatization reflects and promotes this contempt, and therein lies part of its political danger.

Some individual proposals for privatization have considerable merit, but the overall message is clearly to call into doubt the nation's capacity and need for collective provision. The possibilities for change being discussed are not symmetrical. Privatization raises questions exclusively about the adequacy of the public sector; the comparable questions about the private sector do not receive the same attention. Even though privatization is logically distinct from questions of distributive justice, the one-sidedness of the privatization debate puts the advocates of more generous public programs entirely on the defensive. This one-sidedness is why I feel obliged to say I am opposed to privatization. I am opposed to the political consequences that are likely to flow from pursuing privatization as a solution to the difficulties of administering democratic government.

Privatization, as some advocates themselves point out, represents an effort to alter the conditions of political competition by breaking up the coalitions supporting public provision and by promoting more market-oriented political values. In other words, it is an attempt to fix in place the conservative orientation that has emerged forcefully in the 1980s. No one need doubt that public institutions, like private ones, are bases of wealth and power. They are environments that encourage those who work within them to develop different political orientations. To alter the public/private balance is to change the distribution of material and symbolic resources influencing the shape of political life. Privatization ought to be frankly recognized as part of an effort of conservatives to reinforce their own power position. Since I do not share the values for which that power is deployed, I distrust privatization. Ultimately I fear that one form of privatization does entail another—that as we move public provision into the private sector, we move from the realm of the open and visible into a domain that is more closed to scrutiny and access. And in the process, whether or not intending to change, we are likely to narrow our involvements, interests, and vision of a good society and a good life.

References

Ahlbrandt, Roger S., Jr. 1973. "Efficiency in the Provision of Fire Services." *Public Choice* 16: 1–15.

Alchian, Armen. 1965. "Some Economies of Property Rights." *Il Politico* 30: 816–829.

de Alessi, Louis. 1987. "Property Rights and Privatization." In Hanke, 1987: 24–35.

Ariès, Philippe. 1962. *Centuries of Childhood*. New York: Vintage.

Bailey, Robert W. 1987. "Uses and Misuses of Privatization." In Hanke, 1987: 138–152.

Baumol, William J., John C. Panzar, and Robert D. Willig. 1982. *Contestable Markets and the Theory of Industry Structure*. San Diego, Ca.: Harcourt Brace Jovanovich.

Bendick, Marc, Jr. 1982. "Privatization of Public Services: Recent Experience." In Harvey Brooks et al., eds. *Public-private Partnerships*: 153–171. Cambridge, Mass.: Ballinger.

Bennett, John T., and Manuel H. Johnson. 1979. "Public Versus Private Provision of Collective Goods and Services: Garbage Collection Revisited." *Public Choice* 34: 55–64.

Berger, Peter L., and Richard John Neuhaus. 1977. *To Empower People: The Role of Mediating Structures in Public Policy*. Washington, D.C.: American Enterprise Institute.

Borcherding, Thomas, ed. 1977. *Budgets and Bureaucrats: The Source of Government Growth*. Durham, N.C.: Duke University Press.

Braun, Randolph. 1975. "Taxation, Sociopolitical Structure, and State-Building: Great Britain and Brandenburg-Prussia." In Charles Tilly, ed. *The Formation of National States in Western Europe*: 243–327. Princeton, N.J.: Princeton University Press.

Brittan, Samuel. 1985. "The Politics and Economics of Privatisation." *Political Quarterly* 55: 109–127.

Brodkin, Evelyn, and Dennis Young. 1989. "The Political Economy of Privatization." In this volume.

Butler, Stuart M. 1985. *Privatizing Federal Spending: A Strategy to Eliminate the Deficit*. New York: Universe.

Davies, David G. 1971. "The Efficiency of Public Versus Private Firms: The Case of Australia's Two Airlines." *Journal of Law and Economics* 14: 149–165.

Demsetz, Harold. 1967. "Toward a Theory of Property Rights." *American Economic Review* 57: 347–359.

Donnison, David. 1984. "The Progressive Potential of Privatisation." In Julian Le Grand and Ray Robinson, ed. *Privatisation and the Welfare State*: 45–57. London: George Allen & Unwin.

Douglas, James. 1983. *Why Charity?* Beverly Hills, Ca.: Sage Publications.

Ellefson, Paul, Sally Palm, and David Lothner. 1982. "From Public Land to Non-industrial Private Forest: A Minnesota Case Study." *Journal of Forestry* (April).

Elshtain, Jean Bethke. 1981. *Public Man, Private Woman*. Princeton, N.J.: Princeton University Press.

Ferrara, Peter J. 1985. "Social Security and the Super IRA: A Populist Proposal." In Peter J. Ferrara, ed. *Social Security: Prospects for Real Reform*: 193–220. Washington, D.C.: Cato Institute.

Fontana, Andre. "Armed Forces and Neo-conservative Ideology: State-shrinking in Argentina, 1976-81." In William P. Glade, ed. *State Shrinking: A Comparative Inquiry into Privatization*: 62–74. Austin, Tex.: Institute for Latin American Studies, University of Texas at Austin.

Foxley, Alejandro. 1983. *Latin American Experiments in Neoconservative Economics*. Berkeley, Ca.: University of California Press.

Freeman, Alan, and Betty Mensch. 1988. "The Public-prvate Distinction in American Law and Life." *Tikkun* 3 (March–April): 24–30.

Frug, Gerald E. 1980. "The City as a Legal Concept." *Harvard Law Review* 93: 1059–1154.

Furubotn, Eirik G., and Svetozar Pejovich. 1972. "Property Rights and Economic Theory: A Survey of Recent Literature." *Journal of Economic Literature* 10: 1137–1162.

———. 1974. *The Economics of Property Rights*. Cambridge, Mass.: Ballinger.

Galbraith, John Kenneth. 1958. *The Affluent Society*. Boston: Houghton Mifflin.

Glade, William P. 1986. "Sources and Forms of Privatization." In William P. Glade, ed. *State Shrinking: A Comparative Inquiry into Privatization*: 2–23. Austin, Tex.: Institute for Latin American Studies, University of Texas at Austin.

Goodman, John C. 1985. "Private Alternatives to Social Security: The Experience of Other Countries." In Peter J. Ferrara, ed. *Social Security: Prospects for Real Reform*: 103–116. Washington, D.C.: Cato Institute.

Hanke, Steve H., ed. 1987. *Prospects for Privatization*. New York: Academy of Political Science.

Hanke, Steve H., and Barney Dowdle. 1987. "Privatizing the Public Domain." In Hanke, 1987: 114–123.

Hardin, Garrett. 1968. "The Tragedy of the Commons." *Science* 162: 1245–1248.

Hirschman, Albert O. 1970. *Exit, Voice and Loyalty*. Cambridge, Mass.: Harvard University Press.

———. 1982. *Shifting Involvements: Private Interest and Public Action*. Princeton, N.J.: Princeton University Press.

Holmes, Stephen. 1984. *Benjamin Constant and the Making of the Modern Liberalism*. New Haven, Conn.: Yale University Press.

Horwitz, Morton J. 1982. "The History of the Public/private Distinction." *University of Pennsylvania Law Review* 130: 1423–1428.

Huntington, Samuel P., Michael Crozier, and Joji Watanuki. 1975. *The Crisis of Democracy*. New York: New York University Press.

Imray, Linda, and Audrey Middleton. 1983. "Public and Private: Marking the Boundaries." In Eva Gamarinkow et al., ed. *The Public and the Private*: 12–27. London: Heineman.

Kay, John, Colin Mayer, and David Thompson, eds. 1987. *Privatisation and Regulation: The UK Experience*. Oxford: Clarendon Press.

Kelman, Steven. 1987. "Why Public Ideas Matter." In Reich, 1987: 31–54.

Kennedy, Duncan. 1982. "The States of the Decline of the Public/private Distinction." *University of Pennsylvania Law Review* 130: 1349–1357.

Klare, Karl E. 1982. "The Public/private Distinction in Labor Law." *University of Pennsylvania Law Review* 130: 1358–1422.

Krutilla, John V. et al. 1983. "Public versus Private Ownership: The Federal Lands Case." *Journal of Policy Analysis and Management* 2: 548–558.

Kuttner, Robert. 1984. *The Economic Illusion: False Choices Between Prosperity and Social Justice*. Boston: Houghton Mifflin.

Mayer, Colin, and Shirley Meadowcroft. 1987. "Selling Public Assets: Techniques and Financial Implications." In Kay, Mayer, and Thompson, 1987: 322–340.

Musgrave, Richard A. 1981. "Leviathan Cometh—Or Does He?" In Helen F. Ladd and T. Nicolaus Tideman, ed. *Tax and Expenditure Limitations*: 77–120. Washington, D.C.: Urban Institute Press.

Musolf, Lloyd D., and Harold Seidman. 1980. "The Blurred Boundaries of Public Administration." *Public Administration Review* 40: 124–130.

Niskanen, William. 1971. *Bureaucracy and Representative Government*. Chicago: Aldine-Atherton.

O'Higgins, Michael. 1986. "Public-private Interaction and Pensions Provision." In Lee Rainwater and Martin Rein, eds. *The Public-private Interplay in Social Protection*. Armonk, N.Y.: M. E. Sharpe.

Orren, Gary. 1987. "Beyond Self-interest." In Reich, 1987: 13–29.

Reich, Robert, ed. 1987. *The Power of Public Ideas*. Cambridge, Mass.: Ballinger.

Rosaldo, Michelle Zimbalist. 1974. "Woman, Culture and Society: A Theoretical Overview." In Michelle Zimbalist Rosaldo and Louise Lamphere, eds. *Woman, Culture and Society*. Stanford: Stanford University Press.

Runge, Carlisle Ford. 1984. "The Fallacy of 'Privatization'," *Journal of Contemporary Studies* (Winter): 3–17.

Salamon, Lester M. 1986. "Partners in Public Service: Toward a Theory of Government-Nonprofit Relations." In Walter W. Powell, ed. *The Nonprofit Sector: A Research Handbook*: 99–117. New Haven, Conn.: Yale University Press.

Saunders, Peter. 1986. "Public Expenditure and Economic Performance in OECD Countries." *Journal of Public Policy* 5: 1–21.

Savas, E. S. 1987. *Privatization: The Key to Better Government*. Chatham, N.J.: Chatham House.

Sennett, Richard. 1977. *The Fall of Public Man*. New York: Knopf.

Simmel, Georg. 1950. "The Secret and the Secret Society." In Kurt H. Wolff, ed. *The Sociology of George Simmel*: 306–376. New York: Free Press.

Smith, Robert J. 1981. "Resolving the Tragedy of the Commons by Creating Private Property Rights in Wildlife." *Cato Journal* 1: 507–517.

———. 1982. "Privatizing the Environment." *Policy Review* 20: 11–50.

Starr, Paul. 1987. "The Limits of Privatization." In Hanke, 1987: 124–137.

———. 1988a. "Response to Freeman and Mensch." *Tikkun* 3 (March–April): 31.

———. 1988b. "Social Security and the American Public Household." In Theodore R. Marmor and Jerry L. Mashaw, eds. *Social Security: Beyond the Rhetoric of Crisis*: 119–148. Studies from the Project on the Federal Social Role. Princeton, N.J.: Princeton University Press.

———. Forthcoming. "Television and the Public Household." In Michael Rice, ed. *Television in America's Future—A Search for the Right Public Policy*.

Walsh, Annmarie Hauck. 1980. *The Public's Business: The Politics and Practices of Government Corporations*. Cambridge, Mass.: MIT Press.

Webber, Carolyn, and Aaron Wildavsky. 1986. *A History of Taxation and Expenditure in the Western World*. New York: Simon and Schuster.

Weber, Max. 1968. *Economy and Society*. Guenther Roth and Claus Wittich, eds. New York: Bedminster.

Wolf, Charles, Jr. 1979. "A Theory of Non-market Failures." *The Public Interest* 55: 114–133.

Yarrow, George. 1986. "Privatization in Theory and Practice." *Economic Policy* 2: 324–377.

Young, Michael, and Peter Willmott. 1973. *The Symmetrical Family*. New York: Pantheon.

2

The Social Structure of Institutions: Neither Public nor Private

MARTIN REIN

My thesis is that the modern institutions of social protection are neither public nor private in any unambiguous meanings of those terms. The increasing fuzziness of the boundaries and the implications of this blurring are among the major issues in the future development of social welfare in society. These mixed institutional forms must be understood conceptually if we are to understand and design social policy effectively.

My focus is on social services rather than income support, because of the greater complexity of the former. My argument, however, is generalizable to income support and across service sectors.

Intellectual Perspectives on Services

By and large, the literature portrays services in a dualist mode of thinking. What these theories have in common is the idea of a clear separation of parts, which arises because—although there is interaction among the parts—each is driven by a unique organizing principle that gives it its special character. Although I use the word dualist for convenience, three or more segments can be included in the argument without altering the essential nature of the theoretical principles on which this type of argument is premised. Streeck and Schmitter's work clearly illustrates this approach. They argue that three models seem to have virtually dominated philosophical speculation and social science thought. They tend to be identified by the central institution that embodies (and enforces) their respective and distinctive guiding principles: the Community, the Market, and the State (or the Bureaucracy)—although it might be more accurate to label them according to the principles themselves: spontaneous solidarity, dispersed competition, and hierarchical control (1984, pp. 1–2).

Implicit in this type of argument is a posing of the issues which assumes that separation of private from public provision in some sense is the essential or critical distinction that must inform our analysis. Both the liberal and the sociological world views depend on the separation of markets from politics. Dualist thought rejects a more holistic view that focuses on how the parts penetrate and influence each other, not as separate entities but as a unified process.

Public and Private

Since separation of the public and the private sectors and the theme of privatization animates current discussion of service systems, let us start our discussion with this important dichotomy. The underlying assumption is clear: that the government is different from the rest of the world and that a sharp demarcation between government and the other institutions of society can be systematically drawn. When we think of extreme examples, the assumption is not only plausible but self-evident. But when we leave extremes we have more trouble. As Christopher Hood (1984, p. 3) observes in a thoughtful analysis of paragovernmental organization, which includes the nonprofit sector, "To explore the world of para-government . . . is to raise both conceptual and constitutional issues as to how the boundaries of government are to be perceived or defined."

What precisely is government? A surprising answer is proposed by the International Monetary Fund (IMF) in its study of government financing. This five-year-old effort highlights some of the conceptual ambiguities inherent in this question by defining government by its functions. The functions are described as producing nonmarket goods and services and transfer income, which the government pays for primarily with compulsory levies on other sectors. This definition is troubling in that all forms of collective security that do not involve market goods and services are treated as governmental in nature. Such a definition has the obvious advantage of avoiding the problem posed by those situations when government subcontracts to the nonprofit sectors to run its service system. On the other hand, it introduces a daunting new problem. Taken seriously, the definition also implies that households—which provide nonmarket goods and services—must be included in the definition of government. But the household is conventionally regarded as the cornerstone of the private sector. Thus the IMF's efforts to solve one problem produce an even more intractable conceptual puzzle.

Recent efforts by the Organization for Economic Cooperation and Development (OECD) to develop a much broader definition of government encounter other problems. This broader definition includes public enterprises and institutions, public-sector lending and loan guarantees to private borrowers, tax expenditures, and government regulation. The dilemma that arises from this more encompassing concept is clear: The more we press for a definition of government that takes into account its indirect as well as its direct role in the economy—especially as that role is played out through its effects on regulation and the structure of pricing— the less useful becomes the simplistic distinction between the market and the state. Since regulation is the legal recognition of entitlement to economic resources, it must be understood as a part of the "new property" available to individuals. It also shapes the performance of institutions. For example, "The state regulates construction both in private and public hospitals, on the grounds that public funds, in the form of federal, state and private health insurance programs, pay for virtually all capital improvements" (*New York Times*, April 2, 1985, p. B–10). As soon as one enters the field of government regulation, there is scarcely an area of modern economic life able to avoid the direct or indirect influence of government. But if government is everywhere, then we can no longer separate it from nongovernment. Thus, this new convention has the unintended effect of blurring the distinction between the public and the private sectors that the current conventional definition sought to establish.

We can accept, of course, a narrow definition of public (the core of government). This has the advantage of permitting us to draw a clear demarcation between public and private, but it has the disadvantage of excluding much of what we know government is also about. If, however, we also try to understand the multiple roles of government, then we must accept that the definition of government is not merely a social fact, but a social convention. We must also recognize that between government and private must lie a much murkier third terrain that is both public and private. Perhaps modern industrial society is best characterized by the expansion of this fuzzy and ill-defined territory. While there may be problems in establishing a formal definition that unambiguously separates the public and private sector, these problems may not be important if we can establish a clear picture of how the two sectors work in practice. But even here we encounter a rather lively debate between those who see development as state-led and those who see it as market-led (Lindblom, 1977). Like most dualist theories, these also are based on an oversimplification, as we shall see.

In the state-led model, government actively and intentionally makes use of the private interests to achieve governmental aims. Government may directly provide the service itself, or it may actively work through intermediaries, sometimes called paragovernmental organizations. Why should the government choose to do business through these peripheral agencies? In answer, Hood (1984, pp. 8–12) offers five interpretations of what he calls "top-down government." I list them in his rather colorful terms, giving real-world examples of each:

1. "Black motivations," where the government wants to keep its activity secret and uses "front organizations" to avoid detection. The marketing and selling of military equipment is an example, but there may be parallels in social services as well.

2. "Passing the poisoned chalice" to outsiders as a way of taking the political heat off the core institutions of government. Here private institutions are especially useful to deal with controversial questions where government doesn't want to assume the front-line responsibility. Birth-control programs are an obvious example.

3. Bypassing government's stultifying effect on initiative and risk taking. The American War on Poverty was largely motivated by the desire to bypass state government, which was at that time widely interpreted as inhibiting innovation (federalism by contract). But such bypassing of other levels of government was not stable over time. By the 1980s state government became the major conduit for the flow of federal funds through the block-grant program. The state agencies continue to work through these buffer organizations, but the earlier purpose of encouraging risk taking and innovation may no longer apply (state and city contracting).

4. Mobilizing supplementary consent for government action—the well-known device for co-opting interest groups. For example, physicians are given the responsibility for administering a program to ward off their opposition to new legislation.

5. "Load-shedding" of governmental activities. Shedding of the governmental role may either be symbolic (that is, arising from a desire to hide the level of government expenses through subcontracting) or substantive with the intention of devolving administration to independent bodies. For example, the British conservative government discovered after the election of 1983 that the only way to honor its commitment to expand the National Health Service was to increase the number of personnel because health services are so labor intensive. But the government was also committed to decreasing the level of government employment. Subcontracting hospital maintenance, food, and other services to the private sector was one way it could realize this objective. Of course, contracting out could be motivated by the desire to increase efficiency in risk taking.

In the market-led model the starting point is somewhat different, namely, that societies are organized around interests. Sometimes these interests are so strong that a central government cannot effectively function without taking their preferences into account. In an extreme form, seen in some European countries as well as in some cities in the United States, the welfare state seems to exist to serve these private interests. This is especially true in societies that are deeply divided by religion or region. This form of extreme segmentation has been described as "pillarization." Discussing pillarization in Belgium, Jan Vranken (1986, p. 2) offers the following thoughtful observations:

> Pillarization helps to explain why up to now these organizations continue to play an important role in policy making on and in the daily administration of the welfare state provisions, even when the latter have meanwhile been subsidized, made compulsory, guaranteed or financed by the State. For Belgium, one might even argue that not the political authorities but the pillarized organizations have been the prime policy agents, and that not the State as such has been made responsible for providing the Welfare State provisions, but that it has merely been given the responsibility of enabling the organizations concerned to run the Welfare State.

It is not the state that intrudes into civil political learning, but the other way around.

Are these nondominance models a residual category, or are they perhaps the most common way that service systems do business? If the latter is so, we have again discovered the fuzzy demarcation of how the different parts function in practice. We do not have a good understanding of how these models work themselves out in practice, although we can certainly point to examples of each type in both Europe and the United States.

Informal Versus Formal

Informal sectors can be described by the central institution (kin, family, friends, and community) and by the guiding principle these institutions work through, namely, spontaneous solidarity, affection, duty, mutual respect, and so forth. By contrast, the formal institutions are governed by the principle of either dispersed competition (in the case of markets), or hierarchical control (in the case of the state). Theories about the relationship between the formal and the informal caring systems are of two types—those that accept the thesis of substitution between these systems and those that assume that the systems are complementary.

An example of the former is the line of argument that describes the informal care system as the backbone of the "invisible welfare state." When a country spends little on social security, according to this argument, it tends to levy the burden of social care on women (Sundstrom, 1981). The work of care and home production is seen to be mainly women's work. The invisible welfare state becomes visible once there is a movement of women from the informal into the formal economy, after which they no longer perform their historic role to the same extent. The coresidence of aged persons with their children is an example. Shared households often provide the elderly with a higher standard of living; they also create a lower standard of living for everyone else. When the caretaking is eroded, however, as in the case of women entering the formal economy, then the care shifts to formal institutions. According to this theory, it is the pool of caretaking women that influences the size and growth of public social security spending. In this sense, one system substitutes for the other.

The argument has been extended by conservative analysts who favor the expansion of these mediating institutions as well as some formal institutions like the church. They argue that the expansion of the state power is inherently antagonistic to the vitality of the informal sector.

An example of the second type of argument is that the informal care system is essential to the realization of the goals of formal organizations (Litwak, 1985). Informal organizations are particularly needed in three situations: where the tasks to be performed are not predictable, where they are not subdividable, and where there are many contingencies that need to be taken into account. Not all primary groups, however, can be treated as homogeneous. The basic argument is that it is possible to develop a typology of the differences in structure among these primary groups and to match them with the unique services needed to deal with nonuniform events that these informal groups can provide. Moreover, the classification of groups and tasks is based on the same dimension. Thus groups can optimally manage those tasks that are congruent with their structure. Most tasks cannot be fully realized unless formal and informal institutions work cooperatively, because these tasks have uniform and nonuniform dimensions. For example, medical care requires doctors to handle technical problems while primary groups provide emergency first aid, initial diagnosis, and preventive care (Litwak, 1985). Formal organizations are not well equipped to deal with unpredictable events. If an individual has a stroke, which is an unpredictable event, then the informal care system must come into play either to take the victim to the hospital or call an ambulance. The work of a professional specialist comes later. The elaborate system of medical care provided in the formal system is of no use if the individual never arrives in the hospital in the first instance. The more the functions of the informal sector are taken over by the formal sector, the more important is the complementary role of the informal sector.

The interplay between formal and informal care of the elderly is often forgotten by makers of policy that give large resources to substitutes for the family, but only minor support to families. At the same time there is a lot of moralizing about the supposed lack of informal care in the modern family . . . These two kinds of care are interdependent; the one cannot be successful without the support of the other.

Once again the dualist approach is an oversimplification. In this case, however, a theory has been developed that takes explicit account of an important hybrid form.

BETWEEN FORMAL AND INFORMAL: THE LOCAL AMATEUR ECONOMY

The local amateur economy model is most clearly developed in the important but neglected work of Roger Krohn (1977). Krohn developed the theory of the "other" economy in low-cost housing. Housing rent must be understood as not only the purchase of a place to live, but also the purchase of a wide range of services (heating, plumbing, and so on). Krohn argues that there are two economies for the provision of these services. One he calls the professional national economy, and the other the local amateur economy. The professional economy is "conducted by economic sophisticates seeking financial gain through bargained contracts." By contrast, the other economy is private, local, and not legally protected. It is conducted by amateurs who, by avoiding cash outlays where possible, also avoid nationally set interest and wage rates. By using their own resources of capital and especially labor, and sometimes by exchanging labor, skills, information, and advice with relatives and friends, they often provide themselves (and their tenants) with far better housing than could be purchased conventionally (Krohn, 1977, p. 5).

Krohn is proposing a quasi-proprietary model that is a cross between the informal and the proprietary sectors. His study of Britain in the 1960s showed that despite government's efforts to create incentives for housing reconstruction, very few persons were taking advantage of these incentives. Many of the owners were widows, and they did not act as economic "man" is supposed to act. They were members of Krohn's local amateur economy, providing a housing service that was cheap, not up to standards, highly personalized, semi-monetized (that is, not based on the cost of capital in the competitive market, and involving the labor costs of the owner and sweat equity of the tenant). In this model low-cost housing services are achieved because the provider subsidizes part of the cost of the care, largely because he or she does not act as an economic maximizer. When the system is transformed into the for-profit market, or even nonprofit care, the cost will rise.

The Krohn model is generalizable to many service systems other than housing. Many policy analysts, however, fail to distinguish the professional and the amateur proprietary economy and are critical of the entry of capitalism into the service system. The typical argument is that capitalists, acting out of self-interest and the desire to make money, provide inappropriate services at inflated costs and thus represent a threat to the delivery of quality services (Gilbert, 1983).

GOVERNMENT VERSUS NONPROFIT

The bulk of theorizing about the nonprofit/government split is focused on trying to understand the existence of the nonprofit sector and is conventionally presented as a three-sector theory: government, economic or market institutions, and nonprofits. It is possible to identify two schools of thought.

Musgrave (1980) argues that there is no well-developed theory of social goods that can provide a consensual rationale for government's role either as provider or as employer. There is no theory that tells us whether the government itself should undertake the production of such goods and services, or whether it should purchase them from para-public institutions or private firms. He asserts that, "There is no unique feature around which such a theory could be constructed" (pp. 9–10). Salamon (1984) echoes the same disenchantment, identifying five strands of thought that bear on the question, but none provides an adequate theory.

Other analysts, such as Burton Weisbrod (1977) and Henry Hansmann (1980), are much more optimistic that such a theory exists. Weisbrod argues that nonprofit organizations are the outgrowth of both market and government failures. Governments by and large provide services only when there is a demand by a relatively large constituency for these services. Before such demand can be fully developed, the nonprofit institutions provide a unique role in generating the demand for limited clienteles. Eventually, as the demand expands sufficiently, the program is transferred to the public domain.

Hansmann advances a somewhat different theory. Whereas Weisbrod stresses the provision of collective services without full majority support, Hansmann focuses on "contract failure"—where the consumer cannot evaluate the service effectively and thus needs to be protected by the provider. He explains, "The advantage of a nonprofit producer is that the discipline of the market is supplemented by the additional protection given the consumer by another, broader 'contract', the organization's legal commitment to devote its entire earnings to the production of services. As a result of this institutional constraint, it is less imperative for the consumer either to shop around first or to enforce rigorously the contract he makes" (p. 844). Hansmann elaborates the theory of contract failure and tries to show its practical implications.

These theories, which try to assign special standing to nonprofit organizations that are separated from the public and market sectors, either are not convincing or provide evidence of substantial blurring. First, although 35 percent of the overall revenue of nonprofits comes from the federal government, the proportion varies by types of services. For social services, it is as high as 58 percent (Salamon, 1984). Three different tools of government are employed in allocating federal resources: direct grants by the federal government, subcontracting, and reimbursement to individuals for their purchase of service. Reimbursement is the most important tool in health, whereas contracting is more important for social services. Second, all the tools of government require that the nonprofit agencies conform to governmentally imposed standards, which vary in oversight, to insure compliance. But the more the government seeks accountability, the less the autonomy of the nonprofit sector. The erosion of autonomy blurs the boundaries between sectors. More than blurring is involved when policy initiation, financing, audit and oversight, and administration are divided across levels of government and sectors. What is also at issue is governability and the inherent contradictions implicit in this division of labor.

Nielsen (1979) argues that the survival and operation of nonprofits have been thrust into an agonizing transition, a process that is now advanced, but not yet quite complete. "The crucial consequence of these events has been the dissolution of whatever boundaries may have existed in the past" (pp. 184 and 187). Not only the boundary between public and nonprofit has become fuzzy, but also the demarcation of nonprofit and market. In the scramble for resources, exacerbated but not caused by the new concern over fiscal constraint, nonprofits have embraced the principle of cross-subsidization (that is, financing with profits from some services, those services that are nonprofitable). With profits subsidizing nonprofits, the arenas of ambiguity become ever more confusing. Estelle James (1983, p. 359) summarizes the problem as follows:

> As nonprofit organizations face the task of delivering more services, some may find themselves devoting so much effort and energy to their profit-making activities as to alter their fundamental character. Paradoxically, they may operate more like profit-maximizing firms even as they are expected to take on more governmental functions.

Beyond Dualism

As the preceding discussion indicates, dualist theories, rather than elucidating our understanding of the service system, in fact inhibit it. This is because they cannot accommodate institutional realities that are gray areas where the two (or three) parts of a system that the theories take as

separate, in fact overlap. It is also usually the case that those parts that
are identified are narrowly conceived as part of an implicit normative argument that overtly or tacitly is a form of advocacy pleading for the identified segment.

One can see how dualist thinking is born. It starts with the insight that
we can better grasp the infinite complexity of the world by simplifying
the modelings of it into different, separable parts: economy as separate
from society, the private domain as separate from the public. But one can
also see the blurring of the boundaries that dualism fought to establish.

When we contrast dualist theories against an account of institutional
reality, we find that the confrontation with reality destabilizes the dualist
argument. This forces us to invent additional segments that, at the least,
acknowledge the blurring of the elements on which the dualist thesis is
premised. But acknowledging the blurring and going no further is unsat-
isfactory. We must find a way to put some satisfactory structure on the
reality we see.

I propose a two-step process by which we can go beyond blurring: (1)
combine most of the elements of dualism into a broader framework that
builds on the insights of dualist categories without their assumptions; and
(2) assign to government a special standing, one that accepts the intru-
siveness of the state into civil society, not as a normative proposition, not
as a theory of governance, but simply as an acknowledgment of the way
things are.

I would like to start with the dominant historical conceptualization of
the provision of social protection, which dates back to the nineteenth century and was conceived in the context of income security. This is the metaphor of three pillars: a *public pillar*, where government acts directly to
administer and also to finance income support according to some principle of social responsibility; a *personal pillar*, where the individual assumes primary responsibility for asset accumulation (using financial institutions like banks, life insurance, or the real estate market) and the
state plays a minimal role; and a mixed sector, conventionally referred to
as the *private pillar*, where the state acts to influence the behavior of private, profit, and nonprofit enterprises. It does so directly and also indirectly via its capacity to regulate and subsidize the institutions in civil
society. In the field of income support, the major actor within the private
pillar is the firm, acting in the role of employer. Each society creates and
combines these pillars in different ways.

The metaphor that social policy should rest on these three pillars is a
widely accepted ideology in most industrial societies. Its symbolic power
rests on its ability to provide the normative grounding for a division of
labor between the public, personal, and private sectors.

As a stylized picture of social protection, it has certain weaknesses. Although it holds up reasonably well with respect to income support, it does less well with respect to services. Further, the pillars have changed in our time. In particular, some new and potentially important personal pillars—for example, asset accumulation schemes like the Individual Retirement Account (IRA)—are not included in the internationally accepted convention that defines social protection. Finally, although historically the requirements of the private pillar influenced the policies acceptable in the public pillar, the nature of current public policies shapes the size, character, and growth of the private pillar. The state penetrates the private and personal pillars, and reactions within the private and personal pillars cannot be ignored in the actions taken by the state. Thus, the image of stable and free-standing pillars is misleading.

We can keep the image of pillars (or sectors, or segments), however, as long as we supplement it with equally compelling images of penetration and overlap. If we are aware of the limits of our symbolism we can productively proceed.

I find it useful to visualize these pillars as comprising an outer and inner circle. In the outer circle are the pillars on which the private service system rests. In the inner circle is government making use of its tools as best it can. We cannot assume, of course, that government uses these tools to realize a policy objective. Power, tradition, and many other factors play a critical role in why and how government uses these tools. But the outcome, whether through intention or inadvertence, is shaped by government penetration of the institutions in the outer circle. Government can, of course, also be the captive of the outer circle, serving the interests of the private pillar.

THE OUTER CIRCLE: THE BLURRING OF PRIVATE SERVICE FINANCING AND DELIVERY

We can identify at least five pillars on which the outer, private service systems rest: (1) nonprofit organizations, which in turn can be subdivided into professional nonprofit and voluntary nonprofit (the latter relying primarily on volunteers for their staffing); (2) proprietary institutions, which can also be further subdivided into (a) self-employed professional, (b) commercial national chains, and (c) local amateur enterprises; (3) employer-based services (such as counseling, day-care, medical, information and referral, and recreational services directly provided by the firm in which an individual is employed); (4) informal groups (including kinship, neighborhood, friends, self-help, and the like); and finally (5) gray- or black-market social services. The services themselves are not illegal. Their character is gray because they are not administered in full compliance with legal rules. That is, the service providers fail to pay taxes, minimum wages, conform to licensing regulations, and so forth.

Very little attention has been given to the blurring of boundaries within the domain we conventionally refer to as the private sector. I want in this section to make plausible the thesis that even in this terrain there is considerable blurring, much of which is inadvertently brought about by the activities of government.

We can enter the circle at any point. If we start with nonprofit institutions, we find a fascinating pattern where the survival of nonprofit infrastructure seems to depend on its ability to incorporate some proprietary elements such as fee charging. But with the reduction of federal spending, a new and aggressive policy of cross-subsidization has emerged. Cross-subsidization, simply put, means that an agency makes a profit in one part of its operation in order to finance or subsidize another part of its services. Of course, joint production of services makes it difficult to disentangle who is paying for what. Some scholars have tried to document that the fee structure of nonprofit hospitals is redistributive among patients receiving certain services (that is, some patients pay more than the cost of the service). Critics of this practice argue that ". . . those who control the nonprofit hospital exploit the vulnerability of consumers as potential taxpayers. They charge for hospital services at rates that allow some funds to be directed toward research, teaching, favored patients, and favored departments of the hospital; they do not advertise or fully disclose this practice; and they do not give consumers any choice in the matter . . ." (James, 1983, p. 357).

But the practice is more general than redistribution within the enterprise. Indeed, a new phenomenon has emerged. Private for-profit organizations are acting as consultants to nonprofit organizations, advising them how "to become self-sustaining" by developing "New Ventures" (the actual name of one such organization) that permit them to convert their historic assets into current income by profitable market investments.

Many observers have pointed out that self-employed professionals whose profit takes the form of high salaries have a large stake in the existence of nonprofit institutions. This is especially true in the case of the privileges hospitals grant to admitting physicians. In its simplest form, this argument asserts "that the tax treatment and favored legal status of nonprofit hospitals exist in part because they support the economic interests of private physicians." And the argument continues, "citizens and policy makers have been deceived into favoring an organizational structure [nonprofit] that benefits one group—physicians—without providing any net benefit to society at large" (Bays, 1983, p. 377).

The field of housing policy offers yet another example of how public policy contributes to the growth of profit-making operations within the nonprofit pillar. Certain nonprofit housing ventures, such as the Boston Housing Partnership, could make their programs fiscally sound only if they could sell tax shelters. But only a profit-making subsidiary, according to the tax laws, had the legal right to sell such shelters (Robb, 1985).

This brief account of blurring in the nonprofit pillar illustrates how the institutional reality is more complicated than the theory that seeks to assign to this pillar a single overarching principle of organization. The deeper our understanding of each pillar is, the more we can appreciate the scope of blurring. As we extend this argument to the other pillars, further conceptual refinement will be needed if we are to understand the performance of pillars and distinguish terms such as overlapping and parallel functions, and complementary and competitive tasks.

Consider the proprietary pillar. We have already suggested how in some interpretations the self-employed professionals make use of the nonprofit pillar in their service of profit maximization, which takes the form of improved salary position. The argument applies beyond medical care. For example, a profession like social work, which is deeply committed to collective or social purposes, also has an equally strong commitment to the self-employed professional practitioner. Here the tension between governing principles of proprietary and collective ideals contributes to blurring and even suggests a different approach for the analysis of professional practice. By contrast, the local amateur proprietor provides a service to low-income families by keeping housing costs below market. When the amateur service provider is replaced, housing costs increase. There is some empirical evidence that suggests that by absorbing part of the cost of offering housing below the market price, the amateur proprietor plays a significant role in redistributing income. (This role is also generalizable to other social services, including day care.) But at the same time, standards are much lower as well. Indeed, the standards are often far below legal requirements. In this way, the service provided by the amateur is blurred into the black or gray market of service delivery.

A very different aspect of the proprietary pillar is encountered when we turn to the national corporate-investor-owned services. In 1983, 1,200 for-profit hospitals had "asset values in excess of 20 billion dollars" (Simon, 1984, p. 5). Investor-owned hospitals are big business. Most of these multi-unit companies are experimenting with programs that combine health insurance and health delivery. As investor-owned hospitals move into the health insurance business, they will openly compete for patients with the life insurance companies. The proprietary sector will also be competing for health care service in the employer-provided pillar, which covers almost three-quarters of all full-time private sector workers in the United States.

If we view medical care and social services as market commodities, then the employer-provided pillar is simply paying for a service that is administered by another pillar through subcontracting. If we redefine the pillars as market sectors, then blurring is simply market exchange and market competition for a share of the market. The "make/buy" decision (whether to make the product—in this case the service—oneself, or to buy it from another firm) is a decision every actor needs to make in light of the arithmetic of cost-benefit calculation. In this reformulation, all the dualist categories collapse and all the pillars and sectors become profit maximizers. But then we simply rediscover the pillars through the ancient arguments about externalities and market failures.

The final pillar is the informal pillar (community, kin, and family). This informal pillar is perhaps even more complicated than the others, with problems of terminology adding an additional source of confusion. One of the enduring and widely-shared images is that this is the pillar in which self-help initiatives could be fostered. The government and nonprofit pillars periodically mount programs to exploit the essential character of the informal pillar. But even here we find blurring. To illustrate this point I want to cite the experience in the developing countries of low-income housing through personal self-help.

Hugh Stretton's study of contractors in the greater Manila area makes it clear that the dualist impulse to assign self-help to the informal pillar is misleading. In his example, self-help in the informal pillar flows into the proprietary pillar, which is dominated by local amateur paid employment—self-employed artisans working with a gang of laborers and using no equipment.

What stands out particularly in the United States is the way these pillars coexist in society with the other pillars. The conflicting themes of complementarity and antagonism run throughout the history of attempts to explore the terrain within the informal pillar. One important strand in crime prevention, mental health, and poverty reduction policies has been the use of community-based initiatives ranging from self-help, to community organizations, to community activism. These are visible in attempts to formulate policies based on individual therapy supported by the corporate and private foundation sectors (with and without government assistance) to revitalize community as a device for social control and social and personal change. As the informal sector is activated, often with funding from government, it feeds on the entrepreneurial spirit of family and kin and the survival needs of the community organizations they spawned. This indirectly leads to reinforcing a gray service market.

Shifting from the policy to the theoretical level, Alan Silver and others argue that affectional, sentimental, spontaneous, altruistic ties emerge only when the state and market become important. The informal sector is thus constructed by, and a moral concomitant of, the formal sector. If the formal causes the informal to appear and is then used by the formal to realize the aims of social control, we find fresh evidence for blurring in yet a different sense best captured by the term "constitutive."

Blurring has a number of different interpretations depending on which pillar we focus on. Terms such as interweaving, comingling, mutual dependence, complementary overlap, competition, and constitutive are evoked in the attempt to make vivid and specific the imagery of blurring.

THE INNER CIRCLE: THE TOOLS OF GOVERNMENT

Government has an elaborate store of tools it can use in building on and rehabilitating the pillars in the outer circle. A preliminary typology suggests at least the following:

1. Government can subcontract through intermediaries for the purchase of services. The decision to buy rather than make leads to other decisions such as which services are to be purchased; from whom (that is, from which groups); and through what means (cost plus contract, itemized accounting, and so forth).

2. It can make direct cash grants to providers, without subcontracting for specific purchases. For example, direct government subsidies are found in the arts. At the federal level, the Institute for Museum Services provides low-level support for ongoing operations. At the municipal level, about 20 percent of the revenue of the Metropolitan Museum of Art is provided as a subsidy by New York City to cover the cost of guards, maintenance work, heating, and the like.

3. It can reimburse individuals who are free to choose which of the pillars in the outer circle they will use. The use of reimbursement makes the boundary separating cash and services very unclear. For example, in the national accounts, Medicare is treated as a cash program because the individual directly purchases the services and is reimbursed by the government. When the government purchases or provides Medicaid on behalf of the poor, it is defined as a government service program or government consumption.

4. It can also develop regulations and standards that set the conditions under which individuals will be reimbursed and the rules for subcontracts and direct grants. The rule-making and regulatory role of government is, of course, used in combination with the other tools.

5. It can provide incentives for individuals and corporations to purchase or provide certain services. Tax forgiveness is perhaps the most important incentive system. Consider, for example, the system of federal tax exemption where an individual in the proper tax bracket can deduct $480 for child care expenses for one child and $960 for two or more children (based on expenditure of $4800 for the latter).

6. It also disregards earnings in computing benefit levels or in determining income eligibility for public programs. For example, recipients of Aid to Families with Dependent Children (AFDC) who are in the labor force can spend up to $160 a month for day care, and this amount is deducted from their earnings in determining their eligibility for welfare benefits or their benefit level.

7. It can create a system of tax incentives to sponsors of social services. For example, proprietary institutions are permitted to take depreciation allowances on capital investment. The Economic Recovery Tax Act of 1981 permitted employers on a tax-exempt basis to develop a wide range of ways of providing day care to their employees. Such deductions against taxes mean that the enterprise does not absorb the full cost of the services.

8. Finally, government can mandate the provision of services without any reimbursement. For example, the state can mandate that all employers provide medical examinations or vaccinations and leave the cost of these services directly to the firms. This form of mandating is more common in social protection than in services (women's compensation, vacations, holidays, and the like).

It seems plausible to suggest that some of these tools by design or chance encourage the development of some pillars in the outer circle and the neglect of others. The following provides a brief description of how the tools of government contribute directly and indirectly to the size and form of each of the pillars.

Government and the Informal Pillar. It seems plausible to suggest that when tax exemptions and earnings disregards are fixed at a very low level, they encourage, especially for low-income families, the use of the informal service systems. Of course, if the administrative oversight is very weak—and there is very little review to determine whether the money that would entitle an individual to receive these tax advantages was actually spent—then low compliance could have the effect of stimulating self-help. For example, in Britain all severely disabled persons are entitled to some attendants' allowance. The benefit level is minimal, and this may encourage available kin to take care of the disabled individual. In a program with weak oversight, slippage is likely to occur. In this situation, individuals may do without the supplementary service and rely on their own resources, even though, in principle, eligibility depends on the assumption that the individuals are not able to secure these services for themselves.

Government and the Nonprofit Service Pillar. I commented earlier on the role of government in encouraging nonprofit organizations. Salamon estimates that between 1981 and 1982, government's contribution to social services declined by 9 percent (Salamon, 1984). During this time, however, the total real resources spent by nonprofit organizations declined by only 4 percent. This suggests that to some extent nonprofits were able to acquire other resources in absorbing part, but not all, of the losses in government revenue. Fee charging is one of the most important sources of new revenue. Thus, nonprofit organizations appear to pass on the increased cost of doing business to their clients. There is some evidence, however, that since 1982, as a result of the economic recovery, state governments have been willing to pick up some of the program costs lost by the withdrawal of the federal government. As the politics of cost shifting among the multiple institutions took place, it helped to create the nonprofit pillar of the service world. It thus appears that two of the major actors in the politics of cost shifting are the different levels of government and the consumer. These two sources alone account for almost 70 percent of the revenues of nonprofit organizations.

Government and the Proprietary Pillar. To what extent have proprietary social services grown in the last decade? It is difficult to answer this question decisively. A review of the number of persons employed in the hospital industry provides a clue. There is some evidence to suggest that profitization has increased more rapidly than privatization. Between 1966 and 1979, employment in the hospital industry almost doubled (a 98 percent increase). If we take employment growth by sector, we find that nonprofits grew slightly below the average rate (90 percent); government grew by only 58 percent; while the profit-making sector leaped forward by 130 percent (unpublished tabulations from U.S. Current Population Survey and National Income Accounts data).

Another dramatic example of the growth of proprietary agencies is the expansion of nursing homes. Between 1960 and 1970, nursing home facilities increased by 140 percent. Gilbert estimates that close to 80 percent of these facilities are operated by for-profit organizations. The growth of this industry was made possible by the creation of the Medicaid Act of 1965, which provided the resources for a system of reimbursement to individuals. Two-thirds of the revenue of proprietary nursing homes comes from the publicly sponsored Medicaid program (Gilbert, 1984). Gilbert believes that we are drifting in the direction of the substitution of proprietary for nonprofit care, but he cites little evidence to support this thesis. A review of the facts suggests a more complicated story. A study of long-range trends in hospital facilities concludes that "For-profit hospitals accounted for approximately 56 percent of all registered hospitals in the United States in 1910, but now they constitute about 11 percent of all hospitals and only 5 percent of all hospital beds" (Bays, 1983, p. 366).

Nonprofits dominate the field. But the pattern appears to be changing once again.

In the period 1969–1977, for which information for corporate chains as well as the traditional proprietary hospitals is available, the total number of hospital facilities declined slightly. Decomposing this decline by sector suggests that traditional proprietary hospitals declined by 40 percent, while corporate chain hospitals increased by 18 percent. Corporate chain hospitals' share of total hospitals increased from 7.9 to 9.2 percent.

Government policy has contributed both to the dominance of nonprofit hospitals and to the emergence and rapid growth in the late 1970s of for-profit chain hospitals. Bays offers an interesting interpretation of why chain hospitals have grown by citing examples of government bias against proprietaries.

> In some states—a notable exception is California—Blue Cross originally refused reimbursement to for-profit hospitals or reimbursed them at a lower rate than that for nonprofit hospitals. In negotiations between the Social Security Administration and the American Hospital Association regarding the original Medicare legislation, the AHA convinced the SSA to structure the reimbursement formula in such a way as to discriminate against for-profit hospitals. (Bays, 1983, p. 377)

Another form that proprietary care takes is that of the self-employed professionals, such as psychologists, psychiatrists, social workers, and the like. The flowering of a hundred different therapies depends in part on the willingness of government to develop standards that permit these self-employed therapists to get reimbursement from medical insurance. The decision to reimburse draws a sharp line between legitimate and illegitimate therapies. It does so by not enforcing standards with respect to qualification or compensation. Of course, little is really known about which of these therapies are effective or, at the least, not harmful to individuals.

Government policy also influences the growth of local amateur proprietary services, many of which are performed in the gray market, where government does not enforce standards with respect to qualification or compensation. Babysitting is one obvious example of such amateur services. These nannies, babysitters, and *aux-pairs* provide a low-quality service. Its low cost makes it affordable and therefore accessible to low-income families. These amateur service providers therefore must play an important role in some social service systems.

The Government and Employer-Based Programs. The value of fringe benefits can be measured in super dollars that are worth more than nominal dollars, which are subject to tax. Fringe benefits take different forms.

Some provide the individual with reimbursements for the purchase of services outside of the firm that employs them. For example, many universities will pay part of the cost of university education for tenured employees. The university also pays the complete tuition of the children of employees who are students in the university that employs the individual. For some universities, a rather large percentage of its student body are the children of employees who are entitled to full tuition exemption. This has the perverse effect of reducing part of the university's revenue at a time when governmental aid is in decline.

The buy/provide decision is generalizable. The employer must decide whether to provide directly day-care, medical, counseling, or other personal services. The case of university fringe benefits is an example of a policy evolved in one historic period presenting new and special problems in a different time period. But even when an employer elects to provide day-care, medical, counseling or other personal services, it must further decide whether to buy these services from existing sponsors, or to reimburse individuals who purchase their own services. This is, of course, similar to the choice faced by governmental bodies "to buy, to make, or to reimburse."

There is only limited information about what employers actually do, and therefore about the size of the employer-based pillar. A brief review of employer provision suggests that, despite a lively interest in the employer-based pillar, the story is mixed. Day care is an illustration of a field in which there is both federal and state legislation but only very limited development (Kahn and Kamerman, 1987).

On the other hand, the field of corporate education is flourishing. A Carnegie study reports that companies are providing training for nearly eight million people at a cost of about $60 billion. At least eighteen corporations and industry associations award accredited academic degrees. If these figures are accurate, they show that corporate education is as large as the whole array of four-year colleges and universities. Critics argue that these programs provide narrow skills training. Even if this is so, the importance of corporate education must be recognized.

Conclusion

The government and the private sector operate separately and together in numerous ways to provide social welfare services. The state may preempt the whole field, dominate, or peacefully coexist with other actors, work actively in a collaborative or competitive mode, or devolve administration and policy initiative. Whether the state is dominant or passive, its regulatory role permits it potentially always to be a major factor. Private social welfare certainly would exist without government;

but the tools of government influence the size and form of the entire social welfare edifice. Both the conceptual elaboration of theories of the state and the method of doing the bookkeeping for the state (that is, our national and social accounts) underplay this complexity. Dualist and three-sector theories dominate our thinking. Yet they are diversionary because they obscure rather than highlight the penetration into the commingling of government with the institutions of civil society. When theory confronts reality, we retreat into fuzzy boundaries. But by building on the insights of conventional theory, it is possible to develop a framework that goes beyond dualism and more faithfully portrays the public/private interplay in the modern world of social welfare services.

Three empirically relevant policy questions are implicit in this analysis.

1. What precisely is the logic that links a cost shift with a reduction in aggregate expenditure? It is part of the traditional wisdom today that shifting the cost from the public to the private sector would have an effect on the level of expenditures. Two quite different arguments about how such a shift might occur can be identified. They can be discussed in terms of medical care and sickness benefits. The conventional, and certainly dominant, argument in this country is that society should encourage the reprivatization of medical and sickness programs because such a sectoral shift would lead to more effective cost controls. Two of the essential features of this argument are that costs will be reduced because there will be less unnecessary medical care (that is, more efficient allocation of scarce medical care resources) and that we can expect a substantial improvement in the quality of care, because when people or firms pay part of the cost of medical care, they will have a stake in monitoring their own behavior and also that of the medical care system. Hence, cost inflation can be reduced. A similar argument can be found in the field of cash support in the event of sickness. Here it is assumed that sick pay (outlays by the firm) is preferable to sick benefits (outlays by the state) because the firms would have more immediate control over absenteeism, since they have a stake in reducing disruption of the normal work force.

The other argument, much less conventional in the United States, is that a shift from the private to the collective sector would have beneficial effects similar to those postulated for the opposite shift described above. In Sweden, for example, it is believed that if it were possible to reduce the size of the private sector, more effective controls on doctors' reimbursement would be possible. The argument is that a large and invisible private sector acts to set the standards for escalating wages in the public sector. Moreover, costs increase because physicians are given an opportunity to opt out of one system into the other or to participate jointly in both systems. Restricting choice inhibits wage expectations. Hence, the aim of public policy is to reduce the size of the private sector. Such a policy would tend to reduce the aggregate level of expenditures by restructuring the bargaining power of doctors.

2. What effects do different mixes of state provision, regulation, mandating, stimulating, and financing have on the form, quality, and distribution of services? This issue has led to a lively debate in Britain. Some analysts insist that the state must retain its role as provider as well as subsidizer of services if perverse redistribution is to be avoided (LeGrand, 1983). Others feel that a more radical change is needed (Judge et al., 1983). They contend that the state should get out of the service business and only play the more modest role of planner, regulator, and financier. Their argument is that this would improve the quality of service without negative redistribution effects.

Measuring redistributive effects of sectoral shifts is conceptually very difficult because of the problem of assigning a service beneficiary. A student grant or an old-age benefit, for example, may be received by those who would have (perhaps) paid all or part of the tuition for the student or the living costs of the elderly relative. The evidence can be assembled along with the family of counterfactuals (that is, "what if" assumptions) that such an analysis requires. But in the end we must recognize that intellectual perspectives and institutional reality depend on each other—because we need categories to simplify reality and, of course, the reality of practice constrains, at least to some extent, the useful categories we can posit.

Yes, some sectoral or pillar combinations are better than others. But without a consensus on the criterion problem (better as judged by what standards?), cost, and counterfactuals (assumptions about the side effects), it is an illusion to think that empirical evidence will substitute for normative theory.

These comments are not intended to inhibit inquiry, but only to establish its limits. In the absence of a consensus on how to deal with the criterion and slide problems, technical studies observe more than they clarify. But they do have the advantage of calling attention to the issues that the normative debate should more systematically address. A normative debate at the level of social discourse followed by technical analysis is a high priority.

3. How do we resolve the fundamental dilemma between accountability and responsibility? The search for more public accountability is designed to assure a homogeneous product so that people in similar situations do not receive services of different quality. But this may undermine the equally valued principle of autonomous institutions unfettered by regulation and able thereby to experiment and stimulate variety in the pattern of service provision. These conflicts between accountability and au-

tonomy, and between uniformity and variety, pose important dilemmas for policy debate and for the future development of social welfare in society (Lipsky and Thibodeau, 1984).

In a period of financial constraint combined with a continuity of commitment to the ideals of social protection on which the "welfare state" is premised, the one likely outcome will be that the future of the welfare state will be the invention of institutions that are not public and not private. The massive body of literature that pays attention only to the activities of the welfare state will become obsolete as the blurring of the institutions of social protection overwhelm the social landscape. If we are to understand social reality, we must look at all the institutions that provide social protection and not only the institutions of the state.

References

Bays, Carson W. 1983. "Why Most Private Hospitals Are Nonprofit." *Journal of Policy Analysis and Management* 2 (3). Spring.

Gilbert, Neil. 1983. *Capitalism and the Welfare State: Dilemmas of Social Benevolence.* New Haven: Yale University Press.

————. 1984. "Welfare for Profit: Moral, Empirical and Theoretical Perspectives." *Journal of Social Policy.* January.

Hansmann, Henry B. 1980. "The Role of Non-Profit Enterprise." *Yale Law Journal* 89 (5). April.

Hood, Christopher. 1984. *The Hidden Public Sector: The World of Paragovernment Organizations.* Glasgow: The University of Strathclyde, Center for the Study of Public Policy.

James, Estelle. 1983. "How Nonprofits Grow: A Model." *Journal of Policy Analysis and Management* 2 (3). Spring.

Judge, Ken, et al. 1983. "Public Opinion and the Privatization of Welfare." *Journal of Social Policy* 12 (4). October.

Kahn, Alfred J., and Sheila B. Kamerman. 1987. *Child Care: Facing the Hard Choices.* Dover, Mass.: Auburn House.

Kamerman, Sheila B. 1983. *Meeting Family Needs: The Corporate Response.* New York: Pergamon Press.

Krohn, Roger G. 1977. *The Other Economy: The Internal Logic of Local Rental Housing.* Montreal: Peter Martin Associates.

Lampman, Robert J. 1984. *Social Welfare Spending: Accounting for Changes from 1950 to 1978.* Madison, Wis.: The Institute for Research on Poverty, University of Wisconsin.

LeGrand, Julian. 1983. "Is Privatization Always Such a Bad Thing?" *New Society.* April 7.

Lindblom, Charles E. 1977. *Politics and Markets: The World's Political Economic System.* New York: Basic Books.

Lipsky, Michael, and Marc Thibodeau. 1984. "Dilemmas of Utilizing Voluntary Organizations for Public Purposes: The Case of Food Surplus Distribution and Community Feeding Organizations." Paper presented at the annual meeting of the American Political Science Association. September.

Litwak, Eugene. 1985. *Helping the Elderly: The Complementary Roles of Informal Networks and Formal Systems*. New York: Guilford Press.

Musgrave, Richard A. 1980. *Why Public Employment? Public Finance and Public Employment*. Proceedings of the Thirty-Sixth Congress of the International Institute of Public Finance. Jerusalem.

Nielsen, Waleman A. 1979. *The Endangered Sector*. New York: Columbia University Press.

Peattie, Lisa. 1987. "Shelter, Development and the Poor." In Lloyd Rodwin, ed. *Shelter, Settlement, and Development*: 263–278. Boston: Allen and Unwin.

Robb, Christina. 1985. "Nailing Down a Future." *Boston Globe Magazine*. March 31.

Salamon, Lester M. 1984. "Non-Profit Organizations: The Lost Opportunity." In John L. Palmer and Isabel Sawhill, eds. *The Reagan Record*: 261–286. Washington, D.C.: The Urban Institute.

Simon, Herbert A. 1984. *Reason and Human Affairs*. London: Basil Blackwell.

Streeck, Wolfgang, and Philippe C. Schmitter. 1984. "Community, Market, State—and Associations? The Prospective Contribution of Interest Governance to Social Order." Paper for the Working Group on Comparative Economic Systems, European University Institute. Florence, Italy. February 23.

Stretton, Hugh. 1978. *Planning in Rich and Poor Countries*. New York: Oxford University Press.

Sundstrom, Gerdt. 1981. "Informal Care and the Elderly." Unpublished paper. University of Stockholm.

Vranken, Jan. 1986. "Report on the Post-War Development of the Welfare State in Belgium." Paper for a comparative study of welfare state development in Europe. European University, Florence, Italy.

Weisbrod, Burton A. 1977. *The Voluntary Nonprofit Sector, An Economic Analysis*. Lexington, Mass.: D. C. Heath.

3

Welfare: The Public / Private Mix

RICHARD ROSE

To debate whether welfare is or ought to be a public or a private responsibility is to confront two important half-truths. Welfare is not the exclusive prerogative of either the public sector or the private sector, however
these terms are defined. Total welfare in society sums a mixture of actions. From the viewpoint of producers—whether public officials, owners
of profit or nonprofit hospitals, or volunteers providing care without
pay—the differences in the mix are important. But from the viewpoint of
consumers, total welfare in society is of greatest importance.

The public contribution to the welfare mix consists of the goods and
services produced by public agencies—whether federal, state, or local—
or funded by tax revenue, as are Medicaid and Medicare. Social welfare
programs are not the only object of public expenditure. Nor were they
the first. The earliest concern of the state was national security; monar-
chical France and dictatorial Prussia were states in the eighteenth century
because they could defend their territory against external attack and
maintain public order. The second historic concern of the state was economic development. While social welfare programs today consume a substantial portion of public budgets, they are relatively new commitments
(Rose, 1976; Flora and Heidenheimer, 1981).

The *private* contribution to the welfare mix can take two very different
forms. The first is found in the market sector of the economy; agencies
dependent upon selling their services in the market, typically for profit,
are thus differentiated from those that can give their services free of
charge because they are funded by the fisc, that is, the revenue that government collects in taxation. For example, a school charging tuition differs from a public school in its ownership, control, and recruitment of
students.

This paper is part of a program of research on the growth of government in the United
Kingdom, sponsored by British Economic and Social Research Council grant HR 7849/1,
and draws upon research reported in related papers of this program.

The second major source of welfare beyond the state is the household. It is far less subject to public regulation than are private sector hospitals, schools, and pension programs. It is also beyond the market, being independent of the cash nexus that links producers and consumers in the private sector, and public employees and the state in the public sector. In the household, care in sickness and in health is exchanged on the basis of affection and moral obligation. Whereas public and private sector institutions are often involved in recognized interdependencies, as in the government's paying of private sector hospitals, the family is outside this bureaucratized and monetized world. It is private in the sense of being set apart from government and the market.

To think of welfare in either/or terms is to introduce an obsolete dichotomy between the public and the private sectors. There is great interdependence through direct financial provision, regulation, and beneficial legislation such as tax expenditures (Weidenbaum, 1970; Salamon, 1986). Economists refer to welfare services as private goods, because they are provided to individuals (as distinct from collective goods such as defense, which are available to all). But these goods are often paid for by the public purse rather than by the recipient. Welfare services are not private in the literal sense of being withdrawn or solitary; they are profoundly social, depending upon social interaction in the household and with market and state institutions.

The welfare mix, as well as total welfare in society, is continuously subject to change. In the 1960s, the War on Poverty was about increasing total welfare by increasing the public contribution to the welfare mix. In the 1980s the Reagan Administration, consistent with its rejection of big government, emphasized a different theme: reducing the state's contribution to the welfare mix, a move that implies either an increase in private (that is, nongovernmental) sources of welfare, or else a reduction of total welfare in society.

In order to understand the realities underlying the rhetorical polarities, we must distinguish a minimum of three sources of welfare: the state (or public sector), the market (often described as the private sector), and the household. A society's total welfare is the sum of activities in all three sectors; the welfare mix is the contribution each makes to the total. It is more precise to speak of public (state) and nonpublic (market and household) sources of welfare than to speak of private welfare. Strictly speaking, welfare can only be privatized if it has previously been in public hands (for example, the transfer of a school or hospital or prison from state to market, nonprofit, or household hands). Historically, such examples are relatively rare, and the present day instances of the privatization of public services, especially social services, are relatively limited in scale, although often important as political symbols.

The first part of this chapter sets out a model defining these terms and their relationship. The second considers the importance of economic wealth for total welfare, whatever the mix of sources. Current economic strains raise questions about the capacity of the public and nonpublic sectors to finance a continued expansion of monetized welfare. Given these pressures, the final section considers problems for public policy arising from differences in the components that constitute the mix.

Total Welfare in Society

Everyone needs welfare, whether the social institution providing it is the household, the market, or the state. The production of welfare is a social as well as an economic act, for goods and services of value are exchanged between producer and consumer. The American tendency to consider "welfare" as confined to a minority of society is a reflection of a national tendency to regard the state as distant, rather than as the civic embodiment of collective virtues and responsibilities (Allardt, 1986; Glazer, 1986). This is reinforced by the fact that the pioneer tradition tended to stress household self-sufficiency, and immigrants to America were motivated by a desire to flee from a coercive state, relying upon the market to earn the means of welfare.

The welfare products of concern here are those that influence the well-being of a majority of a nation's population—either continuously, such as income or housing, or at a major stage of life, such as education or a pension. Welfare products, like any other good or service, are capable of being exchanged, whether or not an exchange takes place; for example, a meal can be bought in a restaurant, prepared by another member of a household, or by the person who eats it. Excluded are those goods and services that people must produce for themselves, such as eating, sleeping, or exercise.

The primary welfare products that every individual needs on a continuing basis are income, food, housing, and geographical mobility; in addition, individuals at some period of their life need education, health care, and personal social services provided by others.[1] These welfare products can readily be identified empirically; they are not abstractions, as is the

---

[1] The catalogue includes all five primary welfare products identified as central by Wilensky (1975, p. 1), albeit he does not analyze all of them. The additions are personal social services and transportation. Clothing is omitted because of the large element of taste and style; it is similar to food, being a product of the market and the household; it is not provided free by the state. Leisure is arguably another primary welfare need; here, too, the household and the market are dominant, and the state's role relatively limited. Adding clothing and leisure to the above would not alter the overall substantive conclusions about the welfare mix.

idea of a community, nor are they as intangible as subjective feelings of happiness, well-being, or life satisfaction.

Money is not the measure of welfare in society, for welfare is a condition of people rather than a pecuniary sum in a bank account or national income account. Time-budget studies emphasize that a very large amount of time is spent in unpaid work within the household, not least in producing such welfare services as child care (Juster and Land, 1981; Gershuny, 1981; Rose, 1985a). Welfare produced within the home is not sold but given freely; it is priceless in both production and consumption. Many welfare services of the state are mixed: the consumer need not pay for education, health care, or other so-called merit goods, but the producers must be paid by the fisc. Only goods and services produced and sold in the market are fully monetized. Considering unpaid as well as paid labor is consistent with the practice of including nonmonetized as well as monetized labor in the measure of output in Third World countries (Hill, 1979).

In advanced industrial societies, however, we cannot leave money out; it is a necessary input to secure the goods and services that contribute greatly to contemporary social welfare. Richard Titmuss's (1970) famous interpretation of blood donation as a gift relationship in which altruism replaces an economic calculus was only half correct. While blood is often given free by altruistic donors, health service workers who transfer the blood to patients are employees working for money wages. If altruism represents the idealized vision of the proponents of state-provided welfare, then a strike for higher wages by workers administering blood transfusion services is the nightmare vision of its critics.

Four different types of social welfare services can be distinguished, depending on whether the service is monetized at the point of production, the point of consumption, neither, or both (see Table 3.1): market (production and consumption monetized, for example, housing); state (production monetized but not consumption, for example, public education); household (neither production nor consumption monetized, for example, a farmer consuming home-grown food); and barter (exchange without money, for example, a teacher giving lessons to a car mechanic's child in return for car repairs). Given the limits of barter, which quickly leads to the need to reinvent some form of units of account for multilateral exchange, it is not further explored here.[2]

---

[2] The nonprofit production of welfare in schools, hospitals, and other places is only a variant of market provision, not a category on its own. Public employees do not work for nothing; professors in universities, and doctors and nurses in hospitals expect to be paid, as do their suppliers. Since profit is a small portion of the total cost of producing a service, nonprofit services will not differ greatly in cost from those supplied by profit-making organizations. Consumers normally gain access to the services of nonprofit agencies through

TABLE 3.1 Alternative Sources of Welfare in the Mixed Society

	Consumption Monetized	
Production Monetized	Yes	No
Yes	Market	State
No	[Barter]	Household

Total Welfare in Society (TWS) can be described by a simple identity, in which H equals the Household production of welfare; M equals welfare bought and sold in the Market; and S equals welfare produced by the State.

$$TWS = H + M + S$$

The welfare mix of a given society is characterized by the proportion of goods and services produced by these three sectors (Rose, 1986a).

Even though total welfare may be described in summary form, it remains a complex construct not reducible to a single number (as is the gross national product), for the three components producing welfare do not share a common money denominator. But no assumption of total commensurability or total substitutability is necessary in order to make judgments about total welfare in society. Policymakers are accustomed to think in terms of a package of public programs; economists, to think of different goods and services being produced in the market; and spouses, about many different aspects of conjugal relationships. Here we need only keep in mind three different sources of welfare.

Welfare products produced by different sectors of society are not completely substitutable. The personal affection associated with household production cannot be matched by impersonal market or state services. The professionalism of public servants differs from the amateur character of much household activity. Different criteria for access—money as against entitlement—inhibits substitutability between the market and the state.

Different forms of welfare production can be complementary. Eugene Litwak's (1985, p. 253) study of the roles of informal networks and for-

charges paid by themselves or by a third party; Weisbrod (1977) has estimated that 70 percent of all revenue of nonprofit organizations comes from such charges. Nonmonetized services of unpaid volunteers are very limited (Kramer, 1981).

mal organizations in helping the elderly demonstrates that the comparative advantage of a source of welfare varies with the task at hand. There is also a danger of false gestaltism, claiming that differences in a single attribute make a total difference. But an arithmetic teacher will show that two plus two equals four, whether the lesson is provided by the state, the market, or by a parent in the home, and a meal can have the same caloric value whether eaten in the home, bought in a restaurant, or provided in a public institution.

Historically, two great changes have occurred in the composition of the welfare mix. The first was *industrialization*, which brought about a great increase in the monetization of welfare production. Paid employment in a city became the norm rather than work in exchange for shelter, food, and other services in a rural household. A significant portion of the apparent growth in welfare in the past century simply reflects a shift from nonmonetized to monetized production (Sametz, 1968). In this century, the great change has been *fiscalization*, the state's increased capacity to collect large sums in taxation from citizens. The money is used to finance the public provision of education, income-maintenance programs, and health care without a charge to recipients, a form of provision that the market cannot offer.

A theory of a single dominant source of welfare would hypothesize that the household first dominated the welfare mix, until it was replaced by the market, and finally, the state has become the chief or monopoly source of welfare. Alternatively, the program approach to public policy (Rose, 1985b) suggests that the state's contribution to the welfare mix will tend to vary from program to program. The household, the market, and the state can each have a comparative advantage in producing some welfare services, and a comparative disadvantage in producing others.

Of the seven major welfare concerns—income, food, housing, personal social services, education, health, and transportation—some appear well suited to monopoly provision by a single source; others are better produced by a combination of household and market, or household and state, or by all three.[3]

Household monopoly (personal social services). Caring for the young and the elderly occurs in the home as a by-product of family relationships. The family rather than institutional or communal care remains the basic household unit in every industrial nation. Even in Israel, the kibbutz ideal

---

[3] The classification adapts to American circumstances empirical evidence from Britain, which shows the importance of product-specific as against nation-specific attributes of welfare (Rose, 1986b). With a much more restricted definition of secondary consumer income, Lampman (1984) similarly concludes that the role of the state is variable from functional area to functional area.

of collective communal responsibility for care has been falling by the wayside. In the United States, marketed services for the elderly or children are noteworthy, yet remain relatively small by comparison with nonmonetized household care of people of all ages.

State monopoly (education). The provision of education was first among the responsibilities assumed by government in the nineteenth century; democratization and industrialization required a literate population. In the twentieth century the growing complexity of subject matter requires sophisticated instructional facilities, reducing the potential input from the household, and making marketed education increasingly expensive. Concurrently, secularization has much reduced the role of the church, the chief organizational alternative to the state as a source of education. Only in the field of American higher education are not-for-profit universities significant in competition with the state.

Household and market (food). The most basic physical need, food, is sold by the market; it is not treated as a merit good to be supplied without charge by the state. Preparing meals in the household is the norm. Food is only a primary state responsibility in the very exceptional circumstances of wartime, when the state intervenes to ration food as part of a total mobilization of resources for war. The United States is again an exception in having a food stamp program that gives some low-income families vouchers to exchange for food. It is relevant that this program was initially inspired by the problem of disposing of surplus crops generated by farm subsidies, rather than expressing a government intent to regulate diet.

Household, market, and state (income, housing, transportation, and health). Families draw income from a mixture of sources. About half of all persons receiving a regular money income are either public employees or else receive an income maintenance grant such as a pension; the other half work in the private sector. Another substantial block of the population—children and housewives—receive money through transfers within the household (Rose, 1985c: Table 1.17). Housing is bought and sold in the market, but tax subsidies for interest payments affect costs, and some housing is publicly owned. A substantial fraction of housing maintenance is produced by unpaid do-it-yourself household labor. Transportation too reflects a mix of inputs: the market sells motor cars; the state provides roads and often operates railways, buses and airlines; and individuals drive themselves about or walk to many destinations.

Health care is a joint product of the household, the market, and the state, albeit the mix differs in America as against Europe. In Europe the state has the preeminent role in paying for medical and hospital services. The market enters insofar as the services are provided by intermediaries paid by the state, and individuals are often asked to make a token or partial payment for services. The household remains significant in providing care for children and adults who are ill but can be looked after at home rather than in a hospital. In the United States the public sector pays for more than two-fifths of health care through Medicare, Medicaid, and other programs, and the private sector provides the remainder of monetized care. To a significant extent, an individual's health is not the product of any social relationship: it reflects the way a person looks after himself or herself.

The production of major services by private-sector as well as public-sector organizations is pervasive in America, even for services normally regarded as public. The extent is demonstrated by Guy Peters's data of the proportion of public as against private sector employees producing services in the public interest (Table 3.2). While education ranks highest in the proportion of employees in the public sector (almost seven million), even in education private sector employees number more than one million. Highways are publicly maintained, but normally built by private contractors; private delivery services compete with the post office; and tax accountants compete with the Internal Revenue Service. Even the police, in Europe considered a necessary monopoly of government, is supplemented by a host of private security services. A majority employed in producing social services and health care are in the private, not the public sector.

When the basic unit of analysis becomes the consumer of welfare, the interdependence of state, market, and household in welfare production is even more apparent. An individual member of society can receive welfare in a variety of ways: as a consumer in the market; as a citizen entitled to public benefits; and as a spouse, parent, or other member of a family. How one refers to an individual illustrates this variety. To speak of an individual recipient as a citizen is to presuppose that the state's role is monopolistic or preeminent, just as speaking of an individual as a consumer commercializes welfare. An individual has roles in a multiplicity of social subsystems and can consume some welfare in each.

The Size of the Pie

From the perspective of the individual recipient, the size of the pie— that is, total welfare—is of most importance, regardless of the relative contribution of the state, the market, and the household. The limit on total welfare is set by the combined resources of the household and money economy.

TABLE 3.2 Role of Public- and Private-Sector Employees in Delivering
Services in U.S.

	Public Employees	Private Employees	% Public Employees
Education	6,959,000	1,231,000	85
Post office	664,000	250,000	73
Highways	564,000	261,000	68
Tax administration	426,000	280,000	60
Police	627,000	450,000	60
Defense	3,021,000	2,100,000	59
Social services	622,000	1,160,000	34
Transportation	752,000	2,010,000	31
Health	1,674,000	3,987,000	30
Gas., elec., water	314,000	821,000	27
Banking	21,000	1,629,000	1
Telecommunications	8,000	1,376,000	0.5

SOURCE: Peters, 1985, Table 7.7.

From a historical perspective, there have been major changes in the
capacity of the household to produce welfare, arising from changes in
welfare products (hospital care becoming more professional); the technology of production (labor-saving machines in the household); and the
tastes of members of the household (in marriage, family size, and female
participation in the paid labor force). Not all changes have been unfavor-
able to household production; for example, labor-saving devices for
housework have enabled middle-class families to substitute their own efforts for paid domestic servants, and children and parents may visit by
telephone as well as face to face. While the household is changing, it has
not been "crowded out" of a role in the production of welfare. Social
change has altered the definition of household care, but it has not eliminated its significant role in the provision of welfare services. The break up
of traditional stable neighborhoods has been matched by the growth of
"instant" community, for example, in sunbelt villages catering to retired
Americans. Friendships may form more readily, and be stronger when
based on current interest rather than on shared past experiences. Litwak
(1985) demonstrates that much help for the elderly is provided through
the adaptation of informal networks to complement public and market
provision.

The ultimate constraint upon the monetized consumption of welfare is gross national product per capita. Whatever the division between the market and the state, this sets a limit upon the total money resources available in society. The concern of many welfare proponents with the distribution of welfare cannot deny the importance of the gross national product in determining the resources available for distribution.

As an economy, the United States is one of the richest nations in the world. Among Organization for Economic Cooperation and Development (OECD) nations, per capita GDP in the U.S., $16,494, was 79 percent above the mean for OECD nations in 1985, higher than for any other industrial nation. However, the public effort of American government (that is, public expenditure as a percentage of the national product) is below the OECD average. In 1985 American public expenditure was 35.3 percent of GDP (Table 3.3). Whereas the United States ranked first among twenty-one nations in its per capita wealth, it was seventeenth in public effort. When the proportion of the national product spent by government on social welfare programs is examined, the United States is much below average, spending 18.1 percent of the national product on social programs, compared to 25.2 percent as the OECD average.

While trying less, American government spends more on social welfare for its citizens. Because America is well above average in national wealth, total American government spending per capita was 46 percent above the OECD average in 1985. Moreover, whereas the average nation spent $2,273 per citizen on social programs, the United States, thanks to a higher level of national product per capita, spent $2,835, a figure above such historically welfare-oriented governments as Britain. Less tax effort will yield more money for American public policy than many European countries spend as long as America is a wealthier society.

When the amount of money spent on particular social programs is compared with public effort, the importance of America's economic wealth becomes very evident. Government in America makes less effort than the average OECD nation in education, pensions, health, or other social services. It is least below average, 5 percent, in education; it is 20 percent below average in pensions; 23 percent below average in health, and 73 percent below average for other social programs. When attention is turned to the actual amount of money spent, however, a different picture emerges. Government in America spent 64 percent more per capita on education than the average OECD country, and 39 percent more on pensions in 1985. Although public effort is low in health, America's wealth results in total per capita spending by government being 33 percent above the OECD average for health. Total spending for other social services rises too, although it is still below the OECD average.

Health provides an excellent example of how the provision of welfare

TABLE 3.3 Public Expenditure on Social Programs: U.S. in
Comparative Perspective

	USA (% GNP)	OECD (mean % GNP)	USA as % mean	Per Capita Spending		
				USA ($)	OECD (mean $)	USA as % mean
Education	5.2	5.5	95	815	496	164
Pensions	7.2	9.0	80	1,127	812	139
Health	4.3	5.6	77	674	505	133
Other social services	1.4	5.1	27	219	460	48
Total social expenditure	(18.1)	(25.2)	72	(2,835)	(2,273)	125
All other programs[a]	17.2	18.5	93	2,987	1,725	173
Total public expenditure	35.3	43.7	81	5,822	3,998	146

SOURCE: Calculated from OECD 1984 data, as reported in Rose (forthcoming). Program
data for 1984; total, 1985.
[a] Principally defense and debt interest payments.

in American society can be greater than in the average OECD nation, due
to the conjoint effects of national wealth, market, and state. In 1984 the
average OECD nation spent 5.6 percent of its national product on health,
almost one-third more effort than government in America. The United
States thus ranks nineteenth among twenty-one OECD nations in public
spending on health. In the European mixed-economy welfare states, public spending comprises the great bulk of health expenditure in society.

When we examine a society's total health expenditure, America's position is doubly outstanding, because private-sector health expenditure is
greater than public expenditure. Thus, total expenditure on health in
America is 10.8 percent of the national product (OECD, 1985b: Table
4.3). In terms of spending as a proportion of the national product, Americans make more effort to care for their health than any European welfare
state. Because of a higher level of national product, greater social effort is
also translated into more money. Taking public- and private-sector expenditure together, we find that $1,781 is spent on the health care of the
average American, more than is spent in any other OECD nation. In Swe-

den, much greater public effort is offset by much lesser private effort, thus leading to an average expenditure of $1,152. In Britain, less private effort and an economy that has grown much more slowly than the OECD mean result in an average expenditure on health of $492.

The complaint that American government spends too little on social programs often mistakes ratios for quantities; proportionately less effort need not mean absolutely less provision. In fact, government in America spends more money on many social policies than do most OECD nations.[4] The truth in the complaint is that American government makes less effort to raise money than does the average European government. Yet a rich economy with a not-so-rich government can still provide more welfare than a country with welfare-state ambitions but a not-so-rich economy. The American practice of spending more on social benefits through the market and claiming less in taxation to fund public provision is in marked contrast with the Northern European conception of the collective provision of social welfare through the state. The Scandinavian ideal is exemplified by Sweden, which spends 31.3 percent of its national product on state-provided social policies, two-thirds more than American government.

The United States marches to a different drummer than the Scandinavian welfare states—but in no sense does it march alone (Rose, forthcoming). An analysis of twenty-one OECD nations shows a division into four contrasting groups, according to national wealth (a per capita national product above or below the OECD average as measured in 1985 U.S. dollars) and public effort (the proportion of that national product devoted to public expenditure).

By being high in national wealth yet relatively low in public expenditure, *the United States is as representative an advanced industrial society as Sweden*, which is high in both national wealth and public spending. Six OECD nations have the material resources to fund very high levels of welfare through the state but choose not to do so: United States, Japan, Germany, Australia, Switzerland, and Finland. Five relatively wealthy nations also make a major public spending effort: Sweden, Norway, Denmark, France, and Canada. In welfare, people count as well as nations. When people are the measure, America is even more representative. Countries that are rich but have governments making less social welfare effort contain 59 percent of the population of the OECD world, as against 13 percent in the rich, big-spending welfare states.

---

[4] This conclusion is independent of exchange rates used, as demonstrated by testing against very different exchange rates for the dollar since 1981. It also holds when an adjustment is made for OECD calculated Purchasing Power Parities. For details see Rose (forthcoming).

Running Out of Pie

The American approach to welfare emphasizes the importance of the size of the pie, rather than the distribution. The egalitarian concern of many European social policy experts requires the state to dominate the provision of welfare in order to offset the inequalities resulting from the distribution of incomes in the market. By contrast, the American approach accepts a greater role for the market and the resulting inequalities in distribution—as long as the money is there to provide a high standard of welfare for the average American.

The growth of public provision for welfare in America has been a function of the growth in national wealth; this has made more money available for private provision too. For the first three decades of the postwar era, politicians were able to enjoy what Heclo (1981, p. 397) has described as "policy without pain," funding increased welfare expenditure from the fiscal dividend of economic growth. A buoyant economy produced more tax revenue without requiring any increase in tax rates, and an economy subject to inflation saw tax revenues increase at an accelerating rate. Thanks to the fiscal dividend of growth, the state could spend more on education, health, and income maintenance programs and, consistent with the philosophy of a mixed society, individual citizens could also enjoy an increase in take-home pay. There was a change in the welfare mix, too, as the state's role, once small in social security and health, expanded. The proportion of national product spent on social programs went up from 10.9 percent of the national product in 1960 to 18.1 percent in 1981, less than the rise in the average OECD nation, but still an increase.

Since the world recession of the mid-1970s, there has been a slowing down in the rate of economic growth, thus greatly reducing the possibility of increasing total monetized welfare by increasing the size of the national pie. From 1952 to 1960 the American gross domestic product grew at a rate of 2.8 percent a year, and from 1961 to 1972, at a rate of 4.1 percent a year. In the decade since, however, the economy has only grown at an average rate of 1.7 percent a year.

When economic growth slows down, the growth of public expenditure on social programs slows down too. The point is dramatically illustrated by a comparison of growth in major social programs from 1960 to 1975, when the American economy was booming, as against 1975 to 1981, a period of recession (Table 3.4). In the boom period, real public expenditure on social programs grew annually by 7.3 percent in total, and by as much as 10.3 percent in health. Since 1975 the growth rate has fallen by more than three-quarters to 2.0 percent in total, and spending on unemployment compensation has actually fallen in real terms. When account

TABLE 3.4 Annual Rates of Growth in Public Social Expenditure in U.S.:
Boom Time and Bad Time

	Real Expenditure (% annual change)		Adjusted for Demographic Change (% annual change)	
	BoomTime 1960–1975	Bad Time 1975–1981	1960–1975	1975–1981
Education	6.1	0.4	5.0	0.6
Health	10.3	3.8	9.1	2.8
Pensions	7.2	4.4	5.1	1.9
Unemployment compensation	8.3	−9.5	4.4	−8.8
Total	7.3	2.0	5.5	0.9

SOURCE: OECD, Social Expenditures, 1960–1990 (Paris: OECD, 1985), Table 6g.

is taken of the fact that demographic changes can increase aggregate expenditure (for example, more people come of pensionable age), public expenditure has slowed down even more. Since 1975, total social spending by government has grown only 0.9 percent annually in per capita real terms, one-sixth the rate in the boom years.

Given slow economic growth, it is not possible for the market to increase its provision of welfare greatly in compensation for reduced rates of growth or actual cuts in public provision. In times of economic recession, private sector firms will not raise wages much or at all. An increase in unemployment will also affect demand. Moreover, firms will seek to cut costs by reducing fringe benefits, including contributions toward welfare benefits for workers. Pressures for cost containment in health care now come from private sector employers who find that the cost of health insurance for workers is one of their major operating costs.

The household is limited too in the additional resources it can mobilize to augment welfare. At the margin, do-it-yourself labor can be substituted for paid labor for such tasks as simple household repairs or some personal social services, and less money can be spent in restaurants and for convenience foods and more time spent in the kitchen (Rose, 1985a). But major health and education needs cannot be produced at home, and they are expensive to buy in the market. The same is true of transport, for an unemployed person who can no longer afford to run a car suffers very restricted mobility.

The slowing down of rates of growth should not be misperceived as an actual contraction in the economy, or a cut in the real value of spending on health, education, or income maintenance (Rose, 1980). However, once the growth rate of the economy approaches one percent or less, then the overall picture approaches a no-growth pattern (Meyer, 1984).

In a recession, the state cannot easily take on new welfare commitments to compensate for private sector and household problems, because spending on established programs tends to rise in a recession (for example, unemployment benefits and subsidies to business and industry), while tax revenue rises more slowly as the economy slows down.

Public finance today is about policy with pain. The inertia commitments of government insure that major policy commitments are honored in the budget. The statutory entitlements of the welfare state require a Reagan or a Thatcher Administration to maintain retirement security, education, and established health programs. The political commitment to the safety-net features of welfare policies increases in recession, as fewer citizens feel confident that they can make provision for expensive welfare services solely through the market.

Pain arises from the difficulties of meeting the cost of major social programs. In the postwar era, the cost of the two major programs, education and health, has risen faster than the cost of living generally, because they are labor intensive. The relative price effect means that the relative cost of providing services (nursing, teaching, or, for that matter, haircuts) rises, since these labor-intensive services cannot realize the economies of scale and technological innovation achievable through the mass production of capital-intensive goods (Heller, 1981). Social Security costs have risen, as old age benefits have been increased to take into account rising living standards and inflation. Public pensions can thus be more generous (and costly) than private sector pensions.

While costs are rising, public revenue does not rise proportionately in a period of relatively slow economic growth. The "painless" increase in revenue due to the fiscal dividend of economic growth is no longer practicable; real tax increases are often required to achieve major increases in welfare expenditure. Insofar as extra tax revenue means less discretionary income for citizens to spend in the private sector, tax-financed increases in public spending may not lead to an increase of total consumption in society.

The Reagan Administration sought to delay the effects of America's slow growth by financing current consumption through borrowing, particularly, unprecedented borrowing from abroad. Overseas borrowing financed a great increase in imports and harmed exports, creating a trade deficit of more than $150 billion in the year 1987. Very little of the increased imports was devoted to social welfare purposes, either public or private. Simultaneously, the massive cut in tax revenue resulting from the 1981 tax act did not generate the forecast "supply side" growth. Hence, budget deficits rose above $200 billion a year. At one stage, the Reagan Administration was borrowing one dollar for every three it raised in taxes. The borrowed receipts went to finance increased defense spending and the rapidly rising burden of interest payments on accumulated past deficits, as well as a measure of increase in social expenditure. President Reagan resisted any cuts in Social Security, but the tightening of the budget noose by revenue shortfalls and rising expenditures produced a very high opportunity cost, restricting new programs and squeezing rather than expanding other established programs (cf. Marris, 1985).

While economic forecasting inevitably involves uncertainties, one thing appears clear: in order to deal with the foreign-financed double deficits of Reaganomics, a medium-term structural shift will be needed in the American economy. The shift will be from consumption to savings and investment, and from the production of nontradable services, such as health care or primary and secondary education, to manufactured goods for export. When what Peter G. Peterson (1987) has described as the "morning after" effects of Reaganomics are confronted, the brakes will be placed upon the growth of public spending, as reducing the deficit will have a pressing claim on additional revenues. Insofar as this is financed by higher taxes, this may hit the market consumption of non–social welfare goods and services most. But it also means that social programs in the public sector will face what Urban Institute economist John Palmer (1987) describes as the "the inevitability of retrenchment."

Public opinion in the United States is very much more inclined to oppose tax increases than in Northern Europe. This is true even though tax effort (that is, taxation as a proportion of the national product) is substantially lower in America than in most European countries. When surveys ask Britons and Swedes whether they would prefer higher spending on public benefits and higher taxes, the status quo, or lower taxes and benefits, the majority endorse the present high-tax high-benefit regimes of their countries, or favor increasing taxes and benefits (Hadenius, 1985; Rose and Karran, 1987, Table 9.4). In the United States, by contrast, the electorate divides almost evenly between those who favor the status quo, and those who favor reducing public services in order to have lower taxes (ACIR, 1983; Smith, 1987).

The limited room for maneuver in public expenditure is shown by examining the federal budget in terms of its "virtually uncontrollable" programs—income maintenance, defense, debt interest, and health. In the long run these commitments may be modified, by law or other means;

TABLE 3.5 Squeeze of the "Uncontrollable" on U.S. Federal Budget, 1986–1990

	1986 Actual		1990 Estimated	
	$ (billions)	%	$ (billions)	%
Income maintenance	348	34	389	34
Defense	273	27	330	29
Net debt interest	136	13	139	12
Health and Medicare	106	10	131	11
Total "Uncontrollable"	864	84	989	86
All other programs	159	16	167	14

SOURCE: Calculated from Budget of the United States Government: Fiscal Year 1988 (Washington, D.C.: Government Printing Office House Document 99–17, 1987), Table 2–47.

however, in the short run they can hardly be repudiated. Together, these programs accounted for 84 percent of federal expenditure in 1986, and are forecast to claim 86 percent of federal expenditure by 1990. If anything, Table 3.5 underestimates the money required for virtually uncontrollable programs. This is most obviously the case for debt interest, which is officially forecast to fall as a percentage of public spending, even though the size of the structural deficit suggests that it should grow.

State and local governments cannot be expected to find substantial funds for new social programs, for they are feeling the impact of the federal government exporting cuts to state and local government. The federal government has been reducing the real value of broad-based categorical grants, and also proposing to end general revenue sharing (Ladd, 1984; OMB, 1985b: Special Analysis H). State and local government cannot easily initiate new social programs when they must run hard to continue to fund the programs for which they already have fiscal responsibility.

To a very great extent, America is today locked into the present mix of welfare from the state, the market, and the household. Public programs that have survived two terms of a Reagan Administration ideologically predisposed to privatization are unlikely to be repudiated in the future (cf. Palmer, 1987). And the private sector, too, especially such nonprofit agencies as hospitals and universities, has learned the cost to themselves of cutbacks where public funds make a significant contribution to their own revenue mix (Salamon, 1986).

Problems Within the Mix

The provision of welfare from a mix of sources—public sector, private, and household, with major interdependencies between all three—does not dispose of all problems, even in times of prosperity. One problem is perennial—the tradeoff between the individual's access to welfare as a citizen and as a consumer. The other problem is contingent—directing the state's resources at those most in need.

The distinctive characteristic of state provision of welfare is that it makes access depend upon political status (citizenship) rather than market status (purchasing power). Anyone who meets the entitlement qualifications laid down in a public law is able to claim education, health care, or income maintenance benefits. The rationale is political. Citizens are conceived as members of a single national community, deserving benefits by virtue of a common citizenship. In a democracy, such benefits are considered an expression of mutual regard; in a dictatorship benefits are given by the state in order to extract more services from subjects (Flora and Alber, 1981).

Whatever the philosophy about collective care by public servants, the state provision of social benefits is necessarily legalistic, bureaucratized, and, at the point of production, monetized. The access of individual citizens depends first of all upon statutory entitlement. In order for a benefit to be available equally to all citizens, bureaucratic rules are necessary to ensure standardization in service delivery. Because charges are not made and producers have tenured posts, expert producers have a greater opportunity to influence the services that citizens receive than do organizations dealing with consumers in the market (Lipsky, 1980; Rose, 1987).

The distinctive characteristic of the market provision of welfare is that you can get what you pay for. The food a family eats is not dictated by laws or by bureaucratic regulations, but by family tastes and prices in the market. At a given level of expenditure, people can satisfy their tastes for food, housing, and transportation in many different ways. State-funded health care often leaves the choice of doctor to the patient, and public enterprises often provide a choice of goods and services, for example, as between travel by air or rail, or heating a house with electricity or gas.

The limitation of the market provision of welfare is that you only get what you can pay for. Choice is effective insofar as a family has the income to pay for what it wants. Whereas the incomes of families are unequal, their status as citizens is equal. Each citizen can stand as tall as the next in claiming benefits. The state provision of welfare can compensate for income inequalities by providing benefits to those with low incomes, and it can promote equality of access by providing benefits without any test of income.

State and market differ too in the value placed upon uniformity as against variety. Proponents of state action normally promote the idea of a uniform standard of provision for all citizens. The mixing of market and state provision undermines uniformity, and thus equality of treatment, when, as in Britain, 5 percent of the population is educated or given health care outside the state system. Proponents of the market regard differences in welfare provision as nominal, that is, as indicative of different tastes rather than of class differences among citizens. The idea of standardization, with all this implies in terms of monopoly provision from a single source of supply, is anathema to proponents of the market. It is also inconsistent with the pluralism of a federal system of government.

The household remains a barrier against uniformity, for family circumstances differ. State measures can and do discriminate within the life cycle. A family with children benefits from education and a couple without children does not; the elderly receive more health care than the young and active. But the substantial changes in family organization in the past generation—the growth of single-parent families, of cohabitation without marriage, and divorce and remarriage—are likely to alter (and probably reduce) the household's capacity for providing welfare. A divorced parent can probably expect less help from his or her children in old age than a parent who has not been involved in such a disruption. The travail of the AFDC (Aid to Families with Dependent Children) program is a reminder of the limits of the state's capacity to intervene in household matters, even those that directly affect welfare.

The mix of state and market sources of welfare reflects the relative significance of consumer choice as against civic entitlement at a given moment. The American mix today accommodates a substantial state contribution to welfare. The failure of the Reagan Administration to cut the "big ticket" items of social policy emphasizes that there remains much political support for programs that are regarded as part of the American way of life, whether as a consequence of more than a century of tradition (education); two generations (pensions); or more recent innovations (Medicare and Medicaid). These are programs from which everyone can hope to benefit at some stage in life.

But Americans retain a substantial skepticism about the scope for public provision of welfare, and confidence that their efforts in the market and family networks can provide many things that people want and need. American attitudes toward poverty show substantial ambivalence.

People favor action by the federal government on behalf of the poor, they want to spend more, they think the poor have a hard time getting by on what the government gives them. At the same time, they are critical of the poverty efforts, they think they have often failed, and they think poor individuals can and should take more responsibility for themselves

(American Enterprise Institute, 1985). Since the state does not have a monopoly upon the production of welfare, such reasoning is logical. Since America is a relatively rich society, such an attitude is realistic for the majority of the population.

Whatever measure is used, the evidence is that upwards of five-sixths of Americans are above the poverty line.[5] There is neither the political pressure nor the fiscal slack to expand greatly the state's contribution to the welfare mix. For example, to bring public effort for health care up to the relatively low British standard of public spending as a percentage of GDP would add $400 billion a year to the federal budget, at a time when deficits and debt interest costs have produced pressures to keep a lid on public spending. Nor would hospitals, third-party insurance institutions, doctors, and others with a stake in the existing mix of public and private sector services readily abandon established institutions that already meet the health needs of most Americans (Klass, 1985).

Yet it is unrealistic to assume that a rising tide of economic growth will lift everyone out of poverty through success in the market. Even in a period of affluence in the late 1960s and early 1970s, the poor were not helped greatly; the benefits went mostly to those in the work force (Schwarz, 1983). In the 1980s, economic growth can help in some ways, such as reducing unemployment, but it cannot help groups in poverty for noneconomic reasons (Gottschalk and Danziger, 1984).

The segmentation of society, particularly prevalent in America's multiplicity of poverty programs, means that it is not necessary for government to provide benefits for all in order to help many in need. The principle of selectivity is already well established. The taxing of Social Security benefits is an example of a move away from universal or, critics would argue, indiscriminate benefits, toward more selectivity in income transfers. Medicare and Medicaid target financial assistance for health care to those groups most in need—the elderly, because of their physical condition, and the poor, because of their economic condition. In higher education, the principle of subsidized public universities (imposing some charges) coexists with private institutions (receiving some federal funds) to provide mass education by a mix of state and market.

In a mixed society, the guiding principle for budget choices of public policymakers should be to look after those who are least able to meet

---

[5] In international comparisons, there is a fundamental contrast between the definition of poverty in relative as against absolute terms. For example, the Luxembourg Income Study's relative measure of poverty (less than one-half of average posttransfer family income) shows the United States as having nearly double the level of poverty as the average country examined, because of the way in which income is distributed in America. But when GNP per capita is the measure, according to this absolute measure of income, poverty in the United States is hardly so high. Smeeding et al., 1985, Table 5; OECD, 1985a, Table 1; and Rose, forthcoming, Table 1.

their welfare needs through the market (for example, the unemployed) or through the household (for example, single-parent families). In this way, marginal increases in resources can be targeted to those least able to help themselves. Equally important, any cuts (or denials of increases) can be directed at those best able to substitute through the market or the household. In this way, the fisc's allocation of a constrained amount of public money can have the greatest chance of increasing, rather than reducing, total welfare in society.

References

ACIR. 1983. *Changing Public Attitudes on Government and Taxes*. Washington, D.C.: Advisory Commission on Intergovernmental Relations, S–12.

Allardt, Erik. 1986. "The Civic Conception of the Welfare State in Scandinavia." In Rose and Shiratori, 1986: 107–125.

American Enterprise Institute. 1985. "Opinion Roundup." *Public Opinion* 8 (3): 25–31.

Bawden, D. Lee, ed. 1984. *The Social Contract Revisited*. Washington, D.C.: Urban Institute Press.

Flora, P., and J. Alber. 1981. "Modernization, Democratization and Development of Welfare Studies in Western Europe." In Flora and Heidenheimer, 1981: 37–80.

Flora, P., and A. J. Heidenheimer. 1981. *The Development of Welfare States in Europe and America*. New Brunswick, N.J.: Transaction Books.

Gershuny, J. I. 1981. "Changement des Modeles de Loisir, Royaume Uni, 1961–1974/5." *Temps Libres* 4: 115–134.

Glazer, Nathan. 1986. "Welfare and 'Welfare' in America." In Rose and Shiratori, 1986: 40–63.

Gottschalk, Peter, and Sheldon Danziger. 1984. "Macroeconomic Conditions, Income Transfers, and the Trends in Poverty." In Bawden, 1984: 185–215.

Hadenius, Axel. 1985. "Citizens Strike a Balance: Discontent with Taxes, Content with Spending." *Journal of Public Policy* 5 (3): 349–364.

Heclo, Hugh. 1981. "Toward a New Welfare State." In Flora and Heidenheimer, 1981: 383–406.

Heller, Peter. 1981. "Diverging Trends in the Shares of Nominal and Real Government Expenditure in GDP." *National Tax Journal* 34, 1: 61–74.

Hill, T. P. 1979. "Do It Yourself and GDP." *Review of Income and Wealth* 25 (1): 31–40.

Juster, F. T., and K. C. Land, eds. 1981. *Social Accounting Systems*. New York: Academic Press.

Klass, Gary M. 1985. "Explaining America and the Welfare State: An Alternative Theory." *British Journal of Political Science* 15 (4): 427–450.

Kramer, Ralph M. 1981. *Voluntary Agencies in the Welfare State*. Berkeley, Ca.: University of California Press.

Ladd, Helen F. 1984. "Federal Aid to State and Local Governments." In G. B.

Mills and J. L. Palmer, eds. *Federal Budget Policy in the 1980s*: 165–202. Washington, D.C.: Urban Institute Press.

Lampman, Robert J. 1984. *Social Welfare Spending: Accounting for Changes from 1950 to 1978*. New York: Academic Press.

Lipsky, Michael. 1980. *Street-Level Bureaucracy*. New York: Russell Sage Foundation.

Litwak, Eugene. 1985. *Helping the Elderly: The Complementary Roles of Informal Networks and Formal Systems*. New York: Guilford Press.

Marris, Stephen. 1985. *Deficits and the Dollar: The World Economy at Risk*. Washington D.C.: Institute for International Economics.

Meyer, Jack A. 1984. "Budget Cuts in the Reagan Administration: A Question of Fairness." In Bawden, 1984: 33–64.

OECD. 1984. *National Accounts 1960–1983*. Vol. 1. Paris: OECD.

———. 1985a. *Social Expenditure 1960–1990*. Paris: OECD.

———. 1985b. *Measuring Health Care 1960–1983*. Paris: OECD.

OMB. 1985a. *Budget of the United States Government: Fiscal Year 1986*. Washington, D.C.: Government Printing Office.

———. 1985b. *Special Analyses: Budget of the US Government Fiscal Year 1986*. Washington, D.C.: Government Printing Office.

Palmer, John L. 1987. "Income Security Policies in the United States: The Inevitability and Consequences of Retrenchment." *Journal of Public Policy* 7 (1): 1–32.

Peters, B. Guy. 1985. "The United States: Absolute Change and Relative Stability." In R. Rose, ed. *Public Employment in Western Nations*: 228–261. Cambridge University Press.

Peterson, Peter G. 1987. "The Morning After." *Atlantic Monthly* October: 43–69.

Rose, Richard. 1976. "On the Priorities of Government," *European Journal of Political Research* 4 (3): 247–289.

———. 1980. "Misperceiving Public Expenditure: Feelings about 'Cuts'." In C. H. Levine and I. Rubin, eds. *Fiscal Stress and Public Policy*: 203–230. Beverly Hills: Sage Publications.

———. 1985a. "Getting By in Three Economies." In J. E. Lane, ed. *State and Market: The Politics of the Public and the Private*: 103–141. Beverly Hills: Sage Publications.

———. 1985b. "The Programme Approach to the Growth of Government." *British Journal of Political Science* 15 (1): 1–28.

———. 1985c. *Public Employment in Western Nations*. Cambridge University Press.

———. 1986a. "Common Goals but Different Roles: The State's Contribution to the Welfare Mix." In Rose and Shiratori, 1986: 13–39.

———. 1986b. "The Dynamics of the Welfare Mix in Britain." In Rose and Shiratori, 1986: 80–106.

———. 1987. "Giving Directions to Permanent Officials: Signals from the Electorate, the Market, Laws and Expertise." In Jan-Erik Lane, ed. *Bureaucracy and Public Choice*: 210–230. Beverly Hills: Sage Publications.

———. Forthcoming. "How Big and How Exceptional Is American Government? A Political Economy Comparison." *Political Science Quarterly*.

Rose, Richard, and Terence Karran. 1987. *Taxation by Political Inertia*. London: Allen and Unwin.

Rose, Richard, and Rei Shiratori, eds. 1986. *The State's Contribution to the Welfare Mix*. New York: Oxford University Press.

Salamon, Lester. 1986. "Government and the Voluntary Sector in an Era of Retrenchment: The American Experience." *Journal of Public Policy* 6 (1): 1–19.

Sametz, A. W. 1968. "Production of Goods and Services: The Measurement of Economic Growth." In E. B. Sheldon and W. E. Moore, eds. *Indicators of Social Change*: 77–96. New York: Russell Sage Foundation.

Schwarz, John E. 1983. *America's Hidden Success*. New York: W. W. Norton.

Smeeding, Timothy, R. Hauser, L. Rainwater, M. Rein, and G. Schaber. 1985. *Poverty in Major Industrialized Countries*. Walferdange, Luxembourg: Centre d'Etudes de Populations, de Pauvrete et de Politiques Socio-Economiques. LIS-CEPs Working Paper No. 2.

Smith, Tom W. 1987. "Public Opinion and the Welfare State: A Crossnational Perspective." Paper presented at American Sociological Association annual meeting. Chicago.

Titmuss, Richard M. 1970. *The Gift Relationship: From Human Blood to Social Policy*. London: Allen and Unwin.

Weidenbaum, Murray. 1970. *The Modern Public Sector*. New York: Basic Books.

Weisbrod, Burton A. 1977. *The Voluntary Non-Profit Sector*. Lexington, Mass.: D. C. Heath.

Wilensky, Harold A. 1975. *The Welfare State and Equality*. Berkeley, Ca.: University of California Press.

4

Privatizing the Delivery of Social Welfare Services: An Idea to Be Taken Seriously

MARC BENDICK, JR.

Modern philanthropists need to remind themselves of the old definition of greatness: that it consists in the possession of the largest share of the common human qualities and experiences . . . Popular opinion calls him the greatest of Americans who gathered to himself the largest amount of American experience, and who never forgot when he was in Washington how the "crackers" in Kentucky and the pioneers in Illinois thought and felt, striving to retain their thoughts and feelings, and to embody only the mighty will of the "common people."
JANE ADDAMS, *A Modern Lear* (1912)

America has always been a reluctant welfare state. Government-sponsored social welfare services emerged in our history later than in many other market-oriented industrial nations, and they still command a smaller proportion of national income (Trattner, 1979; OECD, 1985). Although political leaders in Bismarck's Germany or Lloyd George's England were advocating the principle of public social welfare services before they were affordable or popularly demanded, in the United States officials still apologetically defend them long after they are in place. From Tocqueville's praise of voluntary groups and Thoreau's paean to self-reliance to Ronald Reagan's anecdotes of kindly deeds from neighbor to neighbor, the American emphasis consistently has been on the local, the pluralistic, the voluntary, and the businesslike over the national, the universal, the legally entitled, and the governmental.

This context—in which "publicization" of social welfare services is viewed as the deviation from the norm—helps to explain the current vogue of proposals to privatize social welfare services. The Reagan Administration did not invent the concept. The idea needs to be treated seriously, not because of who currently holds power in Washington, but because of the perennial fascination it has held for American thought and action.

This chapter attempts that serious treatment. It argues that advocates of expanded social welfare services (I count myself in that category) need to dissect the concept of privatization into two constituent parts. They will thereby discover that what they fear from privatization is associated primarily with arrangements under which government delegates both the delivery of services and the raising of funds to finance those services. However, versions of privatization that delegate the former but leave government responsible for the latter do not inflict the same damages. Instead, they render social welfare services in this country compatible with the dominant American ideology in a way that European social statism is not. Furthermore, empirical evidence indicates that privatized systems, appropriately designed, can deliver many social welfare services as effectively as can public ones. Therefore, the paper concludes that the American social welfare system can best be advanced by making pervasive appropriate forms of privatized delivery.

The Two Faces of Privatization

The logic that leads to this conclusion starts with some definitions. Privatization may be defined as shifting into nongovernmental hands some or all roles in producing a good or service that was once publicly produced or might be publicly produced. A diversity of arrangements falls within this broad approach. One recent survey, for example, lists: contracting out, franchises, grants and subsidies, vouchers, volunteers, self help, use of regulatory and taxing authority, encouragement of private organizations to take over an authority, reducing the demand for services, obtaining temporary help from private firms, using fees to adjust demand, and formation of public/private ventures (Hatry, 1983).

In all these approaches, the "retail level" direct delivery of services is achieved through nongovernmental institutions—nonprofit, for-profit, or even (in the case of self-help) recipients themselves. However, the arrangements fall into two distinct categories along a second dimension, which is the degree to which governmental funding supports nongovernmental service delivery. One category, which may be referred to as "governmental load-shedding," encompasses arrangements under which both the means of financing and the means of delivering a service are divorced from government. In contrast, the second—which may be referred to as "empowerment of mediating institutions"—covers arrangements under which government retains some or all responsibility for funding the service while delegating production and delivery. Budget reductions, user fees, volunteers, and reducing the demand for services fall in the first category; vouchers, contracting out, grants and subsidies, and public/private partnerships fall in the second.

This distinction is important, because, under likely projections of the future, the long-term level of public demand diverges sharply between the two governmental roles. Trends in American society suggest a steady and rising demand for collectively financed goods, and yet a long-term and rising opposition to public delivery. This means that approaches in the "empowerment" category are associated with potential growth, whereas approaches in the "load-shedding" category—as well as traditional government-provided social welfare programs—are not.

The Rising Demand for Collectively Funded Social Welfare Goods

Support for this conclusion derives from the basic economic concept that social welfare services are normal economic goods, which consumers regard in the same way they regard any other good or service that is desirable but not free. In particular, as consumers' incomes rise, individual members of American society demand more of these goods, just as they also want more personal consumption goods (for example, video cassette recorders), more leisure time, and more of other collective goods (such as defense). The formal name for this hypothesis is positive income elasticity of demand, and evidence supports the hypothesis. For example, after adjusting for inflation, per capita private charitable giving in the United States increased at slightly more than 3 percent per year from 1955 to 1983 (*Giving USA*, 1984). In the same period, federal government expenditures—of which social welfare activities claimed a large and growing proportion—increased at about 4 percent a year. Both rates of increase substantially outstripped that of per capita income, for which increases averaged slightly more than 2 percent in the same period.

Ironically, the pullback in voter support for public social welfare spending during recent years—as symbolized in Proposition 13 in California and Proposition 2½ in Massachusetts, as well as federal budget cuts during the Reagan Administration—provides further support for this hypothesis. In the 1975 to 1985 period, reductions in public social welfare spending (as well as in other forms of nondefense governmental outlays) coincided with bleak personal income growth for the average American family. Productivity growth in the overall economy stalled during the 1970s, OPEC price rises and other circumstances triggered galloping inflation, and during the early 1980s the economy endured its longest and deepest recession since the Great Depression. All these together resulted in first a stagnation and then a modest reduction in the average family's real income.[1] Cutbacks in voters' willingness to pay for public social welfare programs should therefore have been expected; these cutbacks coincided with reductions in households' consumption across the board, from new cars to vacations to visits to the dentist.

So long as recent reductions in social welfare expenditures reflect considerations of affordability rather than a sea change in generosity, all is well; affordability is something that time will cure. Despite the mediocre economic performance of the 1970s and early 1980s, long-run prospects for the American standard of living remain bright. In the short run, the economy has recovered—at least partially—from the depths of recession. In the longer run, the continuing process of technological advancement—currently symbolized by the proliferation of microchip devices—suggests a rekindling of the long, steady rise of per capita incomes at the rate of 1 or 2 percent a year, which has prevailed historically (Hulten and Sawhill, 1984). This rise, when mediated by the positive income elasticity of demand previously discussed, should provide a moderate but continuing increase in resources for social welfare services.

Discontent with Public Sector Delivery

The long-term increase in resources for social welfare services could be derailed, of course, if the American citizenry were turned against social welfare services by other considerations. Recent developments in voter attitudes and behavior suggest just such a danger, in the form of widespread distrust, discomfort, and loss of faith in the public sector.

Survey research repeatedly uncovers substantial mistrust of government, a mistrust encompassing both public-sector motives and public-sector competence (Ladd, 1984). When a sample of citizens was asked what proportion of each tax dollar they believe the federal government wastes, the median response was $.48 (Kelman, 1985). Another survey probed the level of public confidence in various major American institutions, and found that only 19 percent of respondents expressed great confidence in the executive branch of the federal government—a figure half as high as for business corporations or local United Ways and one-third as high as for medicine and institutions of higher education (U.S. Senate,

---

[1] For a synopsis of these developments, see Hulten and Sawhill (1984). A further illustration of the same process is provided by the case of "yuppies"—today's young urban professionals whose alleged selfishness led them to support President Reagan and reduced public spending despite their affluence. Statistical analysis reveals that the current generation of persons in their twenties and thirties are generally less affluent than were their parents at comparable stages in their lives, and that therefore their lower levels of support for governmental social welfare measures can be explained as lack of income rather than a lower level of idealism or generosity. See Levy and Michel (1984).

1973). Since at least the early 1970s, the number of survey respondents who favored a decrease in government services and taxes has consistently outnumbered those advocating an increase by four to one (Goodman, 1983).

The same discontent is signaled more directly in voting patterns. The American electorate who selected Ronald Reagan had previously favored Jimmy Carter, who also ran against the Washington establishment. The political advantages of incumbency, formerly much cited by political scientists, have in recent elections proved to be liabilities.

Of course, anti-government attitudes in America are more deeply rooted and permanent than these references to the latest election results or public opinion polls suggest. Rejection of public tyranny was the act that led to the founding of the nation. Concern with limiting government dominated the development of the American Constitution, with its system of separation of powers and explicit Bill of Rights. The preservation of cultural, economic, and political pluralism has been a perennial theme in both American law and American thought—starting with the constitutional protection of states' sovereignty, extending through such historic events as the bending of draft laws to accommodate religious objectors and of public school laws to accommodate conservative religious sects, and continuing currently in developments such as bilingual education and neighborhood school districts.

A second tradition in American thought reinforces our national reluctance to turn to the public sector to solve societal problems—belief in individual initiative and the allocation of rewards to those who work to earn them (Hofstadter, 1955). When we are faced with community problems, this tradition conditions us to turn not to distant government for solutions, but to personal voluntarism and community self-help organizations. Starting with Tocqueville's famous discussion of the "principle of association" in American life in the 1830s, the origins of this approach have been attributed to reliance on volunteer groups of neighbors among pioneers settling the American frontier (Schambra, 1982).

I do not cite these hoary traditions to imply that social arrangements never do change or never should change. My point is that as societal needs evolve and new societal arrangements must be constructed, those arrangements should conform to the response style that a society has consistently favored.

Given such a consistent pattern of anti-government bias in the American response style, it is unfortunate that much of American social policy has looked to Europe for models of both specific programs and general approaches. Reflecting political, social, economic, and intellectual circumstances very different from those in the United States, most European nations have evolved an approach to social welfare services that is strongly state centered.[2] The American nation was formed in revolt against tyranny. European nation-states typically emerged when central governments imposed national unity on independent feudal states. Although class conflict has bred significant voting support in Europe for socialist and semisocialist political parties, the comparable portion of the political spectrum virtually does not exist in the United States. From such historical roots grew European political systems—and social welfare systems—in which government was simply presumed to be the logical instrument for meeting community needs.

When presented explicitly to the American public, the European welfare state approach has won few adherents outside academic circles. Consider, for example, the political drubbing of George McGovern in the 1972 presidential race, resulting in no small part from the public's swift rejection of his proposed guaranteed annual income "demogrant." Other examples include the recurrent failure of the political process to provide comprehensive national health insurance and the chronic absence of a children's allowance in the American system. In contrast, legislative and public support for successful American social welfare initiatives has been mobilized by deemphasizing their governmental nature and pretending that they conformed to more traditional American values. The characterization of Social Security retirement benefits as insurance rather than income transfers is the most prominent example; the practice of justifying social services for low-income families in the name of preparation for self-support is another.

The Dilemma of Public Goods Provision

Why did we link social welfare services to the public sector in the first place? The explanation may be found by reference to another concept from economic theory, that of "public goods" and their undersupply by the private, for-profit markets (Olson, 1965).

Economists define a public good as one that confers consumption benefits on a number of individuals simultaneously. A private good—such as a candy bar—is consumed by me alone, but the national defense protects the whole nation at the same time. So, too, social welfare programs benefit a range of persons simultaneously. Donations to a charitable cause benefit not only the donor and the recipient, but also other concerned citizens.

Economists argue that private, profit-seeking markets will produce the

[2] Partial exceptions may be observed in the Federal Republic of Germany and the Netherlands, where delivery of social welfare services through private nonprofit agencies is the norm.

socially efficient quantity of private goods, such as candy bars, by responding to consumer demand. But public goods present special problems in accumulating consumer demand to provide a market for profit-seeking producers. Although I benefit from your charitable donation, you have no way to make me pay for that benefit. If I behave in a selfish and rational manner—which is what economists assume—then I maximize my well-being by playing the "free rider" on your charitable behavior—enjoying the benefit without contributing anything myself. But then, you would reason the same way and not make your donation. Thus, the private market will have little or no effective demand to respond to by producing public goods, even though substantial actual demand is going unsatisfied.

Faced with this dilemma, economists traditionally suggest compulsory taxation as the only way to accumulate your and my demand for public goods and thereby to assure their production in socially desired quantities. This is the basic logic behind assigning public goods—including social welfare services—to the governmental sector.

Of course, moving from economic theory to the real world, we observe that the provision of public goods outside of government is not zero. Nonprofit institutions—such as private charities—operate in the United States on the scale of many billions of dollars per year (Weisbrod, 1977). Nevertheless, there are real limitations to nongovernmental arrangements for funding public goods such as social welfare services, and that multi-billion-dollar scale may be assumed to underrepresent society's full demand for those services.

To make matters worse, the fund-raising difficulties that handicap the nongovernmental financing of social welfare services as public goods are growing over time, reflecting major social and economic trends in the late twentieth century. At the root of these growing difficulties is that the success of nongovernmental, nonprofit fund-raising is typically dependent on personal relationships. A sense of personal identification between donor and donee helps to overcome the rational tendency to play the free rider. So does peer pressure among donors. Thus, the more close-knit and homogeneous the society, the more successful fund-raising is likely to be. But modern community life is increasingly impersonal and heterogeneous. We no longer live in small, scattered frontier settlements and join together in neighborhood barn raisings such as those Tocqueville observed. Most of the American population lives in urban areas with relatively little face-to-face contact with the majority of fellow community members. A high rate of geographic mobility means that relatively few of us live in communities to which we have lifelong ties. Perhaps most tellingly, there is an ever-increasing divergence in personal characteristics between recipients of social welfare services and potential donors, particularly along dimensions such as race. In such circumstances, charitable acts tend to become less self-motivating; direct personal contact and personal identification give way to impersonal acts, such as writing a check to an institutional cause. These are precisely the circumstances where the free-rider problem operates most virulently.

Another fact influencing the level of donations—particularly those of in-kind volunteer time—is demographics. Future levels of volunteer time may be expected to be affected adversely by the shrinking proportion of the American population in categories that traditionally contribute disproportionate amounts of volunteer effort. The youth population (age 15 to 19) in the year 2000 is projected to be only 7.1 percent of the national population, down from 9.3 percent in 1980; working-age females not employed outside the home are projected to decline to 16 percent from 17.1 percent in 1980; and the younger retired population (age 65 through 74) is projected to fall to 6.6 percent from 6.9 percent in 1980.[3]

The upshot of these considerations is that, throughout the last years of the twentieth century, the absolute level of resources generated privately for public-regarding purposes such as social welfare will probably increase modestly, but the relative ability of such activities to fund themselves will continually decrease. Voluntarily financed provision of social welfare services will continue to play some role in the American system of social problem-solving, but a gradually decreasing one.

Load-shedding under
the Reagan Administration

From this set of circumstances comes terror on the part of advocates of social welfare services in the face of much of Ronald Reagan's rhetoric about private-sector initiatives. Reagan's dominant approach to privatization can appropriately be placed within the category of load-shedding—that is, turning over to the private sector both the delivery and the financing of social welfare services.

Among several bits of evidence supporting the characterization in the previous paragraph, the most straightforward is that President Reagan's public statements on the subject have consistently praised private projects that provide the type of services for which federal funds simultaneously were being substantially cut—by 38 percent over a three-year period in a sample I examined in an earlier paper (Bendick and Levinson, 1984). More to the point, his cuts in programs in which the government acted to empower private service deliverers have been as deep as those in pro-

---

[3] See Bendick and Levinson (1984). That reference also discusses parallel changes in the business community, which is another important source of charitable giving.

grams in which government both financed and delivered services. Examples of these "empowerment" programs include the federal agency Action (which provides technical assistance, training, research and development, publicity, and other services in support of such volunteer-based programs as Foster Grandparents, Young Volunteers in Action, and Volunteers in Service to America); the Urban Development Action Grant program (which provides financial subsidies to make private inner-city economic redevelopment commercially feasible); postal subsidies for nonprofit organizations (which are central to nonprofit fund-raising efforts); and federal financing to encourage private adoptions in place of publicly supervised foster care.

Unfortunately, privatization in the sense of load-shedding is equivalent to a reduction in the quantity of service provided. There is simply no way that private sector initiatives will voluntarily replace the funding removed by these cuts.

This point was well illustrated in an Urban Institute study of the financial support given nonprofit organizations such as hospitals, universities, social service agencies, and neighborhood organizations (Salamon and Abramson, 1982). The study estimated that such organizations stood to lose approximately $33 million in federal support over fiscal years 1982 to 1985, if President Reagan's then-current budget proposals had been adopted. To maintain current service levels, private giving would have had to grow over that period at a rate of 30 to 40 percent per year, three times more rapidly than it had grown over the previous several decades. At the same time, if these organizations were to expand to fill gaps in services left by an additional $115 billion in proposed cuts in federal programs in the same fields, it would have been necessary for private giving approximately to double during these years, a rate eight times greater than the highest rate of growth ever experienced. The likelihood of that occurring is slim.

Load-shedding would not only result in substantial reductions in the total quantity of social welfare services but would also generate adverse effects in terms of the nature and distribution of those services.

One problem arises in matching needs and resources over time and space. As discussed earlier, private charitable donations drop during a recession—just at the moment when the need for social welfare services grows along with the unemployment rate. Similarly, volunteers are most plentiful in affluent suburbs, while social welfare needs are most abundant in low-income, inner-city locales. The federal government can run a countercyclical deficit to expand its expenditures during recession and also can redistribute resources from affluent areas to poor areas. Nonprofit sources of funds typically are not well situated to do either.

A further problem with reliance on nonprofit fund-raising arises in the form of differences in values or culture between donors and recipients. Affluent donors often set different priorities in how resources are to be spent than do low-income recipients.[4] Thus, for example, corporations are more likely to fund a program to bring low-income children to hear the symphony than they are to fund a low-income community advocacy agency, whereas the preferences of the low-income community might well be the reverse.

Furthermore, in typical public programs, if a recipient can demonstrate eligibility for assistance, then he or she is legally entitled either to benefits or at least to due process and the absence of discrimination in competition for benefits. Privately financed programs, in contrast, more typically take the legal form of gifts, so that if a recipient behaves in some manner of which the donor disapproves, withholding assistance offers a powerful means of coercion. President Reagan's speeches frequently describe a world in which an indigent individual might depend on a volunteer doctor for medical services, a local church for food assistance, and a corporation for a college scholarship. The potential loss of individual freedom and dignity in such situations is substantial.

In sum, governmental load-shedding in social welfare services—such as that in which the Reagan Administration has engaged—is potentially disastrous from the point of view of meeting urgent social welfare needs. The total quantity of services, their targeting, and their effectiveness are all at risk.

The Efficiency of For-Profit Service Delivery

But suppose that we separate the two aspects of the provision of goods and services—financing and delivery. Do these dire predictions for privatized financing extend to programs involving public financing but privatized delivery—arrangements labeled "empowerment of mediating institutions" earlier in this chapter? To answer this question, I turn to empirical studies of what differences delivery systems make, starting with arrangements that utilize the profit-seeking private sector.[5]

CONTRACTING

Consider, to begin, what is in many senses the simplest privatization arrangement—contracting out. Much of the impetus for for-profit contracting out of social welfare services comes from the analogy to government contracting in general, where it is in fairly widespread use. A 1973

---

[4] See Brown (1984); Bendick (1978); Bendick and Levinson (1983).
[5] This section draws heavily on my earlier paper: Bendick (1982b).

survey of more than two thousand municipalities, for example, found that each of twenty-six types of public services were contracted out by at least 1 percent of sampled cities, and four types of services—refuse collection, street lighting, electricity supply, and engineering services—were contracted out by more than 10 percent of cities (Kirlin, Ries, and Sonenblum, 1977).

Minimizing cost is the usual reason cited for the use of privatization in such cases. The potential for cost savings is seen as arising from several sources: competition among firms that may create pressure for efficiency not present in a monopoly municipal department; a relative freedom from "red tape" and other procedural constraints; and the ability of private firms to hire, fire, compensate, and therefore motivate and utilize workers with greater flexibility than can government departments constrained both by civil service rules and strong unions.[6]

Empirical experience generally supports these contentions. When controlled evaluations have been undertaken, verifiable cost savings were observed, if not universally, more often than not. For example, in refuse collection, two independent studies have estimated cost saving at about 25 percent (Savas, 1982). A 1981 survey found that 69 percent of local governments in California reported that contracting out led to reduced costs, while only 17 percent reported increased costs. The survey also revealed that 41 percent of the municipalities indicated service quality improved under the contracting arrangement, as opposed to 18 percent noting poorer service quality (Hatry, 1983).

In extrapolating from these generally favorable findings to social welfare services, it is important to note the nature of the services encompassed within this pool of experience. Contracted-out municipal functions are predominantly straightforward, immediate, measurable, amenable to monitoring, and technical in nature—such as refuse collection, data processing, and streetlight maintenance. As one moves from such examples to (relatively rare) examples of contracting out for the more complex, undefinable, long-range and "subjective" services characteristic of the social welfare field, the record of successful experience rapidly thins.

One interesting example is provided by the growing phenomenon of privatized correctional services. The for-profit private sector has long occupied a small role in the operation of detention facilities in such forms as contracted-out laundry or food services. Nonprofit agencies have also

[6] On the other hand, costs could increase in a contracting-out arrangement if the administrative costs of letting and monitoring contracts are large; if private bidders are so few that little competitive pressure exists; if union, civil service, or other constraints prevent the public agency from reducing its own labor force and costs when some functions are contracted out; or if corruption arises in the contracting process.

been active in providing juvenile housing and remedial treatment. However, a dramatic expansion of these roles is now being attempted in the form of contracting out the entire operation of adult correctional facilities to for-profit corporations. Currently, about two dozen privatized detention centers exist in the United States, and the number is expected to double in the next two years.[7]

As with the previous examples, the main benefit of privatization in correctional services seems to be that of saving time and money. For example, a private detention center run by the Corrections Corporation of America for the Immigration and Naturalization Service (INS) was built in six months, whereas officials estimate that construction within the public sector would have required five years. Once in operation, the facility charges the INS $23.84 per inmate-day, a figure 10 percent lower than the $26.48 average cost in the INS's own facilities.

How are these cost savings achieved? Part of the answer seems to be found in ways that do not directly affect inmate welfare. For example, staff compensation paid by the corporation averages $500 per year lower than the comparable federal civil service scales, and employee benefits are more limited. Other sources of saving, however, may be assumed to be more at the expense of the "quality" of jail services experienced by inmates. For example, the Corrections Corporation of America provides each employee with 160 hours of training, most of it on the job; each federal jail employee receives 240 hours of formal full-time training before commencing work. Other services, such as a resident psychiatrist, are also less common in privatized facilities.

Parallel outcomes were observed in the largest single experience with contracting out for the delivery of complex human services—experiments with educational performance contracting during the early 1970s (Gramlich and Koshel, 1975). The concept is to delegate classroom instruction in regular public elementary and secondary schools to for-profit firms, allowing these firms considerable freedom in instructional methods. Typically, contractors implemented a variety of proprietary learning systems, computerized instruction, incentive pay to students, and other techniques not in widespread use in public schools. The firms were compensated not on the basis of costs, but on the basis of students' educational gains as measured on standardized achievement tests.

More than one hundred school districts experimented briefly with educational performance contracts using their own funds, and the federal government financed a more carefully controlled study in twenty localities. The experience was universally disappointing. In the controlled studies, test scores in subjects for which firms were paid showed only modest

---

[7] This information and that in the following paragraphs are drawn from "Trends in Private Jails—Controversy Breeds Studies," *Urban Outlook* 7 (March 15, 1985): 1–3.

gains (for example, about 7 percent in language and mathematics). At the same time, scores fell in subjects for which firms were not paid. Consistent with these results, none of the participating school districts chose to renew their contracts, the private firms lost money, and relations between contractors and school boards often closed on an acrimonious note.

VOUCHERS

Moving from contracting arrangements for the privatization of service delivery to the use of vouchers makes the situation even more problematic. In the context of public programs, a voucher may be defined as a transfer of income to a citizen to enhance that person's ability to purchase a specified type of good or service. The rationale for using vouchers instead of unrestricted cash transfers is that taxpayers wish to restrict the use of their donations to activities they approve of. The rationale for using vouchers instead of direct governmental provision of the good or service is, first, that recipients should be allowed some consumer choice among goods or services within the eligible category, and, second, that goods can be provided at lower cost.

One recent demonstration program illustrates both the strengths and the weaknesses of the voucher approach. The Experimental Housing Allowance Program (EHAP) was a social experiment (complete with control group) conducted with 30,000 households in twelve cities during the 1970s.[8] Housing allowances—vouchers intended to increase housing consumption by low-income families—were being proposed as an alternative to direct governmental provision of housing, such as in public housing projects.

On questions of housing costs and housing quality, the empirical findings of EHAP were encouraging. For example, the average cost of providing a standard quality two-bedroom housing unit in Pittsburgh in 1974 was estimated to be $4,155 a year for units provided through government-operated public housing. A comparable unit provided by the private market and paid for by a housing allowance cost $1,869 annually, only 45 percent as much. Low-income families generally proved to be efficient shoppers, obtaining good value for their money and needing little assistance in searching for or negotiating for units. Landlords proved generally cooperative, and no major supply bottlenecks or price inflation was evident. Control of the program could be maintained for relatively modest administrative costs (between 10 and 20 percent of total program costs). At least in the majority of housing markets, vouchers seemed better for everyone—taxpayers, recipients, and housing suppliers—than public construction and operation of low-income housing.

[8] The following discussion is based on Bendick (1982c); and Struyk and Bendick (1982).

While housing vouchers thus seem a success in terms of cost, efficiency, and straightforward aspects of housing quality, the story becomes more complex and the lessons more cautionary when other program objectives are considered. The reason housing vouchers were provided rather than cash was that taxpayers wished the additional purchasing power to be used only for housing. In practice, recipients elected primarily to substitute their vouchers for money they were already spending on rent and thus, in effect, to divert their new income to other uses. Only about 20 percent of the face value of vouchers went toward increased housing expenditures. This substitution was legal. The nonhousing uses made of the money often were of the sort that taxpayers might approve (additional food, clothing, and medical and dental care, for example); nevertheless, the objective of controlling recipient behavior was not achieved.

The principle this example illustrates is that provision of social welfare services through the voucher mechanism is a double-edged sword. On the one hand, harnessing the efficiency of private markets may lead to lower costs, better quality, or both. On the other hand, the more consumer control is given to voucher recipients, the less taxpayers are able to impose their own preferences on the behavior of recipients. Use of the private market through vouchers may thus be efficient in narrow terms but ineffective in more ambitious terms.

The housing voucher experience is not an isolated example. Other voucher experiences follow a parallel pattern. For example, the Special Supplementary Food Program for Women, Infants, and Children (WIC) provides a limited range of nutritious foods to low-income pregnant women, nursing mothers, infants, and young children. Distribution of these foods via vouchers at commercial grocery stores costs about 10 percent less than distributing foods at public health clinics. But the voucher system provides less control in restricting foods to allowable items rather than more popular but less nutritious ones, and it also is less successful in linking recipients and their families into the health care system (Bendick, 1978).

Similarly, on the one hand, it has been estimated that health care can be delivered by private physicians working on a fee-for-service basis at about 40 percent less cost than by government physicians working in the National Health Service Corps. On the other hand, Corps physicians have been successfully placed in medically underserved areas that were unable to attract private physicians even with voucher (Medicaid, Medicare, and other) funding available (Hadley, 1980).

SUBSIDIES

This limited ability of privatized systems to tackle the most difficult cases or to pursue the most complex objectives is also typical of the experience of many subsidy-type privatization initiatives. The concept behind such programs is to provide profit opportunities to private firms by subsidizing some of their production inputs—those the governmental sector would like to see employed. Two major examples of such initiatives are wage subsidies to encourage the hiring of disadvantaged workers and capital subsidies to encourage firms to locate plants in economically distressed locales.

The premise is that providing subsidies to encourage private employers to hire hard-to-employ workers is a cost-effective alternative to having these workers idle and dependent on unemployment insurance or public assistance and that it is preferable to creating public-sector jobs through programs such as the Depression-era Civilian Conservation Corps or the more recent Public Service Employment Program under the Comprehensive Employment and Training Act.

The most current experience with a large-scale wage subsidy program is that of the federal Targeted Jobs Tax Credit (TJTC). Under TJTC, private firms can claim a credit against corporate income tax liabilities for up to $4,500 in wages paid to workers hired from such difficult-to-employ groups as ex-convicts, welfare recipients, the handicapped, and disadvantaged youth. The objective is to expand employment opportunities for these groups by making them relatively cheap compared to other workers and compared to the purchase of capital equipment that will substitute for labor.

Despite the generous size of the subsidy and extensive (although spotty) efforts to advertise the program, the response of the business community has been persistently disappointing. Only a small proportion of firms participate, and credits are claimed for only a small proportion of potentially subsidized workers. More significantly, about two-thirds of the claims filed are retroactive in the sense that firms hire workers without determining whether they are TJTC-eligible and then later have them certified. In such circumstances, it is presumed that the subsidy had no effect on the hiring decision (Ripley et al., 1982).

There are many reasons why employers are reluctant to participate in this program, but they can all be summarized by saying that the employers evidently feel the costs outweigh even a relatively generous subsidy. Employers may fear employees who may be unreliable, unproductive, or even disruptive (for example, ghetto teenagers). They may also anticipate extra training or supervisory costs, or union opposition. In some cases, these fears may be justified; even when they are not, they are difficult to overcome. Even larger subsidies—of which both the political and budgetary feasibility are questionable—would probably face similar unresponsiveness.

Parallel patterns of business unresponsiveness are characteristic of state, local, and federal experience with programs to encourage businesses to locate in economically distressed locales. Virtually every one of the fifty states uses a rich variety of economic development incentives to solicit new businesses in such locations and to retain and encourage expansion of existing firms. These include interest-subsidized industrial revenue bonds; tax exemptions, credits, or moratoriums; and free or below-market provision of goods and services ranging from prepared plant sites to worker training. Many local governments (often using federal funds such as Urban Development Action Grants) have become financial partners in new business ventures located in decayed parts of their cities.

The general experience with such incentives has been that their cost-effectiveness in eliciting significant change in business behavior is low. For one thing, when states and localities offer competing incentives, competitors' offers cancel each other. Then too, many of the incentives are badly designed, offering firms little value per dollar of costs borne by government (Rasmussen, Bendick, and Ledebur, 1982). But most important, in making locational decisions, firms typically are much more concerned with the production costs, risks, and convenience of a location than with special incentives. No special incentives will overcome the perceived disadvantages, for example, of an inner-city plant site that is too small to allow construction of a modern, single-story industrial building; that does not offer sufficient safety for employees, goods, or facilities; or is too far from the firm's markets, raw materials, or specialized labor pool (Bendick and Rasmussen, 1985; Schmenner, 1981). Little evidence is available to show significant amounts of job development in declining regions or distressed inner cities as a result of extensive federal, state, and local attempts at industrial location incentives (Bendick, 1982a).

These examples illustrate that economically distressed locations and hard-to-employ job seekers that for-profit firms have largely chosen to abandon are not made easily attractive. Their real or perceived drawbacks are substantial, so the size of an effective compensatory incentive would have to be quite large. Finding efficient ways to provide such subsidies is not easy, and many firms will not cooperate even when offered generous incentives. Privatization offers no simple solutions to problems that have proved resistant to public programs.

Designing Programs
for For-Profit Privatization

From all this we may conclude that, in terms of efficiency gains in a simple productivity-enhancing or cost-cutting sense, for-profit privatization has only a modestly impressive record. It does a somewhat more efficient job in simple cases where goals are neatly specifiable and amenable to monitoring; it does not produce noticeably better or worse results than public provision when problems are complex—as is typical for many social welfare programs, where program goals are often ambitious and production processes not well understood.

This conclusion suggests two strategies for making more extensive use of for-profit providers in the delivery of publicly financed social welfare services.

The first is to examine each social welfare program in terms of the feasibility of specifying performance standards and goals. Only those programs or activities amenable to explicit, arms-length monitoring and control should be selected for such privatization. In some cases, an entire program may fall within this category. For example, many low-income housing rehabilitation programs have been successfully contracted out to private building contractors. For many other social welfare programs, however, only certain program activities can be readily delegated. Currently, the potential for contracting out activities within programs is greatly underexploited. For example, the Basic Educational Opportunity Grants program has used a private computer contractor to process applications for income-conditioned student financial assistance. Why could eligibility determination not be similarly contracted out for Food Stamps, Aid to Families with Dependent Children (AFDC), and other public assistance programs?

An alternative strategy for preparing to privatize service delivery is to alter the design of programs themselves, simplifying their structure and goals so that they become more readily monitored and managed. I believe that such modifications would also improve the effectiveness of many programs. For example, in my judgment, eliminating discretionary special needs payments and detailed budgeting would improve both the administrative efficiency and the equity of public assistance programs such as AFDC (Bendick, 1980; Bendick, 1986). Similarly, in my opinion, attempts to constrain how recipients of in-kind programs use program benefits are counterproductive (Bendick, 1978). However, not all persons concerned with social welfare policy share these opinions. The net effect of this consideration, therefore, should be to make the social welfare community reexamine the value of program complexities and explicitly to defend their necessity when it truly exists.

The Efficiency of Nonprofit Delivery

Yet another strategy for privatization of social welfare programs having goals that are inherently complex is to turn to the nonprofit sector. Research indicates that nonprofit service deliverers have a distinctly better record than for-profit firms in providing services in the interest of clients beyond what is precisely specifiable in contracts. For example, a recent examination of regulatory records in the state of Wisconsin revealed that complaints are lodged against for-profit nursing homes at a significantly higher rate than against either governmental or nonprofit homes. Similarly, a 1976 survey was conducted among family members concerning the care their institutionalized relatives were receiving in nursing homes, psychiatric facilities, and facilities for the mentally handicapped. They consistently expressed higher levels of satisfaction with governmental and nonprofit institutions than with for-profit ones (Weisbrod, 1983).

For such reasons, the use of nonprofit contractors to deliver social welfare services has precedents going back well into the nineteenth century. It has proliferated into a major approach in recent decades. Church-based social welfare agencies place and supervise children in publicly financed foster care; disadvantaged workers are trained for employment opportunities under government contracts to community-based organizations such as the Urban League; federal contracts for social welfare research are awarded to nonprofit universities; and patients are cared for in nonprofit hospitals with their bills paid by Medicaid or Medicare. In fiscal year 1980, federal support accounted for 58 percent of total revenues for nonprofit social service agencies (Salamon and Abramson, 1982). In 1979, purchase of services was estimated to consume 55 percent of expenditures in publicly financed personal social services (Hatry and Durman, 1985).

Those who advocate service delivery through the nonprofit sector usually argue that delivery will be both more efficient (provided at a lower cost) and more compassionate and effective. Innovation in private efforts, the absence of expensive and unnecessary bureaucracy, the ability to identify accurately the "truly needy" through local or personal knowledge, the utilization of "costless" volunteers or donated materials, and the managerial expertise of the private sector—all these usually are seen as contributing to these results.

Rigorous comparisons between nonprofit delivery and public sector delivery in terms of production efficiency are relatively scarce. One of the few recent studies on this subject compared state agencies and United Way agencies in terms of their implementation of the Emergency Food and Shelter Program created during the 1981–1982 recession to supplement ongoing food and shelter assistance programs for the unemployed. The two modes of delivery proved equally satisfactory in terms of program quality, targeting, and costs, but United Way programs were implemented more rapidly than counterpart state-run systems (Burt and Burbridge, 1985).

In many cases, however, such direct comparisons of cost or efficiency are largely beside the point. The major objective in using nonprofit channels is not to be more efficient in delivering a service that could be delivered in any case, but rather to reach clients or to fulfill roles that a public agency could not serve at all. For example, ethnically based nonprofit refugee groups can sometimes deliver services to new immigrants in culturally relevant styles that are difficult for public agencies to adopt. In response to a recent survey among fifty-five social service agencies in the San Francisco Bay area, approximately as often as they listed cost savings, agency directors listed flexibility, the availability of specialized expertise, and the ability to reach difficult-to-reach clientele as major advantages in contracting with nonprofit agencies (Terrell and Kramer, 1984).

The same idea has been espoused as a general approach to delivery of public services by the American Enterprise Institute under the rubric of "mediating structures." These structures are various community-based, grass-roots institutions such as neighborhoods, families, churches, and voluntary associations. Through their small scale, nonbureaucratic nature, local knowledge, and personal relationships, they can respond rapidly, accurately, and in a more acceptable manner to local and individual needs in ways that large, formal institutions such as government agencies cannot (Berger and Newhaus, 1977; Meyer, 1982). It is perhaps not always realistic to assume that nonprofit institutions can simultaneously remain as local and personal as the American Enterprise Institute envisions and also perform effectively and professionally in the purchase of service business. Nevertheless, the grain of truth remains relevant.

In summary, though empirical evidence is far from abundant, we are probably safe in concluding that nonprofit privatization is a feasible approach to the delivery of many complex social welfare services for which for-profit privatization would be risky because of the inability to specify precisely program goals and performance standards. Some efficiency gains might be achieved by empowering nonprofit mediating institutions as the delivery system; but, whether or not efficiency is enhanced, we can expect gains in service targeting and quality.

The Interaction of Delivery with Financing

But why, you may ask, do I give the benefit of the doubt to privatization? The record just reviewed in terms of efficiency—which was what got discussions of privatization started—suggests gains are not nonexistent but neither are they overwhelming. Why do I persist in suggesting ways to implement it? Is it really worth the bother?

Part of the answer is to be found in those relatively modest potential gains in efficiency just referred to. Even a 5 or 10 percent saving in production costs would represent billions of dollars, given the vast scale of the American social welfare system. Then, too, there are various improvements from the clients' point of view in terms of greater choice, enhanced personal dignity, greater cultural accessibility, and reduced complexity.

But the answer ultimately more important than any of these is that the questions of total quantity and mode of service delivery cannot be separated as I have done so far. History teaches that there is a very strong interaction—one that those who are trying to reduce the total quantity of public social welfare services have recognized in their strategy of privatization through load-shedding. Now is the time for those who seek to preserve and to expand the social welfare system to recognize that, when privatization takes the form of the empowerment of mediating institutions, it can be mobilized to have the opposite effect.

The first step is to unlink the popular charitable instinct from the politically unpopular governmental establishment. Analysts commenting on public opinion data frequently refer to what they consider a paradox— that in response to one set of questions, citizens regularly call for less government, but in response to other questions they demand more of the sorts of services that government typically provides (Ladd, 1984). I have emphasized that this result is neither paradoxical nor inconsistent. By restructuring social welfare programs to empower mediating institutions— both for-profit and nonprofit—we can offer exactly the combination these poll results indicate the American voting public desires.

Expanded social welfare services also can be promoted by drawing service suppliers into the political constituency that advances and defends public programs. The continual growth of the American defense industry provides a relevant model here, with large-scale and effective political support provided to the Department of Defense by military contractors.

Within the social welfare field itself, the example of New York City is an instructive one. There, most publicly financed social services programs are delivered through contracts. In turn, private suppliers—most notably well-established human services agencies, both secular and religiously affiliated—have provided much of the political lobbying in support of the city's human services activities. These, by no coincidence, are among the most generous in the nation.

A related lesson in the practical politics of social welfare services is provided by the relative popularity of in-kind assistance programs as compared to cash assistance programs. Over the decade between 1965 and 1975, for example, the proportion of total federal social welfare expenditures accounted for by in-kind transfers rose from 3 percent to 20 percent (Lynn, 1977). Food Stamps, WIC, Medicaid and Medicare, Low-income Home Energy Assistance, and tax credits for day care are several examples of in-kind programs that in recent years have been created or have experienced extensive growth, or both. During the same period, the real value of benefits in cash programs such as AFDC has steadily eroded, and broad-scale welfare reform proposals that would have cashed out many of the in-kind programs have remained stalled. It is no coincidence that each of the in-kind programs has some large provider lobbies behind it. WIC, which has both the food production industry (producers, manufacturers, and distributors) and the medical establishment behind it, has been a particular prodigy (Rauch, 1984; Bendick, 1978).

Conclusion: A Strategy for Advocating Social Welfare Services

Current discussions of privatization of social services typically start as though what is at stake is a simple question of production efficiency: can service x be produced some percent cheaper by switching from public to private? In this chapter, my thesis has been that the choice of delivery mode is part of a more general balance affecting program quality and quantity as well as efficiency. These other effects make a case for privatization that efficiency gains alone do not.

This conclusion, in turn, implies that advocates of expanded social welfare services in the United States need to rethink their stance toward privatization. They should become fervent and creative advocates for its implementation throughout the social service delivery system. A new, privatization-based strategy for seeking the expansion of the American social welfare system would encompass three major thrusts.

The first thrust concerns how to defeat proposals for load-shedding such as proffered by the Reagan Administration. The typical current approach is to defend the budgets of existing, government-delivered programs. Instead, my logic calls for co-opting the political momentum for privatization by suggesting that empowerment versions of privatization substitute for the load-shedding versions.

The second element of the strategy is to learn to make common cause with the new political allies created by privatized social welfare programs. Suppliers can be mobilized into effective political coalitions to defend and to increase program funding.

The third element consists of investing in efforts to make the nongovernmental delivery system work. Public agencies need to be reoriented to perform skillfully as contract managers.[9] The service delivery institutions being empowered need to be strengthened to make them efficient—particularly in terms of managerial skills within nonprofit organizations.[10] And, as discussed earlier, social welfare programs need to be redesigned

[9] For one useful agenda here, see Salamon (1981).

[10] Programs such as Columbia University's joint MBA–MSW would seem to be an ideal preparation for many future managers. For in-service training needs of the current generation of managers, see Egan and Bendick (1977).

to make feasible the privatization of either entire programs or elements of them.

From such roots could grow a flourishing and politically secure social welfare system in this country—flourishing and politically secure because, for the first time, it would constitute a distinctly American welfare state.

References

Bendick, Marc, Jr. 1978. "WIC and the Paradox of In-Kind Transfers." *Public Finance Quarterly* 6 (July): 359–380.

———. 1980. "Quality Control in a Federal-State Public Assistance Program." *Administration in Social Work* 4 (Spring): 7–20.

———. 1982a. "Employment, Training, and Economic Development." In John R. Palmer and Isabel V. Sawhill, eds. *The Reagan Experiment*: 247–269. Washington, D.C.: Urban Institute.

———. 1982b. "Privatization of Public Services: Recent Experience." In Harvey Brooks et al., eds. *Public-Private Partnership*: 153–172. Cambridge, Mass.: Ballinger.

———. 1982c. "Vouchers versus Income versus Services: An American Experiment in Housing Policy." *Journal of Social Policy* 11 (3): 365–377.

———. 1986. "Targeting Benefit Payments in the British Welfare State." In Jerome McKinney and Michael Johnston, eds. *Fraud, Waste, and Abuse in Government*: 49–59. Philadelphia: Institute for the Study of Human Issues.

Bendick, Marc, Jr., and Phyllis M. Levinson. 1983. *How's Business in the Reagan Era?* Washington, D.C.: Urban Institute. Chapter 6.

———. 1984. "Private Sector Initiatives or Public-Private Partnerships?" In Lester M. Salamon and Michael S. Lund, eds. *The Reagan Presidency and the Governing of America*: 455–479. Washington, D.C.: Urban Institute.

Bendick, Marc, Jr., and David W. Rasmussen. 1985. "Enterprise Zones and Inner City Economic Revitalization," In George Peterson, ed. *Reagan and the Cities*: 97–129. Washington, D.C.: Urban Institute.

Berger, Peter L., and Richard John Newhaus. 1977. *To Empower People: The Role of Mediating Structures in Public Policy*. Washington, D.C.: American Enterprise Institute.

Brown, Angela C. 1984. "The Mixed Economy of Day Care: Consumer versus Professional Assessments." *Journal of Social Policy* 13 (3): 321–331.

Burt, Martha R., and Lynn C. Burbridge. 1985. *Summary, Conclusions, and Recommendations, Evaluation of the Emergency Food and Shelter Program*. Washington, D.C.: Urban Institute.

Egan, Mary Lou, and Marc Bendick, Jr. 1977. "Management Training for Public Welfare Agencies." *Administration in Social Work* 1 (Winter): 359–367.

Giving USA. 1984. Annual Report. New York: American Association of Fundraising Counsel.

Goodman, John L. 1983. *Public Opinion During the Reagan Administration*. Washington, D.C.: Urban Institute.

Gramlich, Edward M., and Patricia P. Koshel. 1975. *Educational Performance Contracting*. Washington, D.C.: Brookings Institution.

Hadley, Jack. 1980. "The National Health Service Corps." In Jack Hadley, ed. *Medical Education Financing*: 268–272. New York: Prodist.

Hatry, Harry. 1983. *A Review of Private Approaches for the Delivery of Public Services*. Washington, D.C.: Urban Institute.

Hatry, Harry P., and Eugene Durman. 1985. *Issues in Competitive Contracting for Social Services*. Falls Church, Va.: National Institute of Government Purchasing.

Hofstadter, Richard. 1955. *Social Darwinism in American Thought*. Boston: Beacon.

Hulten, Charles, and Isabel V. Sawhill, eds. 1984. *The Legacy of Reaganomics, Prospects for Long-Term Growth*. Washington, D.C.: Urban Institute.

Kelman, Steven. 1985. "The Grace Commission: How Much Waste in Government?" *Public Interest* 78 (Winter): 62–85.

Kirlin, John J., John C. Ries, and Sidney Sonenblum. 1977. "Alternatives to City Departments." In E. S. Savas, ed. *Alternatives for Delivering Public Services*: 111–145. Boulder, Colo.: Westview Press.

Ladd, Everett Carl. 1984. "The Reagan Phenomenon and Public Attitudes Toward Government." In Lester J. Salamon and Michael S. Lund, eds. *The Reagan Presidency and the Governing of America*: 224–227. Washington, D.C.: Urban Institute.

Levy, Frank, and Richard C. Michel. 1984. *Are Baby Boomers Selfish?* Washington, D.C.: Urban Institute.

Lynn, Laurence E. 1977. "A Decade of Policy Developments in the Income Maintenance System." In Robert H. Haveman, ed. *A Decade of Federal Antipoverty Programs*: 55–117. New York: Academic Press.

Mancur, Olson. 1965. *The Logic of Collective Action*. Cambridge, Mass.: Harvard University Press.

Meyer, Jack A., ed. 1982. *Meeting Human Needs, Toward a New Social Philosophy*. Washington, D.C.: American Enterprise Institute.

OECD. 1985. *Social Expenditures 1960–1990*. Paris: OECD.

Rasmussen, David W., Marc Bendick, Jr., and Larry Ledebur. 1982. "Evaluating State Economic Development Incentives from a Firm's Point of View." *Business Economics* 17 (May): 23–29.

Rauch, Jonathan. 1984. "Women and Children's Food Program Is 'Off Limits' to Reagan Budget Cutbacks." *National Journal* (November 17): 2197–2199.

Ripley, Randall et al. 1982. *The Implementation of the Targeted Jobs Tax Credit*. Columbus, Ohio: Ohio State University.

Salamon, Lester M. 1981. "Rethinking Public Management: Third Party Government and the Changing Forms of Public Action." *Public Policy* 29 (Summer): 22–35.

Salamon, Lester M., and Alan Abramson. 1982. *The Federal Budget and the Nonprofit Sector*. Washington, D.C.: Urban Institute.

Savas, E. S. 1982. *Privatizing the Public Sector*. Chatham, N.J.: Chatham House.

Schambra, William A. 1982. "From Self-Interest to Social Obligation: Local Communities v. the National Community." In Meyer, 1982: 105–130.

Schmenner, Roger, 1981. *The Location: Decisions of Large, Multiplant Companies*. Washington, D.C.: U.S. Department of Housing and Urban Development.

Struyk, Raymond J., and Marc Bendick, Jr., eds. 1982. *Housing Vouchers for the Poor*. Washington, D.C.: Urban Institute.

Terrell, Paul, and Ralph M. Kramer. 1984. "Contracting with Nonprofits." *Public Welfare*: 36 (Winter): 5–12.

Trattner, Walter I. 1979. *From Poor Law to Welfare State*. New York: Free Press.

U.S. Senate. 1973. *Confidence and Concern: Citizens View American Government*. Washington, D.C.: Committee on Government Operations. December.

Weisbrod, Burton A. 1977. *The Voluntary Nonprofit Sector: An Economic Analysis*. Lexington, Mass.: D. C. Heath.

———. 1983. Effectiveness, Efficiency, and the Evaluation of Social Policy Programs. Manuscript.

5

Making Sense of Privatization: What Can We Learn from Economic and Political Analysis?

EVELYN Z. BRODKIN AND DENNIS YOUNG

Our essay offers a rough guide to an analysis of privatization viewed from the perspectives of economics and political science. We map what we think are key features of the conceptual landscape relevant to privatization and point out some possibilities and hazards in following alternative paths of analysis. In setting out to make a manageable tour of this vast analytical territory, we have encountered many of the frustrations of the overly ambitious traveler committed to seeing eight countries in only five days. We hope, however, that even a selective and vastly simplified map of the analytical terrain will contribute to clarification of the policy debate and critical thinking about directions for future research.

As the preceding chapters make clear, discussions of privatization are complicated by the term itself, which, perhaps, has more coherence as a political symbol than as an analytic construct (see Paul Starr's discussion in Chapter 1). Added to the complexity of the construct itself is the fact that there are a variety of private organizations to which service responsibility can be delegated and a variety of arrangements under which such delegation can take place. Moreover, the borders between public and nonprofit organizations and between nonprofit and profit-making organizations are not clean lines but rather gray areas inhabited by hybrid organizations (see Martin Rein's discussion in Chapter 3). Similarly, there are various ways in which private sector organizations may be engaged in public service provision. These include outright delegation of responsibility to the private sector ("load-shedding"), regulation of the private market, contracting with private providers, and subsidization of private suppliers or consumers of their services, or both (see Marc Bendick's discussion in Chapter 4). Nor are the implications of privatization the same for different state functions, as the case studies in Part II of this book demonstrate.

We begin by discussing how standard economic theories define the appropriate places for government intervention in the market and the mechanisms for maximizing efficiency in the production of public goods. We then attempt to place privatization in political perspective, describing analytic approaches that treat privatization as part of a battle to define the American welfare state. We conclude with some brief observations about the analytic paths we have mapped.

Economic Perspectives on Privatization

Musgrave (1959) describes three basic responsibilities of government: stabilization of the economy, distribution of wealth, and allocation of resources to their best uses. Gassler (1986) adds two more functions: the environmental function, which includes shaping the values of the citizenry and supporting research leading to changes in the technology by which goods and services are produced; and the systemic function, which represents government's responsibility for maintaining the legal and institutional framework that allows the market to operate.

The stabilization, systemic, and environmental functions have not been major focuses of contemporary discussions of privatization, although privatization may very well have implications for the efficacy with which government carries out these functions.

For example, it is conceivable that privatization could destabilize the economy by reducing the size and thus leverage of government in modulating periods of boom and bust. Similarly, privatization could affect the systemic function if parts of the legal system are turned over to private hands. Indeed, some argue that this may already be happening with the use of private police forces or the operation of correctional or detention facilities by private contractors. Privatization could also impinge on the environmental function. For example, the participation of religiously affiliated nonprofit organizations in the provision of residential care or education services may profoundly influence the values of those in their charge. And public support of research in private universities may lead to changes in the technology utilized in the economy at large.

The distribution function, in contrast to the three functions already mentioned, is a prominent concern in the privatization debate. There is considerable suspicion that privatization, particularly of the load-shedding variety, makes the distribution of income more unequal. In particular, reducing government's role as a provider of services that benefit primarily the poor exaggerates rather than ameliorates existing inequalities in income and wealth. While this may seem obvious, it is useful to refer to theory for its underpinnings.

As government phases down its redistributive activity, two other mechanisms remain for changing the distribution of wealth and income: the private marketplace and charitable giving. Economic theory suggests that the first of these mechanisms is likely to be regressive and the second is likely to be a weak substitute for governmental action.

In concept, the competitive marketplace is neutral with respect to the distribution of income and wealth; it can operate (efficiently) with almost any initial distribution of individual "endowments." Moreover, such endowments include not only physical and monetary resources but also human intelligence, skill, unique talents, and personal determination. Conceptually, therefore, the market can just as well make poor people rich as rich people poor. Overall, however, the market in pure form favors those with more favorable initial endowments (whether rich or poor) and neglects those with poor initial endowments. From this we can infer two things: first, that since poor people are more likely to have small initial endowments they are more likely to be hurt or less likely to prosper in the market than those born to greater advantage. Second, the market is liable to increase the extremes of wealth and income distribution by favoring the competent and well-endowed and neglecting the poorly endowed. Thus, even if there is some interchange of members among these extremes, the market is likely to create both rich and poor.

A market economy also allows for voluntary redistribution through philanthropy. But economic theory argues that such charity is likely to be a weak substitute for governmental redistribution. The main component of this line of thought is collective action theory, largely associated with the work of Mancur Olson (1965). In this view, an "equitable" distribution of income or wealth, or the maintenance of some subsistence level under which members of society should not be permitted to sink, can be viewed as a "collective good" in the following sense: Everyone in society can simultaneously enjoy the benefits of this good while no one can be excluded from enjoying those benefits. Collective action theory demonstrates that goods with such characteristics will not be provided in optimal amounts because of individuals who enjoy benefits of the good without voluntarily paying for it. This is the free-rider problem. Thus individuals in the society who "want" (that is, are theoretically willing to pay for) redistribution will hold back and let their compatriots pay instead. As many people behave like this, the argument goes, voluntary distribution fails as a mechanism to provide the level of distribution theoretically desired by the society. Government is thus needed to effect redistribution through the use of coercion (taxes), that is, the police power of the state.

It is also worth mentioning that the state itself may not always redistribute resources in a progressive way. This assertion too is supported by parts of economic theory, in particular by the "public choice" school. The normative public finance literature (Musgrave, 1959) assumes that government undertakes redistribution for the purpose of reducing inequality. Public choice economists such as Buchanan and Tullock (1962), in contrast, demonstrate that under assumptions of direct or representative democracy using less than unanimous voting rules, "controlling coalitions" will form that will induce government to undertake programs that generate private benefits to coalition members at the expense of those outside the coalition (for example, a controlling coalition of farm states will generate subsidies to farmers supported by the nation as a whole). As there is no reason to believe that controlling coalitions are necessarily dominated by the less affluent members of society, this mode of governmental redistribution is as likely to be regressive as progressive. Thus, it is conceivable that privatization might even have a progressive effect by reducing such exploitive activity in the public sector.

The remaining function—the allocation function—is even more prominent in the privatization debate than the distribution function. Allocation is the function of ensuring that economic resources are put to their best uses, given some initial distribution of wealth, technology, and individual tastes and preferences. It is the allocation function that is judged by the criterion of "efficiency." And it is within this realm that most of the discussion concerning the appropriate roles of the public, private, and nonprofit sectors is found.

Broadly speaking, the relevant components of economic theory fall into a general class labeled "failure theories." These consist of a broad literature on "market failure" and much more specialized literatures on "government failure," "voluntary failure," and "organizational failure." These failure theories identify the conditions under which particular institutional forms fail to achieve economic efficiency, thus providing a normative perspective on the appropriate functions undertaken in each sector of the economy.

MARKET FAILURE

Since our subject is privatization, it may seem logical to begin with a review of "government failure." However, the overall economic paradigm on which all failure theories are built focuses on the operation of the competitive marketplace. Therefore, we begin with a discussion of markets and market failure.

Most of the analysis stems from a mathematically elegant theory of a simple perfectly competitive economy. In this economy it is assumed that all firms seek to maximize profits and are small relative to their industries; there are no restrictions on firms wishing to enter an industry; consumers are well informed and have well-defined preferences about alternative products and prices; all goods and services are private in nature; production technologies are well known; and both consumer preferences (utility functions) and production characteristics (production functions) are of a certain "well-behaved" (convex) mathematical form. The fundamental theorem states that under these conditions of perfect competition, a state of economic efficiency—called Pareto efficiency or Pareto optimality—is achieved, which has the following defining character: "No individual can be made better off without making someone else worse off."

In this state, all goods have been produced just to the level where someone in the society is willing to pay what it cost to produce the last unit; all trades have been made that could improve the welfare of any possible trading partners; all firms are producing at peak internal efficiency and are maximizing their profits; all consumers are maximizing utility; and all abnormal profits have been competed away. Truly a pristine state of affairs!

One implication of this result is that industries whose characteristics come reasonably close to the theory's assumptions presumably ought to be organized through an unencumbered private sector, at least as far as efficiency considerations are concerned. This observation probably does little to explain current privatization initiatives, since most such industries are probably already privately organized. An implication of equal importance, however, is that industries that depart from the assumptions of the simple theoretical model may require some other mode of organization. Thus, classical microeconomic theory examines what is called market failure (that is, conditions that cause markets to depart from Pareto optimality). Scholars have approached this subject in various ways (Bator, 1958; Wolf, 1979; and Douglas, 1983). Even so, the analyses can be grouped in terms of two broad categories of effects: externalities and market imperfections.

Externalities may be thought of as benefits or costs that are not appropriable for trade and therefore not captured by the price system. If I keep the sidewalk in front of my house clean, my neighbors benefit but it would not be feasible for me to charge them for that benefit. As a result, I may not keep the sidewalk as clean as I might if the neighbors could contribute to the upkeep. Thus, we depart from Pareto optimality since gains from trade are foregone (my labor in return for added benefits of a cleaner sidewalk). Moreover, my neighbors are all likely to feel the same way and so we may all refrain from keeping the sidewalks clean. In this case, a "public good"—a cleaner neighborhood—is foregone despite the fact that, as a group, my neighbors and I value that good more than it would cost us to produce it. Externalities and public goods are essentially the same phenomenon. As noted earlier, a public good is shared by everyone simultaneously and no one can be excluded from consuming its benefits. These are the characteristics that restrain individuals from appropriating the good and trading it in the marketplace.

Market imperfections consist of various other characteristics of goods, services, and markets that cause those markets to depart from the model of perfect competition. These characteristics include the following:

Imperfect information: consumers may not have good information about products and prices or may not be competent to judge the quality or cost of those products.

Barriers to entry: large capital costs, regulatory requirements, or other factors seriously inhibiting new firms from entering the industry and keeping it competitive.

Increasing returns to scale: costs continue to decline as production volumes increase, providing a competitive edge to large-scale producers and leading to monopoly (one producer) or oligopoly (a few producers) in a market.

Risk: industrial projects involve very large-scale risks or long-term payoffs, leading private-sector producers to be reluctant to enter the market.

Instabilities: some markets may be disrupted by "boom and bust" effects (farms) or panic (banks, stock markets).

Each of these conditions undermines the Pareto optimality of competitive markets. Increasing returns and barriers to entry restrict competition, leading to overpricing and restriction of outputs. Risk problems impose high barriers to entry (for example, in space programs or research on exotic technologies) that may negate the possibility of voluntary market activity entirely. And, imperfect information or instabilities preclude consumers or producers from competently exercising choice and thus bringing about effective competition.

Classical market failure theory stops short of prescribing precisely what to do about these problems except to indicate that it may be desirable to have "the government do something." In fact, a wide array of institutional responses is available to deal with the various sources of market failure. Very broadly speaking, there are three possible sets of solutions: collective provision of services by government; government regulation of the private providers; and shift of responsibility to private institutions other than profit-making firms.

Consider, for example, the case of nursing homes for the elderly. Nursing home services could be provided by profit-making firms in the unfettered marketplace. Market failure theory suggests, however, that this market may entail imperfections. In particular, consumers have imperfect information. This would be the case if the primary users of the service (the elderly parent) could not adequately inform the purchaser of the service (the children of elderly parents or third-party payers) of the quality of care provided. One remedy is to have the government regulate nursing homes. As Krashinsky (1984) indicates, regulation addresses market imperfections by standardizing the implicit contract between producers and consumers (that is, by specifying service characteristics) and by providing more efficient centralized information and enforcement. Krashinsky (1986) suggests and Weisbrod and Schlesinger (1986) demonstrate that there are two aspects of service quality that government can attempt to regulate: Type I attributes, which are easy to monitor (for example, floor space per patient, sanitary conditions, or patient/staff ratios), and Type II attributes (such as the humaneness or competence of medical or mental health care), which are difficult to monitor. But because government must set objective, measurable standards, it can only effectively regulate Type I attributes. This leaves room for profit-making nursing homes to increase their profits by cutting back on expenditures that affect Type II attributes, which neither government nor consumers can adequately discern or control.

While regulation of the profit-making marketplace may be inadequate for nursing homes, it may be a more satisfactory alternative in other cases of market failure. For example, market imperfections are associated with the provision of taxi service or consumer products such as pharmaceuticals or children's toys. Here, even competent consumers cannot be completely informed of all aspects of product safety, reliability, or price; however, governmental regulation can substantially control problems in these areas.[1]

In general, the idea of regulation is to modify the incentives of profit-making producers—through sanctions, subsidies, taxes, service requirements, and pricing policies—so that profit maximizers, acting in their own best interests under the new rules, take into account externalities and imperfections. If that can be done, more direct government involvement may be unnecessary. Further, governmentally provided services with such characteristics may be safely privatized from an efficiency standpoint.

Where externalities are pervasive, however, or where market imperfections are severe, other institutional alternatives may be preferable. For

---

[1] Other examples of markets where regulation can be effective are natural monopolies (for example, utilities), inherently unstable industries (for example, securities, agricultural markets), high-risk industries (for example, high technology requiring patents to protect research and development investments). All these reflect aspects of market failure that government may ameliorate by imposing fairly clear-cut and enforceable requirements on the marketplace that presumably assist those markets to work more satisfactorily.

example, where markets exhibit imperfect information and consumer competence problems, an alternative to conventional government regulation of profit-making suppliers may be to put the industry in the hands of "more trustworthy" private institutions. The idea here is to identify institutional forms that, because of their unique constitutions or by virtue of their presumed integrity, can be relied upon not to exploit imperfect information or consumer incompetence. Professions and nonprofit organizations are two such institutions. But on what theoretical grounds are such institutions to be considered trustworthy and capable of overcoming market imperfections?

Consider again the case of nursing homes for the elderly. Even within the profit-making context, the fact that some important services within nursing homes are provided by professionals (for example, doctors, nurses, and social workers) presumably affords some protection against market imperfections that would otherwise accrue to the detriment of the consumer. Economists have not paid much direct attention to this issue, but there are at least two strands of economic theory that appear to apply. First, restriction of service provision to certain classes of professionals is simply an extension of the framework of governmental regulation. To the degree that aspects of provider competence can be measured and monitored, consumers can be protected by providing licenses only to those that qualify.

The viability of professionals as an institutional response to market failure does not rely solely on governmental regulation and licensing, however. Indeed, some would argue that such licensing is intended more to serve the professionals (through restriction of entry and hence enhancement of income) than the public at large. Rather, the efficacy of professionalization relies more heavily on the self-policing incentives of professionals themselves.

This perspective can be understood in the framework of "exclusive groups" as described by Olson (1965). An exclusive group is one whose members share a benefit that is of limited supply, such as the (total) income available for doctors' services. Exclusive groups require two conditions in order to maintain high levels of benefit: (1) they must have 100 percent membership, else benefits can be drawn away (services undersold) by unlimited competition from the outside; and (2) they must keep the group as small as possible so that each member's share is as large as possible. These conditions, in turn, create incentives for self-policing. First, high standards and tough entry requirements are desirable so as to satisfy condition (2). Second, peer review is useful so that the quality of services delivered by members is maintained above a level that might invite severe public criticism and hence undermine the group's sanctioned monopoly position, that is, condition (1). It is also to the members' mutual advantage, however, to protect each other from negative exposure to the outside world, for this will also undermine condition (1). Thus, professionals can be expected to tolerate a certain amount of incompetence as long as it can be hidden from view.

Another obvious limitation of the professionalization alternative for addressing market imperfections is the fact that professionals often do not operate as free agents (that is, solo practitioners) but rather as employees of organizations; hence they are subject to the incentive structures of those organizations in addition to the behavior code of the profession. Thus certain contributions to theory address the possibility of utilizing service delivery agencies that are presumed more trustworthy than profit-making organizations, namely nonprofit organizations.

Some theorists have argued that nonprofit organizations are more "trustworthy" than for-profits. In particular, Hansmann (1980) focuses on conditions of "contract failure" that occur when consumer information or competence are problematic. Under these conditions, Hansmann argues, nonprofit organizations are preferable to profit-making organizations because the former are subject to the "nondistribution constraint." That is, although nonprofit firms are not precluded from generating financial surpluses (profits), they are prohibited from distributing those surpluses to those who govern or control the organization. As a result, nonprofit firms have much weaker incentives to exploit consumers by defrauding them (failing to deliver on promises), by cutting quality, or by overcharging.

While in practice the effectiveness of the nondistribution constraint can be called into question (what is to prevent the siphoning of surplus revenues into bloated salaries and kickbacks on purchases?), Hansmann's argument is buttressed by at least two related considerations. First, the state provides some policing machinery in the form of chartering procedures, enforcement by the IRS, and regulation within particular service delivery systems. Second, a process of self-selection and screening will attract less pecuniary-minded managers and staff to nonprofit organizations, hence lessening the danger of exploitation for greedy purposes (Young, 1983, Weisbrod, 1983, and Hansmann, 1980).

Although the trustworthiness theory of nonprofits provides some guidance on the circumstances in which private nonprofit organizations may be preferable to profit-making organizations if services are left to voluntary provision, the theory still leaves puzzling questions. For example, if nonprofits are trustworthy, why is it often necessary for government to regulate them? Here the theory is murky, although it is worthwhile citing ideas contributed by several different scholars. According to the theory of "exit and voice" advanced by Albert O. Hirschman (1970), all organizations have a tendency to build up internal slack and experience losses in the quality or cost of their services if not kept accountable by outside forces. Thus, while nonprofits may not intentionally cut corners or exploit unwary consumers, they may become slack, inattentive, or preoccupied by other goals. Indeed, Krashinsky (1984) suggests that the same disincentives that restrain nonprofits from cutting corners also make them less inclined to keep costs down; hence they have a tendency to become less efficient.

External regulation presumably helps keep such deterioration in check. Weisbrod and Schlesinger (1986) found that (because of profit incentives) profit-making nursing homes were actually less likely than (less efficient) nonprofits to commit Type I violations of regulations that were monitored by government. They were more likely, however, to commit Type II offenses that government could not regulate and thus required a greater degree of trustworthiness on the part of the provider organization.

Another puzzle is whether private nonprofit organizations are necessarily more trustworthy than governmental organizations for delivering services subject to market failure. After all, government, too, presumably operates under a nondistribution constraint. Although the Hansmann theory fails to address this issue directly, it does imply answers to this question. First, private nonprofit organizations are generally more limited in their scope than government. As a result, clients of a private nonprofit institution have a stronger sense of what their money is spent on or, indeed, if their contributions are expended on agency services at all. Governments tend to be large and multifunctional, with individual agencies subject to budgetary decisions of the government as a whole. Hence, a contributor to a government agency may have little assurance that his dollar will be used for the agency's intended purposes rather than effectively used to reduce taxes or fund other functions. This might help explain, for example, the greater reluctance of individuals to give to public universities than to private ones. Add to this other theoretical arguments—that the generally smaller scale of nonprofits makes consumers more at ease in using their services compared to government (Berger and Neuhaus, 1977), that governmental corruption may discourage reliance on governmental services (Rose-Ackerman, 1978), and that government's monopoly position makes it more difficult for consumers to exert their influence in comparison to a regime of multiple nonprofits (Nelson and Krashinsky, 1973)—and you have various possible justifications for favoring nonprofits over public institutions. To the contrary, however, one could argue that consumers should be less trusting of private institutions because they are less open to public scrutiny than public institutions.

In summary, the trustworthiness theory suggests that if privatization is applied to services strongly characterized by Type II attributes then it may be efficient to avoid profit-making organizations, even if regulated, in favor of nonprofits, or to rely on the involvement of professionals, or both. Moreover, the theory also hints at some reasons why private nonprofits may engender greater trust than government.

The trustworthiness theory of nonprofits presumably applies to choices between for-profits and nonprofits regardless of whether government funding is involved. It does not directly address the question of whether service should be provided within a purely voluntary regime of service delivery or whether governmental subsidy is justified. This question has two important parts: whether government should provide (that is, finance) a given service and, if so, whether it should deliver that service directly or arrange to have it delivered by a third party (for example, by contracting out). Theories of "voluntary failure" address the former; theories of "organizational failure" address the latter.

VOLUNTARY FAILURE

The theoretical justifications for governmental provision emanate directly from the public goods and externalities aspects of market failure. In cases of pure public goods, or where externalities are pervasive, it is clear that society will incur serious problems of underprovision unless government supports service provision through tax subsidies. To understand this, Olson (1965) explores the circumstances under which public goods may be provided under voluntary arrangements. He shows that in small groups in which substantial social pressure can be exerted, or in so-called privileged situations—where some individual member of the group finds it personally worthwhile to provide some of the good for himself—then some (suboptimal) level of the good may be provided voluntarily. However, in so-called latent situations—where groups are large and no individual receives such a large fraction of the total benefit that it is worthwhile to undertake individual provision—none of the good may be produced voluntarily at all. In these situations, Olson concludes, one of two mechanisms is needed: selective incentives or coercion.

Coercion, of course, refers to governmental provision using taxation and the police powers of the state. Selective incentives are the tie-in of private benefits that can only be received if one contributes to the public good (for example, the uniquely emblazoned tote bag one receives by supporting a public television station). Selective incentives, of course, facilitate the provision of public goods in a regime of voluntary provision where the provider has some monopoly control over the private benefit. In such cases, the monopoly profits can be used to subsidize the public good.[2]

---

[2] There is sometimes available an even more radical alternative than either coercion or

Olson's arguments for failure of voluntary action ignore the possibility of purely philanthropic motives for supporting public goods (Douglas, 1983). Clearly people do give to worthwhile causes without coercion or demanding selective private benefits in exchange. Indeed, Sugden (1982) argues that philanthropy can be explained by moral imperatives that motivate individuals to give. Still, it is questionable that philanthropy alone can support efficient levels of public goods.

The work of Lester Salamon (1985) expands on why purely voluntary arrangements for provision of public goods may not be efficient. Salamon formulates a theory of voluntary failure that includes the limits to the nonprofit sector's ability to raise resources. He calls this "philanthropic insufficiency," which includes the free-rider effect as well as the inability of the voluntary sector to allocate funds countercyclically (for example, to spend during recessions, as government can, to address social problems when they are most severe). To this failing, Salamon adds "philanthropic particularism"—that the voluntary sector is inevitably balkanized with needs and resources unevenly distributed among self-defined communities of interest (religious or ethnic groups and the like). As a result, some groups manage fairly well for themselves while others cannot. Moreover, groups are liable to behave competitively and to duplicate one another's services. This leads to inefficiencies and failure to exploit potential economies of scale in production. For these reasons, Salamon argues that governmental intervention in the form of financial support, regulation, or possibly direct service provision may be necessary.[3]

Salamon's arguments are complementary to the work of scholars who have examined the behavior of nonprofit organizations. James and Rose-Ackerman (1986), for example, review a number of behavioral analyses of nonprofit organizations which indicate that such organizations tend not to pursue any pure conception of public goods or collective interests.

---

selective incentives—an alternative suggested by the famous "tragedy of the commons" (Hardin, 1968): the conversion of a public good to a private one in order to exploit market incentives for more efficient usage. The proclivity of modern governments to sell off public assets and service functions may be so motivated, though such policies also seem driven by ideological commitments to "smaller government" or the need to raise revenues to address budget deficits.

[3] Salamon also cites two voluntary failings that fall outside the efficiency dimension: First, "philanthropic paternalism" refers to the fact that voluntary social welfare arrangements are controlled by the wealthy, who decide who is deserving and who should be served. Social goods are viewed as charity rather than as a "right" in this regime. This is seen as undesirable because it creates resentment and dependency of the poor on the rich. Second, "philanthropic amateurism" is the concern that volunteer-based activities may employ a variety of idiosyncratic and unprofessional approaches to service delivery (for example, providing social services coupled with religious exhortation in the belief that moral turpitude is the cause of social problems) and in any case may not be able to mobilize the level of resources required to support a professionally based service system.

For example, the management or staff of nonprofit organizations are alternately seen as cross-subsidizing between services they intrinsically prefer and those that can generate revenues to support the former services (James, 1983); as pursuing quality or prestige for its own sake (Newhouse, 1970); as maximizing budgets (Niskanen, 1971); or as exploiting their organizations as indirect sources of income (Pauly and Redisch, 1973).

These theories of the behavior of nonprofit organizations correspond only imperfectly to the more idealistic theoretical rationales for these institutions. Hence the clarity with which it can be argued that nonprofits can address the manifestations of market failure (or government failure, see below) is reduced. At the least, behavioral theories suggest that nonprofits may require public oversight or regulation.

The foregoing theory of voluntary failure focuses on the circumstances under which voluntary sector activity requires substitution or supplementation by government. But it is of equal interest to ask if there is theory to suggest where substitution of profit-making for nonprofit activity may be efficient. Indeed, "profitization" is as much of interest as privatization in contemporary policy debate in areas such as health care and even social services. The review of nonprofit organization behavior models by James and Rose-Ackerman (1986) reveals this to be a complex question, with few simple answers.

Briefly, the issue turns on three factors—externalities, competition, and discretionary revenues. Assume that all revenues derive from sales cost curves that are the classical U-shape, there are no barriers to competition, and nonprofits maximize their outputs. Under these conditions, economic analysis shows that where there are no externalities, nonprofits are less efficient in the short run than profit-maximizing firms, because they produce too much output (that is, they continue to produce to the break-even point even though the costs of the marginal units exceed the benefit as measured by market price). In the long run, however, as price is driven down and excess operating margins are competed away, there will eventually be no difference between nonprofits and profit-makers. Both will produce at minimum unit costs and at efficient levels of output.

Bringing externalities, imperfect competition and managerial discretion, grants and contributions, multiproduct firms, and other subtleties into the analysis introduces greater complexity and results in less clear-cut conclusions.

Suffice it to say that under certain conditions economic theory indicates that profit-making firms can efficiently replace nonprofit firms. Those conditions, however, tend to reflect optimal conditions for the production of private goods, where markets work well and are free of externalities, barriers to entry, and the informational problems (market imperfections) discussed earlier. Under less pristine circumstances it is a matter of trading off one set of inefficiencies for another.

Organizational Failure

Having previously established the case that market failure may not be completely ameliorated by regulation or by the employment of private, trustworthy institutions (professions or nonprofit organizations), one arrives at the conclusion that, from an efficiency point of view, provision of public services by government is often required. Further theoretical inquiry, however, is necessary to determine where it may be desirable for government to deliver services directly and where it may be preferable for government to provide its services through contractual arrangements with other (private) organizations.

In this connection, it is useful to review the third-party government perspective of Salamon (1985). Salamon argues that the contracting aspects of privatization are nothing new, and that government provision through the engagement of third-party delivery agents has been common in the United States for a long time. He argues that the popular view that the welfare state is a constantly expanding and monolithic bureaucracy that has grown at the expense of voluntary institutions is simply incorrect. Rather, he sees government and the voluntary sector as partners in service delivery and the use of contractual arrangements revealing of intrinsic American preferences and philosophy (see also the Bendick discussion in Chapter 4 of this volume). In particular, Salamon argues that third-party delivery reflects American skepticism toward large bureaucracies; that it serves the purposes of a pluralistic society by allowing for an adaptation of services to local community styles; and that it may often be cost-effective where there exist diseconomies of scale. In short, third-party contractual arrangements permit a partnership that overcomes the problems of both direct government provision and the elements of voluntary failure previously discussed.

The work of Oliver Williamson (1975) on markets and hierarchies helps put some of these considerations into a more general perspective. Williamson is concerned with the question: When is it efficient to conduct economic activities (or transactions) within the context of a formal organization (for example, government) rather than to conduct them in the open market place? In the best tradition of the economics profession, he begins by supposing that all transactions are initially carried out through the market and then asks what factors will cause markets to fail, leading to the formation of hierarchical organizations. Then, having established the rationale for organizations, he asks under what conditions organizations will fail, leading to the use of the market (for example, contracting) rather than to the extension of internal organizational activity. The conditions that Williamson identifies as favoring internal organization are those that mitigate against contracting out; the conditions that limit the efficiency of internal organization indicate when contracting out is efficient.

Williamson identifies three principal considerations that lead to the rationale for organizing activities internally: bounded rationality; opportunism and small numbers conditions; and information impactedness. Bounded rationality refers to limits on human cognitive capabilities, including computational capacity and the ability to communicate through language. Bounded rationality, in conjunction with complexity and uncertainty in the environment, favors internal organization because such organization "permits the parties to deal with uncertainty/complexity in an adaptive, sequential fashion without incurring the same types of opportunism hazards that market contracting would pose" (p. 25). Opportunism consists of the "strategic manipulation of information or misrepresentation of intentions" (p. 26). Small numbers conditions obtain when a market has few effective traders (either initially or after rounds of bidders for contracts have effectively divided bidders into incumbents and outsiders).

In small-numbers circumstances, Williamson sees internal organization as curbing opportunism in three ways: by attenuating the incentives to behave opportunistically; by providing for more effective auditing of each party's performance and fulfillment of promises; and by providing more efficient means of dispute resolution. Finally, internal organization may be more efficient than markets where "information impactedness" exists. This is defined as obtaining where "true underlying circumstances relevant to the transaction . . . are known to one or more parties but cannot be costlessly discerned by or displayed for others" (p. 31).

Williamson analyzes all these conditions, and his analysis informs the privatization discussion by identifying the pitfalls of contracting. Contracting is seen to be problematic both where there are few potential bidders and also where the number of bidders is effectively reduced at the contract renewal stage by the "insider" advantages of incumbency. Williamson's work suggests that in-house activity can be superior in these situations.

The case of nursing homes for the elderly again helps illustrate the point. Government may contract for such care with private suppliers. There may be many bidders at the outset but significantly fewer in subsequent rounds of bidding: many initial bidders may have dropped out for lack of business, incumbents will have learned the nuances of the delivery system, and government may have become familiar and deceptively comfortable with them. A small-numbers condition then obtains. Moreover, information impactedness may exist because the contractors, who deal with service and operations on a day-to-day basis, are likely to have much better information on costs, quality of care, and patient needs and conditions than their government overseers, especially as some of these parameters are difficult to measure. All this makes it more difficult (less efficient) for government to exert control than if services were delivered by government in-house.

But Williamson also addresses why internal organization can fail. He argues that the relative advantage of organizations declines as organizations become larger and more complex. Moreover, he concludes that organizations, particularly in the nonmarket sectors, have tendencies to overextend themselves, to persist in nonproductive activities and to suffer from communications and incentives difficulties as they become larger.[4] A very large social service bureaucracy, therefore, may indeed increase efficiency by contracting out for nursing home care, whereas a small government bureau may more efficiently deliver such care itself.

GOVERNMENT FAILURE

As Williamson points out, one condition under which government supply is inefficient (that is, when government "fails") is when government overextends itself rather than contracts out. Williamson does not, however, inform us about what types of organizations are best for government to contract with.

The question of what types of contractors government should do business with may be addressed by referring back to the Hansmann (1980) theory of nonprofit organizations and to our earlier consideration of regulation. Essentially, the same arguments used to describe nonprofits as more trustworthy vis-à-vis donors and consumers can be used to suggest that nonprofits are less likely to cut corners or dilute quality in connection with governmentally contracted services. Moreover, as our earlier discussion indicates, for hard-to-measure attributes government will have a difficult time monitoring contractors just as it does regulating firms in the

---

[4] The tendencies of organizations to expand beyond efficient size is not a new idea. The public choice school of economics has long underwritten this view with formal analyses such as Niskanen's (1970) budget-maximizing model of public bureaus. Williamson (1975) explains that indeed public (budget-based) organizations are not only more inclined to expand but also more likely to persist in obsolete or otherwise unproductive activity, because budget-based support for such activity is less likely to be withdrawn than is market-derived revenue. In addition, Williamson indicates that the managerial incentive problem is more disturbing in public than private organizations: ". . . a basic distinction between the business firm and bureaucracies . . . [is that] . . . incumbent managements can be displaced more easily [by stockholders] though . . . effecting displacement in the large firm is not always easy . . ."

marketplace generally. Thus, where difficult-to-discern attributes characterize services (as they do in nursing homes or day care), theory suggests that nonprofits may be the preferable alternative. On the other hand, the general theory of competitive markets implies that where services are not difficult to discern, efficiency would be served by utilizing profit-making suppliers.

Wider perspectives on government failure are given by Charles Wolf (1979), James Douglas (1983), and Burton Weisbrod (1977).

Wolf's work identifies the following aspects of government provision and public services that lead to inefficiencies and other shortcomings: inadequacy of governmental provision, internalities, redundant and rising costs, and derived externalities. Internalities are the manifestation of private goals of individuals in nonmarket organizations. Redundant and rising costs result from a number of public sector phenomena. One is the problem of internalities. Another is the political process that sometimes causes governments (politicians) to articulate and pursue unrealistic and sometimes conflicting goals such as "finding a cure for cancer by 1980" or "minimizing unemployment while maximizing earnings." Redundant costs may also result from the difficulty public agencies have in measuring and monitoring outputs or terminating programs that outlive their usefulness.

Derived externalities consist of unintended side effects of government interventions in market processes—for example, the economic or foreign policy losses associated with tariffs or import restrictions, or the incentives for public utilities to make inefficient substitutions of capital for labor created by the rate of return method of rate regulation. Thus, Wolf argues that when government acts to correct market failures, it often creates new inefficiencies of its own.[5]

In contrast to Wolf, who focuses on the new inefficiencies created by governmental action, Douglas (1983) and Weisbrod (1977) focus on constraints that inhibit government from fulfilling public demands for service. Douglas identifies five sources of restraint that suggest a role for private nonprofit organizations in the provision of public services:

1. The "categorical" constraint derives from the requirement that government provide services in a uniform and universal way. This leaves unsatisfied those individuals in the population who have demands for public service that differ from the norm. Moreover, the need for universal pro-

---

[5] Wolf also argues that "distributional inequity" may be an outgrowth of governmental activity because public policy puts power in the hands of officials who may abuse it or use it arbitrarily, thereby transferring wealth in a perverse way. More generally, public policies are seen often to produce "larger public subsidy or a more protective regulatory policy for the benefit of 'constituencies' that are well organized."

vision precludes small scale innovation and experimentation that may be needed before a given service can be wisely or economically adopted more widely.

2. The "majoritarian" constraint reflects the possibility that multiple, conflicting conceptions of the public good may exist that cannot all be pursued or resolved by government. This too leaves a category of unsatisfied demand for public goods or services.

3. The "time horizon" constraint reflects the short tenures of politicians and thus the likelihood that government will neglect long-term consequences of public policies or societal problems.

4. The "knowledge" constraint reflects the notion that government, because of its relatively monolithic nature, cannot be expected to generate all the relevant information and research it needs intelligently to formulate and administer public policy. As a result, nongovernmental knowledge (research) centers and advocacy groups are required to supplement government's information base.

5. The "size" constraint reflects the observation that government organizations are commonly large, impersonal, and difficult to approach; hence, "mediating structures" are required as liaison between government and people (Berger and Neuhaus, 1977).

Each of these complaints implies a niche for the nonprofit sector as a source of voluntary provision of collective goods. Each is a source of unsatisfied demand for public goods that can only be satisfied by voluntary organizations that mobilize subgroups of the citizenry for the purpose of self-provision—though in the case of the latter three constraints at least, government conceivably may recognize the difficulties and contract out with such organizations for the necessary services.

Weisbrod's (1977) theory of the nonprofit sector focuses mainly on the categorical constraint. Weisbrod argues that in providing a public good, government must select a uniform level of service and a corresponding tax rate or tax-price that reflects the preferences of the swing voter. For example, under majority rule, voting theory demonstrates that the preferences of the median voter will be followed (Black, 1971). Whoever the key voter is, Weisbrod's point is that only that voter will be fully satisfied with government's level of provision. Voters with weaker preferences for the particular public good will feel they are paying too much, and voters with stronger preferences for the good will want more service at the given tax price. The former voters can only move somewhere else if they are sufficiently unhappy. The latter, however, can supplement government service with voluntary provision of their own, through the nonprofit sector. Thus, for example, in a community with widely divergent preferences for police services, high-demand groups may organize their own supplementary security arrangements on a voluntary basis.

A Recap

The overall picture that emerges from this collage of failure theories is of an economy that may be best described in ecology-like terms. Various arrangements and combinations of profit-making, nonprofit, and public organizations may be seen as niches into which different goods and services fit so as to provide those goods and services in the most efficient way. Accordingly, privatization policies may be seen as means of making appropriate institutional adjustments so that services can be moved from niches where they are less efficiently provided to niches where they are more efficiently provided.

Political Perspectives on Privatization

The analytical map of privatization detailed thus far begins with the objective of determining how to achieve a more efficient mix of services and providers and uses the tools of economic analysis toward this end. Although this is no simple task, economic analysis is well suited to the problem of finding an optimal way of achieving specified ends.

But what if the ends of privatization are not as obvious as we have initially assumed? What if the debate about privatization is in part a debate about the ends of the welfare state? If this is the case, then it is inappropriate to think only in terms of optimal solutions and efficiency criteria. Questions of ends are inherently political, involving conflicts over values, power, and social relationships. It is worth recalling Max Weber's classic commentary on social policy: "The distinctive characteristic of a problem of social policy is indeed the fact that it cannot be resolved merely on the basis of purely technical considerations which already assume settled ends. Normative standards of value can and must be the objects of dispute in a discussion of a problem of social policy because the problem lies in the domain of general cultural values" (Weber, 1949, pp. 56–57).

We now extend our analytical map of privatization by considering what ends beyond efficiency are at stake in efforts to restructure the provision of public and, particularly, social goods and services. We draw on political theories of the welfare state to explore in broad terms *what* the movement to privatize is about. Then we consider *how* privatization provides a means to those ends, focusing analytic attention on its strategic contribution to a fundamentally political struggle.

The "Ends" of Privatization

Efficiency, while clearly important to anyone concerned with the conservation of limited resources, is not everything. Nor would most economists insist that it is. From a political vantage point, a great deal more is at stake in privatization. Privatization has direct implications for the boundaries of the state and indirect implications for the distribution of political power, social benefits, and values.

The balance between individual interests and social interests is a central issue in the politics of the welfare state. Harold L. Wilensky once wrote that "throughout history the determination of what rightfully belongs to Caesar has been one of the fundamental challenges facing all social institutions. In the field of social welfare there has been a recurrent quest for principles that would maintain a balance between the state and the interests of the individuals and groups comprising it" (Kramer, 1981, p. xxiii). The state's boundaries are not constitutionally fixed or permanent; rather, they expand or contract as issues and activities are redefined politically to be within either the social or private domain. These boundary changes both reflect and influence the strength of competing groups within the polity.

In market economies, for example, state institutions often function as an instrument of countervailing power for those disadvantaged by the market. The growth of the welfare state is associated with an expansion of the public sphere into both economic regulation and social protection. This expansion involves more than a reallocation of functions. It is also associated with a reallocation of political power from capital to labor. Briggs (1961, p. 228) defined the welfare state as "a state in which organized power is deliberately used (through politics and administration) in an effort to modify the play of market forces in at least three directions— first, by guaranteeing individuals and families a minimum income irrespective of the market value of their property; second, by narrowing the extent of insecurity by enabling individuals and families to meet certain 'social contingencies' (for example, sickness, old age, and unemployment) which lead otherwise to individual and family crises; and third, by ensuring that all citizens without distinction of status or class are offered the best standards available in relation to a certain agreed range of social services."

The welfare state can empower citizens to resist market exploitation by guaranteeing them a minimum level of public support in the form of family allowances, income transfers, health care, housing, education, and so forth. Of course, there is considerable variation across welfare states in the provision of these minimums, with the U.S. typically among the most limited.[6] The welfare state also empowers citizens to restructure the mar-

---

[6] There is a rich comparative literature on the politics of social welfare states. See, for example, Wilensky and Lebeaux, 1965; Heclo, 1974; Offe, 1984; Rimlinger, 1971; Skocpol and Ikenberry, 1983; Flora and Heidenheimer, 1981; Furniss and Tilton, 1977; and, on the

ket through the regulatory instruments of the state or through direct state provision of certain products; for example, housing or health care.

Further, the institutions of the state provide a means, however flawed or limited, for asserting democratic control over the economy and social relations. Thus, as Starr and Immergut (1987) contend: "In democratic states, to move something from the private to the public sphere is to subject it, however imperfectly, to open discussion and the will of majorities. And in social democratic and other welfare states, such a shift moves an issue into an arena where equality is a more significant aim or standard than it is in the private market. The public and private spheres afford different opportunities for collective and individual choice. Hence the battle over whether a set of problems is properly public or private typically calls forth a combination of material interests and ideological commitments."

For the U.S., the issues of the state's boundaries and the substance of the welfare state itself have been particularly resistant to political settlement. Although there have been expansionary surges that dramatically extended the boundaries of the welfare state, these periods of advance have generally been followed by periods in which only some of these advances were consolidated, while others were retracted or reduced. Some scholars, reexamining significant growth periods, such as the New Deal and the War on Poverty, raise questions about the apparent elasticity of American welfare state boundaries and how far (or how little) they seem to stretch even at peak moments.

For example, Skocpol and Ikenberry (1983) describe the New Deal as path-breaking in bringing state regulation to the market and social guarantees to citizens. But they also stress that state interventions in both areas were limited, fragmented and, to some extent, impermanent. Similarly, they characterize the surge in social welfare programs during the late 1960s and early 1970s as limited in scope, particularly in relying on means-tested, categorical programs for the so-called "undeserving poor" and decentralized, intergovernmental policy mechanisms. Piven and Cloward (1971) have argued that there is a give-and-take character to American social welfare politics—giving during periods of social unrest and taking back during periods of social quiescence.

Yet, periods of expansion have produced new institutions that provide opportunities for citizens to make increasing demands on the state for economic and social protection. This situation was regarded with alarm in the 1970s by those who feared that political institutions were too weak to resist increasing demands. Some scholars predicted that the result

reluctant development of the American welfare state, see Hartz, 1964; Piven and Cloward, 1971; Patterson, 1981; and Karl, 1983.

would be an "overload" and a "governability crisis" (Huntington, 1975; King, 1975; Sundquist, 1980). Others viewed these new institutions more positively, favoring the establishment of welfare state institutions that strengthened the political voice of relatively disadvantaged groups (Katznelson, 1981; Piven and Cloward, 1982).

This disagreement reflects divergent preferences for the distribution of political power—a distribution influenced by changing boundaries of the state. As Furniss and Tilton (1977, p. 39) assert, "the liberal fears concentrated political power and tries to restrict the scope of the political; the social welfare statist, while respecting the notion of a balance of social powers, tries to democratize authority rather than privatize it. In short, the social welfare statist's conception of human welfare differs from the liberal view in espousing a more organic concept of society, a more egalitarian concept of justice, and a more democratic solution to the problem of political power."

Normative questions of privatization's ends have more than theoretical interest. They also have implications for the selection of evaluative criteria used to assess specific proposals. While value judgments cannot be removed entirely from this selection process, analysis can seek to assure that the range of criteria is more inclusive than exclusive and extends beyond the limited reaches of efficiency to include political, social, and organizational criteria.[7]

Even if, as we have argued, the ends of privatization are more far-reaching than we at first assumed, it is conceivable that its impact could be relatively modest. Privatization does not propose to sweep away the major institutions of the welfare state. Nor, as we have noted, are these institutions either fully public or private to begin with. Further, the changes we are discussing are apt to be incremental, shifting only gradually the balance of public and private. However, even incremental changes, over time, can have significant consequences that merit serious scrutiny (Lindblom, 1979).

---

[7] In one interesting effort to extend the boundaries of analysis, Alan Walker criticized evaluations based on the "least-cost notion of efficiency . . . achieved 'when the value of what is produced by any set of resources exceeds as much as possible the value of resources' " (Walker, 1984, p. 32). He contrasted that notion with "social equity" criteria focusing on "the distribution of resources, status and power between different groups in society. A socially equitable policy is one that maximizes equality within this framework. It is not simply a matter of distributional justice in the spread of incomes and wealth; the distribution of status and power too should be subject to the same criterion" (Walker, 1984, pp. 32–33). Thus far, too few analyses of privatization have given in-depth consideration to the multiple values at stake in this debate, perhaps in part because it is so difficult to grapple with abstract questions of value. One empirical approach is to undertake comparative research that examines the quest for efficiency in countries that give primacy to differing values. For example, a comparison of efficiency-minded reforms in U.S. and Swedish social programs might provide insights into the role of political values in shaping these efforts.

PRIVATIZATION AS A BATTLEGROUND

With the development of American welfare state structures, opportunities for claims to be made upon the state increased. But the state's capacity to regulate these demands did not. Nor did an expanded welfare state indicate a stable political resolution of disagreement as to the appropriate size and scope of the state's welfare role. As costs and fiscal pressures intensified in the 1970s and 1980s, so too did opposition to the state's growth. Privatization, and the Reagan Administration's efforts to reduce the federal role in regulating public and private life, can be understood, at least in part, as a response to these pressures and as a political strategy for reducing demands on the state and limiting its growth by changing the structure of social provision.[8]

We begin with the premise that when there is fundamental disagreement over the ends of social policy and the capacity of the state to achieve agreement is weak, then policy disputes may occur on many battlegrounds and in many forms. In their concluding chapter to this volume, the editors suggest that "privatization is best understood as a battleground, rather than as satisfactory policy for our day or as nostrum." That is, privatization may be viewed, not only as a policy end, but also as a battleground on which disputes over the ends of the social welfare state are being fought. But not all battlegrounds are alike. They differ in how they establish the terms and arena of battle, what kind of tactics they facilitate, and how they are linked to the world of realpolitik.

The terms and arena of battle are critical elements in the structure of political conflict, because, as E. E. Schattschneider (1960) explained, they influence the scope and character of participants. As participation changes, so too does the likelihood of various outcomes. Thus, for disadvantaged minorities, it is strategically important to expand the scope of conflict, perhaps utilizing broad themes that appeal to a larger constituency (for example, defining the rights of blacks as civil liberties or even human rights). For more powerful elites, it may be equally important to limit the scope of conflict, keeping choices about the closing of a factory, for example, as private matters within the discretion of the firm rather than public matters involving the community residents whose jobs are at stake.

The terms on which issues achieve agenda status and how these terms shape and define political opportunities also have received considerable attention under the rubric of "agenda setting." Cobb and Elder (1983)

---

[8] We should note that in adopting this perspective, we do not assume that all proponents of privatization fully share these ends or that other objectives are unimportant. Nor do we assume that privatization—to the extent it has been implemented—has proven to be an effective strategy for limiting the welfare state. We do seek to describe analytic approaches that facilitate an exploration of the poltical dimensions of this issue.

assert that "control over how the issues of conflict are defined means control over the choice of battlefields upon which a conflict will take place. A group will always select a battlefield that gives it an advantage in terms of potential support." In this sense, the terms, arena, and scope of conflict are related. For example, the issue of day care formulated as a question of social rights is apt to be pushed into the national political arena, whereas day care as a question of private consumption is more appropriately a matter for individual families and the market.

Thus, development of the welfare state is generally accompanied by a politicization of formerly private matters. This is apt to be viewed as desirable by those emphasizing the ends of equality, solidarity, and security (three ends of the welfare state noted by Furniss and Tilton, 1977). It is seen as undesirable by those emphasizing the ends of the liberal state (among them, individualism and freedom from overly large government).

If one can risk characterizing an issue as complex as privatization, it would appear to have developed along two rather different lines—one that frames the issue largely in technical terms of efficiency and the other in terms of "empowering" communities and, reciprocally, curtailing the development of large public bureaucracies (Meyer, 1982; Berger and Neuhaus, 1977).

In the first instance, privatization is treated as primarily a technical or administrative concern. Although there is much more at stake than efficiency, by posing the privatization issue in relatively technical terms, rather than as a matter involving the distribution of political power or material benefits, it is theoretically possible to narrow the scope of conflict.[9] Strategically, defining an issue as technical tends to limit discussion to "experts" and obscure its nontechnical dimension.

But privatization is not strictly an administrative concern, nor have arguments in its behalf been strictly technical. To the contrary, the "empowerment" argument offered in behalf of privatization invokes a normative preference for reducing the size of government and utilizing smaller, decentralized policy delivery systems. Further, it is argued that privatization would enable social programs to be produced more efficiently and responsively. This line of argument does not overtly challenge the importance of social welfare programs; in fact, it appears to accept their importance.

Implicit in these arguments is a definition of a social policy problem to which privatization is posed as the solution. In order to assess the solution, however, it is first necessary to consider the problem definition. Es-

[9] For discussions of the participation-limiting consequences of technically defined policy issues see, for example, Brooks, 1984; Cobb and Elder, 1983; Offe, 1979; Thomas and Bailar, 1984.

sentially, the problem as presented is twofold. First, big government and big bureaucracy are undesirable. They contradict deeply held beliefs in individualism, freedom from state intrusion, and liberty. Second, large-scale public programs do not work, in part because they require bureaucratic implementation and, in part because they undermine individual initiative and responsibility.

James Q. Wilson drew attention to the bureaucracy problem (1967) at the height of the activist government period of the late 1960s. He argued that "inherent limits to what can be accomplished by large hierarchical organizations" make them unsuitable vehicles for achieving social welfare aims. From this perspective, the enduring dilemmas of bureaucracy make reformist and managerial solutions to social policy failures virtually pointless. Under these circumstances, Wilson commented, "one might be forgiven if one threw up one's hands and let nature take its course." Others have pursued analysis of alternatives to government social programs based on similar assumptions of bureaucratic failure. For example, Nathan Glazer (1983) proposed that the solution to the problems of efficiency and responsiveness in the welfare state might lie in turning away from government bureaucracy and "towards a self-service society."

If one accepts bureaucratic failure as the definition of the problem, it follows logically that a nonbureaucratic, nongovernmental alternative might be preferable. (Not all nongovernmental alternatives are nonbureaucratic, however.) But what if one disputes this definition of the "social policy problem"? Alternative perspectives lead in different directions. For example, Paul Starr and Gosta Esping-Anderson (1979), point out that many programs criticized for failing to solve social problems were pursued through mixed means, ranging from grant-supported local government programs to private activities only indirectly subsidized by tax subsidies (as in low-income housing). From their perspective, the "problem" with the social programs of the 1960s and 1970s was not too much public bureaucracy, but too little. They describe a policy dilemma in which government, needing to amass political support for social policies, offers pieces of the action to an assortment of public and private organizations. Fragmented and indirect modes of provision create cost inefficiencies and difficulties in accountability that, eventually, undermine public support. The implications of these two arguments for the privatization solution could hardly be more disparate.[10]

Further, the "bureaucracy problem," to which privatization is proposed as a partial remedy, like other political symbols tends to highlight some "facts" and mask others (Edelman, 1977). It does speak more to

[10] One might also challenge the view that the social policies of the 1960s and 1970s were largely unsuccessful. See, for example, Levitan and Taggart, 1976.

the matter of the ends of social policy than do economic arguments. However, it deals largely with only one set of ends—those attached to concern over the size of the state and centralization of its functions. It does not illuminate "facts" relevant to other "ends," for example, distributional equality, solidarity (building an organized constituency for the general social welfare), and other matters germane to privatization.

Once privatization is viewed as a battleground, then the terms of battle become important features of the analytical landscape. So, too, do the tactics by which participants seek to gain political advantage. In certain respects, privatization may usefully be assessed as a political strategy analogous to other administrative strategies that attempt to avoid or at least limit direct conflict over contentious social policy objectives (Brodkin, 1986; Lipsky, 1984; Nathan, 1983; Stone, 1984).

In general, administrative strategies limit conflict over policy issues by defining issues in nonpolitical terms, for example, as questions of "better management" or "efficiency." In addition, these types of strategies limit conflict by locating it in the administrative arena, avoiding, as much as possible, legislative activity that potentially broadens its scope. Further, administrative strategies may limit conflict by making policy indirectly, through alterations in bureaucratic structure or practice that are less visible than policy changes made through formal, legislative, or rule-making processes (Brodkin, 1987–1988). These strategic elements are interactive and inseparable.

For example, disability policy, as Stone describes, entails difficult political and social judgments—how to balance work against welfare, help against handouts, and cost against demand. She argues that potential conflicts over these dimensions of disability policy have been defused, in part, by converting political questions into technical ones and delegating them to medical experts for resolution. In this process, physicians become gatekeepers, at times widening and at times narrowing definitions of entitlement. In this way, Stone contends, it has been possible to redefine the scope and generosity of disability programs without subjecting them fully to the politics of the policy process.

Social policy delivery is not cut and dried. It involves considerable discretion on the part of those who deliver social programs, from welfare to day care. When discretion is intrinsic to program delivery, then the individuals or organizations that deliver policy effectively make policy and give it concrete meaning as they interpret and operationalize it. Consequently, decisions about who will deliver programs are also in part decisions about how discretion will be exercised and what criteria, norms, and biases will be applied to the interpretation of policy.

There is ample evidence of the importance of bureaucratic discretion in social policy implementation.[11] For example, Martha Derthick (1975) vividly demonstrated how changing the locus of discretion within the Department of Health, Education, and Welfare had major consequences for the outflow of social services grants to states. In that case, when authority shifted from social service professionals—who held states to a strict, informal, standard—to less experienced administrators, these informal standards were abandoned, and the former trickle of grants to states became a flood.

In different policy contexts, studies of social services and welfare also highlight the policy effects of choices about administrative systems. In the case of social services, Lipsky found that when institutional responsibility for problems facing families and individuals was divided among multiple public and private agencies, the information and effort required to match a given set of family problems to an appropriate set of institutional actors was often beyond the capacity of those needing help (or even of those trying to help them). One may reasonably argue that decentralization in this case, as in the case of privatization, has virtues in terms of its flexibility and variety. However, it also may establish a structural obstacle course that effectively negates these virtues by making ostensibly available support virtually unobtainable.

Even so-called "entitlements," such as public assistance, may be restricted by the administrative arrangements developed to deliver them. In the case of welfare, administrative reforms implemented in the 1970s to reduce erroneous payments, in practice, created systematic procedural and bureaucratic barriers preventing many poor families from obtaining the assistance they were ostensibly promised by law (Brodkin, 1986). Significantly, the rationing of assistance in this case occurred not as a matter of declared policy but as a bureaucratic by-product of institutional changes initiated for a manifestly different purpose.

A critical common feature of the disability, social services, and welfare examples is that social provision was limited not directly by changing policy regarding eligibility for assistance but indirectly by changing the structure of the delivery system and the institutional incentives that influenced the exercise of discretion by bureaucrats at the front lines of the delivery system (claims evaluators, social workers, medical examiners, and the like).

As these studies demonstrate, choices about policy delivery are choices about public policy. These choices, however, may be made for reasons apparently unrelated to their ultimate policy effects. In the case of social services, for example, one need not argue that bureaucratic fragmentation

[11] See, for example, Bardach, 1977; Derthick, 1972; Lipsky, 1980; Lowi, 1979; and Pressman and Wildavsky, 1973.

was intended to limit access to benefits in order to demonstrate that it had that effect. The lesson to be derived from these studies is that analysis of changes in the policy delivery system, such as those proposed under the rubric of privatization, must cast a wide net—assessing impacts beyond those manifestly intended.

Privatization would reorganize the delivery of social policy, shifting the balance from public to private institutions, each with a different set of incentives, constituencies, internal norms, standard operating procedures, and reference groups. Depending on one's point of view, the studies cited previously have either disturbing or promising implications for privatization. They suggest that privatization, potentially, provides a way of altering social policy without formally subjecting policy provisions to political debate. The precise effects of privatization, however, will depend on the type of organizations to which social policy delivery is transferred. Thus, analysts have appropriately begun the task of distinguishing among the types of organizations that might assume these responsibilities. The effects will also depend on how these organizations are influenced by their relationship with government, conceivably even becoming more like the public bureaucracies they replace.[12] The meaning of privatization for social policy, as delivered, is an important question for future research.

In addition to terms and tactics, analysis of privatization as a battleground requires that it be considered as realpolitik. While this dimension of analysis is related to those previously discussed, it focuses attention more directly on how dominant interests seek to institutionalize their powers (Redford and Blissett, 1981) and on an assessment of those interests. Although privatization's effects, ultimately, are problematic, its origins in the recent debate are more evident. During the Reagan Administration, the policy constructs that seemed to provide a framework for building an American welfare state came under attack in a variety of ways as the Administration sought to reduce accumulated government responsibilities.

In social welfare, in particular, the Administration pursued reductions through two major strategies. One was by cutting social programs outright. This strategy produced initial successes in the early phase of budget cutting, especially in cuts made through the Omnibus Reconciliation Acts in the first two years of the Reagan Administration. As a variety of observers have noted, however, this strategy left intact much of the policy

---

[12] Community organizations, forced to compete for funds and constituents, encounter a variety of dilemmas that influence their behavior and strategies. Wilensky expresses concern that "the new alliance between voluntarism and vendorism . . . does not threaten agency autonomy as much as it deflects resources to the scramble for subsidies and then to rituals of reporting and accountability—the often meaningless counts of 'outputs,' such as number of interviews, hospital days, or meals served" (Wilensky in Kramer, 1981, p. xvii).

structure that has provided a scaffolding for social welfare state development (Katznelson, 1981; Piven and Cloward, 1982).

Privatization rose to the political agenda as another element in a multidimensional assault on the structures and content of the welfare state. In this context, it may be analyzed as an instrument of the "administrative presidency." Richard Nathan (1983) coined this term to describe intentional presidential efforts to achieve administratively policy objectives that have been or are likely to be unattainable legislatively. Key instruments of the administrative presidency include bureaucratic reorganization and placement of critical personnel. Privatization, both by load-shedding and by decentralizing discretion in the delivery of social policy, can be viewed as an administrative tactic for reducing the power of the federal social welfare bureaucracy and, potentially, for diffusing political demands for social benefits. Whether privatization has been or will yet become a successful administrative strategy for defusing opposition to social welfare cuts is an empirical question still to be answered.

Conclusions

In this review of approaches to privatization, we have followed two distinct analytical paths. Although these paths are not necessarily dichotomous, we have treated them as if they were, at least in part to highlight their differences in assumptions, problem conceptualization, and analytic task.[13] The main economic approaches described above assume that the purpose of privatization is to improve efficiency in the provision of public goods and services. The problems they seek to address stem from institutional and market failures in the existing "mixed economy of welfare." The analytic task is to redesign this mix in order to improve efficiency.

In contrast, the political approaches sketched above do not assume privatization's purpose; they question it. The problems the political approaches seek to address stem from unresolved conflict over the scope and content of the American welfare state. The issue of privatization is viewed as a manifestation of and strategy in that conflict. The analytic task is to assess privatization's implications for social welfare politics—how it defines the agenda, channels conflict, and distributes political and material benefits.

These strands of analysis can be joined to clarify the privatization debate by considering tradeoffs between economic efficiency and other values of equity, justice, or social solidarity. Alternative institutional arrangements can be better understood by considering their responsiveness

---

[13] As previously noted, Hirschman (1970, 1982) has made several contributions in both these areas but they have not been tied to mainstream theory.

to both economic and political factors. Also, political and economic perspectives can jointly illuminate distribution and stability issues.

In the normative sphere, the nexus of economic and political analysis seems to contain some of the most interesting and potentially most productive lines of inquiry. Economic analyses directed mainly toward questions of efficiency and the allocation of resources may be used to evaluate political claims to the benefits (or harms) of privatization. By reaching beyond the political rhetoric, such analyses can usefully inform political debate and advance alternatives to current forms of policy delivery. Conversely, political analysis can expand the terms of economic analysis by directing the focus toward the political environment within which privatization proposals are advanced and by assessing the prospects for winning political acceptance. It also can suggest the feasibility of achieving the implementation of particular options, as well as consider a range of consequences beyond that of efficiency. In addition, political analysis can raise questions about the broader meaning of privatization as it relates to the advancement or contraction of the welfare state.

Political and economic analyses, when each is informed by the other, may conceivably lead to a clearer appraisal of privatization options. Further, they can contribute to defining new possibilities that can be productive in terms of efficiency, politically feasible, and cognizant of longer-term welfare and institutional implications.

References

Allison, Graham T. 1971. *Essence of Decision*. Boston: Little Brown and Company.

Bardach, Eugene. 1977. *The Implementation Game*. Cambridge, Mass.: MIT Press.

Bator, Francis M. 1958. "The Anatomy of Market Failure." *Quarterly Journal of Economics*: 351–379.

Beer, Samuel. 1965. *British Politics in the Collectivist Age*. New York: Knopf.

Berger, Peter, L. Berger, and Richard J. Neuhaus. 1977. *To Empower People*. Washington, D.C.: American Enterprise Institute.

Black, Duncan. 1971. *The Theory of Committees and Elections*. Cambridge University Press.

Briggs, Asa. 1961. "The Welfare State in Historical Perspective." *Europaisches Archiv für Soziologie* 2: 21–258.

Brodkin, Evelyn Z. 1986. *The False Promise of Administrative Reform: Implementing Quality Control in Welfare*. Philadelphia: Temple University Press.

———. 1988. "Policy Politics: If We Can't Govern, Can We Manage?" *Political Science Quarterly*. Winter.

Brooks, Harvey. 1984. "The Resolution of Technically Intensive Public Policy Disputes." *Science, Technology and Human Values* 46.

Buchanan, James M., and Gordon Tullock. 1962. *The Calculus of Consent.* Ann Arbor, Mich.: University of Michigan Press.

Burnham, Walter Dean. 1978. "Great Britain: The Death of the Collectivist Consensus?" In Maisell and Cooper, et al. *Political Parties: Decline and Decay.* Beverly Hills, Ca.: Sage.

———. 1980. "American Politics in the 1980s." *Dissent* 27.

Cobb, Roger W., and Charles D. Elder. 1983. *Participation in American Politics: The Dynamics of Agenda-Building.* 2nd ed. Baltimore, Md.: Johns Hopkins University Press.

Dahl, Robert. 1956. *A Preface to Democratic Theory.* University of Chicago Press.

Derthick, Martha. 1972. *New Towns In-Town.* Washington, D.C.: Urban Institute.

———. 1975. *Uncontrollable Spending for Social Services Grants.* Washington, D.C.: Brookings Institution.

Douglas, James. 1983. *Why Charity?* Beverly Hills, Ca.: Sage.

Edelman, Murray. 1977. *Political Language.* New York: Academic Press.

Evans, P., D. Rueschemeyer, and T. Skocpol, eds. 1985. *Bringing the State Back In.* Cambridge University Press.

Flora, Peter, and Arnold J. Heidenheimer. 1981. *The Development of Welfare States in Europe and America.* New Brunswick, N.J.: Transaction Books.

Furniss, Norman, and Timothy Tilton. 1977. *The Case for the Welfare State.* Bloomington, Ind.: Indiana University Press.

Gassler, Robert Scott. 1986. *The Economics of Nonprofit Enterprise.* Lanham, Md.: University Press of America.

Glazer, Nathan, 1983. "Towards a Self-Service Society?" *Public Interest.* Winter.

Hansmann, Henry B. 1980. "The Role of Nonprofit Enterprise." *Yale Law Journal* 89 (April): 835–901.

Hardin, Garrett. 1968. "The Tragedy of the Commons." *Science.* December.

Hartz, Louis. 1964. *The Founding of New Societies.* New York: Harcourt, Brace, World.

Heclo, Hugh. 1974. *Modern Social Politics in Britain and Sweden.* New Haven, Conn.: Yale University Press.

Hirschman, Albert O. 1970. *Exit, Voice and Loyalty.* Cambridge, Mass.: Harvard University Press.

———. 1982. *Shifting Involvements.* Princeton, N.J.: Princeton University Press.

Huntington, Samuel P. 1975. "The United States." In M. Crozier, S. P. Huntington, and J. Watanuki, eds. *The Crisis of Democracy.* New York University Press.

James, Estelle. 1983. "How Nonprofits Grow: A Model." *Journal of Policy Analysis and Management* 3 (Spring): 350–363.

James, Estelle, and Susan Rose-Ackerman. 1986. *The Nonprofit Enterprise in Market Economies.* Chur, Switzerland: Harwood Academic Publishers.

Kahn, Alfred E. 1970. *The Economics of Regulation: Principles and Institutions.* New York: John Wiley & Sons.

Kamerman, Sheila, 1983. "The New Mixed Economy of Welfare: Public and Private." *Social Work.* January–February.

Karl, Barry. 1983. *The Uneasy State*. University of Chicago Press.

Katznelson, Ira. 1981. "A Radical Departure? Social Welfare and the Election." In Ferguson and Rogers, eds. *The Hidden Election*. New York: Pantheon.

King, Anthony J. 1975. "Overload: Problems of Governing in the 1970s." *Political Studies* 23 (2): 162–174.

Kramer, Ralph M. 1981. *Voluntary Agencies in the Welfare State*. Berkeley, Ca.: University of California Press.

Krashinsky, Michael. 1986. "Transactions Costs and a Theory of the Nonprofit Organization." In Susan Rose-Ackerman, ed. *The Economics of Nonprofit Institutions*: 114–132. New York: Oxford University Press.

Lampman, Robert J. 1974. " 'What Does It Do for the Poor?' A New Test for National Policy." In E. Ginzberg and R. Solow, eds. *The Great Society: Lessons for the Future*. New York: Basic Books.

Levitan, Sar A., and Robert Taggert. 1976. *The Promise of Greatness*. Cambridge, Mass.: Harvard University Press.

Lindblom, Charles E. 1965. *The Intelligence of Democracy*. New York: Free Press.

———— 1979. "Still Muddling, Not Yet Through." *Public Administration Review*. November–December.

Lipsky, Michael. 1980. *Street-Level Bureaucracy: Dilemmas of the Individual in Public Services*. New York: Russell Sage Foundation.

————. 1984. "Bureaucratic Disentitlement in Social Welfare Programs." *Social Service Review*. March.

Lowi, Theodore J. 1979. *The End of Liberalism: The Second Republic of the United States*. New York: W. W. Norton.

Meyer, Jack A. 1982. "Private Sector Initiatives and Public Policy: A New Agenda." In Meyer, ed. *Meeting Human Needs: Toward a New Public Philosophy*. Washington, D.C.: American Enterprise Institute.

Musgrave, Richard A. 1959. *The Theory of Public Finance*. New York: McGraw-Hill.

Nathan, Richard P. 1983. *The Administrative Presidency*. New York: John Wiley & Sons.

Nelson, Richard R., and Michael Krashinsky. 1973. "Two Major Issues of Public Policy: Public Subsidy and Organization of Supply." In Dennis R. Young and Richard R. Nelson, eds. *Public Policy for Day Care of Young Children*. Lexington, Mass.: Lexington Books.

Newhouse, Joseph. 1970. "Toward a Theory of Non-profit Institutions: An Economic Model of a Hospital." *American Economic Review*. March: 64–74.

Niskanen, William A., Jr. 1971. *Bureaucracy and Representative Government*. Chicago: Aldine-Atherton.

Offe, Claus. 1979. "The State, Ungovernability and the Search for the 'Non-Political'." Paper presented at the Conference on the Individual and the State.

————. 1984. *Contradictions of the Welfare State*. Cambridge, Mass.: MIT Press.

Olson, Mancur. 1965. *The Logic of Collective Action*. Cambridge, Mass.: Harvard University Press.

Patterson, James. 1981. *America's Struggle Against Poverty—1900–1980*. Cambridge, Mass.: Harvard University Press.

Pauly, Mark, and Michael Redisch. 1973. "The Not-for-Profit Hospital as a Physicians' Cooperative." *American Economic Review* 63 (March): 87–99.

Perrin, Guy, 1969. "Reflections on Fifty Years of Social Security." *International Labour Review* 99.

Piven, Francis Fox, and Richard Cloward. 1971. *Regulating the Poor*. New York: Random House.

———. 1977. *Poor People's Movements: Why They Succeed, How They Fail*. New York: Random House.

———. 1982. *The New Class War*. New York: Pantheon.

Pressman, Jeffrey L., and Aaron Wildavsky. 1973. *Implementation*. Berkeley, Ca.: University of California Press.

Redford, E., and M. Blissett. 1981. *Organizing the Executive Branch*. University of Chicago Press.

Rimlinger, Gaston V. 1971. *Welfare Policy and Industrialization in Europe, America, and Russia*. New York: John Wiley & Sons.

Rokkan, Stein. 1974. "Dimensions of State Formation and Nation Building." In Charles Tilly, ed. *The Formation of National States in Western Europe*. Princeton, N.J.: Princeton University Press.

Rose-Ackerman, Susan. 1978. *Corruption: A Study in Political Economy*. New York: Academic Press.

Salamon, Lester. 1985. "Partners in Public Service: Toward a Theory of Government-Nonprofit Relations." The Urban Institute. August.

Savas, E. S. 1982. *Privatizing the Public Sector*. Chatham, N.J.: Chatham House.

Schattschneider, E. E. 1960. *Semi-Sovereign People*. New York: Holt, Rinehart, and Winston.

Scherer, F. M. 1973. *Industrial Market Structure and Economic Performance*. New York: Rand McNally & Co.

Shubik, Martin. 1982. *Game Theory in the Social Sciences*. Cambridge, Mass.: MIT Press.

Skocpol, Theda, and John Ikenberry. 1983. "The Political Formation of the American Welfare State in Historical and Comparative Perspective." *Comparative Social Research* 6.

Starr, Paul, and Gosta Esping-Anderson. 1979. "Passive Intervention." *Working Papers*. July–August.

Starr, Paul, and Ellen Immergut. 1987. "Health Care and the Boundaries of Politics." In Charles S. Maier, ed. *Changing Boundaries of the Political: Essays on the Evolving Balance Between State and Society, Public and Private in Europe*. Cambridge University Press.

Steiner, Gilbert. 1971. *The State of Welfare*. Washington, D.C.: Brookings Institution.

Stone, Deborah A. 1984. *The Disabled State*. Philadelphia: Temple University Press.

Sugden, Robert. 1982. "On the Economics of Philanthropy." *Economic Journal* 92 (June): 341–350.

Sundquist, James. 1980. "The Crisis of Competence in Our National Government." *Political Science Quarterly* 95.

Thomas, Stephen, and John Bailar III. 1984. "What Are We Doing When We Say We're Doing Risk Analysis?" Paper presented at the conference of the Association of Public Policy Analysis and Management. New Orleans, La. October 1985.

Walker, Alan. 1984. "The Political Economy of Privatisation." In J. LeGrand and R. Robinson, eds. *Privatisation and the Welfare State*. London: Allen and Unwin.

Weber, Max. 1949. "Objectivity in Social Science." In *On The Methodology of the Social Sciences*: 49–112. Edward A. Shils and Henry A. Finch, eds. and trans. Glencoe, Ill.: Free Press.

Weisbrod, Burton A. 1977. *The Voluntary Nonprofit Sector*. Lexington, Mass.: Lexington Press.

————. 1983. "Nonprofit and Proprietary Sector Behavior: Wage Differentials Among Lawyers." *Journal of Labor Economics* 2 (3): 246–263.

Weisbrod, Burton A., and Mark Schlesinger. 1986. "Nonprofit Ownership and the Response to Asymmetric Information: The Case of Nursing Homes." In Susan Rose-Ackerman, ed. *The Economics of Nonprofit Institutions*: 133–151. New York: Oxford University Press.

Wildavsky, Aaron. 1966. "The Political Economy of Efficiency: Cost-Benefit Analysis, Systems Analysis, and Program Budgeting." *Public Administration Review* 26 (4).

Wilensky, Harold. 1975. *The Welfare State and Equality: Structural and Ideological Roots of Public Expenditures*. Berkeley, Ca.: University of California Press.

Wilensky, Harold L., and Charles N. Lebeaux. 1965. *Industrial Society and Social Welfare*. New York: Free Press.

Williamson, Oliver E. 1975. *Markets and Hierarchies*. New York: Free Press.

Wilson, James Q. 1967. "The Bureaucracy Problem." *Public Interest*. Winter.

Wolf, Charles, Jr. 1979. "A Theory of Nonmarket Failure: Framework for Implementation Analysis." *Journal of Law and Economics*. April: 107–139.

Young, Dennis R. 1983. *If Not For Profit, For What?* Lexington, Mass.: Lexington Books.

II

CASE STUDIES

6

Social Welfare and Privatization: The British Experience

MICHAEL O'HIGGINS

David Donnison has argued that " 'privatization' is a word invented by politicians and disseminated by political journalists. It is designed not to clarify analysis but as a symbol, intended by advocates and opponents of the process it describes to dramatize a conflict and mobilize support for their own side. Thus it is a word which should be heavily escorted by inverted commas as a reminder that its meaning is at best uncertain and often tendentious" (1984, p. 45). Yet it is also a term describing a mechanical process that can be clearly defined as a decrease in the proportionate or relative role of one or more of state production, finance, or regulation in the supply of a good or service.

The difference between the two interpretations—the symbolic and the mechanical—highlights the confusion and the complexity of the privatization debate. Part of the origins of this confusion, particularly in Britain, lie in the statist perspective within which the provision of social welfare services has tended to be analyzed. Although the reality of provision has always been that of a "mixed economy of social welfare," with public and private (for-profit and nonprofit) institutions existing alongside an informal network of family, community, and voluntary services, "this complex reality remained obscured largely because of the restricted construction of social services as public services, [a restricted construction] which dominated social administration until very recently" (Walker, 1984, p. 23).

Ironically, much of this restricted construction owes its origins to Titmuss's social division of welfare, wherein he identified the two nonpublic elements of his welfare triad—occupational and fiscal welfare—as being inegalitarian and therefore detrimental to broad social welfare aims (1963). This led to the assumption that public had to replace private in order to advance the aims of social policy. Little attention was paid to alternative strategies of seeking to shape or regulate the provision of services—whether public or private—in order to achieve a balance or package that more effectively advanced the broad goals of social policy.

Just as importantly, the Titmuss thesis led to an analytic focus on state provision, an assumption that social policy analysis was the analysis of government social provision. Thus, Webb argues that "one of the major past defects of social policy has been the tendency to treat social welfare as an end in itself and therefore to concentrate on resource inputs as symbols of progress and commitment—to the neglect of outputs" (1985, pp. 54–55). This focus conflates the idea of the state as an agent of social responsibility and the state as the mechanism whereby any such responsibility is implemented. In turn, this conflation leaves one analytically less well prepared to distinguish policy changes that represent reductions in the extent to which the government is accepting or acknowledging a social responsibility, from those that represent shifts in the form whereby this responsibility is being implemented.

Privatization and Motivation
Instruments and Ideologies

One view of privatization thinks of it as a changing of methods or procedures that has no necessary or a priori outcome consequences and that should be judged in the light of the actual outcome according to whatever criteria of policy purpose or impact are in use. The focus is on effects, not methods of provision. Included in this category would be those arguments that emphasize the efficiency with which a service can be provided, or its effectiveness, in such terms as the proportion of a client group that is reached or the likelihood that a service will be in line with and responsive to the needs of its users.

An alternative view would deny that instruments can be separated from outcomes in this way. The traditional welfare socialist perspective on this is summarized by Walker: "Once one set of services based on values such as social integration and community is replaced by another reflecting different values, such as self-interest, the nature of the service and its social consequences will have been transformed" (1984, p. 41). Privatization thus represents "an attempt not only to shift the demarcation line between public and private services and establish a 'new balance' between them, but also, thereby, to change the character of those services, particularly those in the public sector" (1984, p. 24).

The assumption underlying this view is not, however, confined to the political left; it is implicit in Murray's *Losing Ground*: "A moral dilemma underlies the history of social policy from 1950 to 1980, an anciently recognized dilemma that in the enthusiasm of the 1960s we dismissed as fusty and confuted. It is indeed possible that steps to relieve misery can create misery . . . [Traditionally] the dilemma was taken for granted. The very existence of a welfare system was assumed to have the inherent, intrinsic, unavoidable effect of undermining the moral character of the people . . . a welfare system was perpetually in danger of tilting the balance in favor of the easy way out" (1984, pp. 9 and 16).

Despite the wide practical divergence between these perspectives, both view the argument about the form and nature of provision as being concerned with more than short-term consequences (such as the unit cost of provision or the percentage of the poor who receive assistance). Each believes that the form of provision has important dynamic consequences. One ideological perspective may condemn privatization "as one manifestation . . . of the increased importance given to individualistic values" (Walker, 1984, p. 27) and because it increases the emphasis on market relations, at the expense of values of social responsibility, community, and human relations. Another may support it because it promotes values of self-reliance and of individual and family responsibility, which are seen to be the only foundation for lasting prosperity and social well-being. But both share a belief that the form of provision has longer-term consequences, which may not be detectable or "provable" as social science evidence, but which are more fundamental than the short-term or static effects that may be captured by impact analysis. In this sense, ideology is a belief in dynamic effects that are a matter of faith rather than proof.

The more limited instrumentalist view is not then the whole story and may lead us to ignore important social forces and beliefs if we rely solely on it. But neither is the ideological view adequate on its own: We need the instrumentalist approach to allow us to measure and assess the more immediate costs and benefits arising from the implementation of the ideological arguments. Even taken together, however, they do not provide an adequate framework for analyzing privatization because each ignores the importance of the context in which changes may take place: The instrumentalist view focuses only on a narrowly defined set of outcomes; the ideological view presupposes that the outcomes are unaffected by the political or economic context in which they take place and also ignores the implication of the current reality of a mixture of public and private provision.

In the next section I propose a third alternative, one that I term a strategic approach to analyzing privatization.

A Strategic Approach to Privatization

A strategic approach to privatization is one that is more sensitive to the political economy of social welfare than instrumentalist approaches, but less deterministic than ideological approaches. It draws upon a number of features of the existence of both a mixed economy and a mixed polity of social welfare and in so doing indicates the inadequacy of the other two approaches.

The first feature is that the mixed economy of social service provision means that the government already has only a partial role in the provision of any particular service: It may therefore be possible to advance social welfare aims by reallocating or redistributing roles or tasks within that mixed economy. Privatization in one area may allow socialization in another.

For example, one of the policy areas in Britain where the role of the state is most comprehensive is health care: More than 90 percent of the population routinely use the National Health Service (NHS). Yet even here there are a multiplicity of roles for and areas of private provision. It may apply to some individuals (the rich), to some operations (abortion, plastic surgery, heart transplants), to some proportion of costs (prescription charges, deductibles and co-insurance), to some preventive strategies (checkups, self-help health groups), to some times of the week (no elective surgery at public expense on weekends), or to some associated facilities (privacy, visiting times, communication and entertainment systems). Each of these aspects of private provision are parts of the territory within which the NHS must determine its dimensions and mark out its boundaries. It cannot convincingly be argued that the existing dimensions of the public role must necessarily be optimal in all respects.

The second feature reinforces this argument. The mixture of provision is located within a dynamic policy environment, so that even if the optimal balance was once achieved, circumstances may have changed. Constraints on spending levels may change; new priorities may emerge for demographic, technological, or other reasons; or the relative income levels of different population groups may alter, leading to shifts in their relative need or perceived relative claim on public resources in certain programs. (For example, it might be argued that the recent rises in the relative income levels of the elderly in the United States and similar prospective rises in the United Kingdom may allow a greater proportion of their increasing health and social care needs to be financed from their own resources, allowing a higher priority for family-oriented programs in the use of public resources.) Any of these factors may mean that the privatization of certain responsibilities may be part of a welfare-improving shift in public policies and priorities.

These arguments suggest, therefore, that the role of public policy is not to set out policies in a vacuum, but to design policies that will, as appropriate, take advantage of, accommodate, or nullify existing types of nonpublic provision. This implies seeing public policy within a dynamic interactive framework where the object is to intervene in social welfare provision, financing, or regulation so as to move the overall package as far as possible towards social welfare objectives. This perspective therefore moves toward an instrumentalist view of privatization but within a wider structure of strategic planning than the narrow instrumentalist view identified earlier.

The third feature is logically part of the second, but merits particular attention. Even if all existing public provision could be preserved, any significant further development of social provision may need to incorporate private elements. In this context, the long period of economic growth after World War II, coinciding with and permitting the development of social provision, may be seen to have brought the "mature" welfare state in many West European countries. (In the United States, the argument might be expressed by saying that the combination of the New Deal and the Great Society had introduced some social institutions that are now in a mature state, such as Social Security and Medicare.) Therefore, the recent reassessment of the social role of the state in most developed countries, though hastened and exacerbated by the depth and length of the recessions of the late 1970s and early 1980s, would have occurred anyway, as an inevitable reaction to this maturing.

Among the arguments buttressing this view are that the relative growth of social spending in the economy could not continue indefinitely; that the resulting deepening of the tax burden on lower income groups was having counterproductive and perverse results, negating many of the redistributive aims of welfare provision; and that the mature existence of large welfare institutions was also revealing unanticipated problems of inflexibility, unresponsiveness, self-interest, and rigidity that suggested a case for having any future growth take place outside the government sector (Weale, 1985). Without implying any fixed limits to the relative size of government spending or production, the argument suggests that the appropriate pattern of service and financing development from a mature social welfare basis may be different from that followed during the period of establishment and consolidation.

These first three features suggest weaknesses in the ideologically negative view of privatization. A fourth feature points up a weakness in the instrumentalist position. Many of the supposed virtues of privatization rest upon the flexibility and adaptability of market or voluntary structures of provision. To some extent this is a function of small size, rather than of public or private location (Judge and Knapp, 1985). It is also, however, often conditional upon the marginality of those private structures—that is, upon their playing only a relatively small role in the total provision package. "Much of the attraction of the private sector depends on its marginality. To the extent that the private sector replaces the public sector, there is a risk that it may also reproduce its weaknesses, its rigidi-

ties, its unresponsiveness and its administrative costs—with the bureaucracy of regulation taking the place of the bureaucracy of management"
(Klein, 1984, p. 28). Webb makes the same point with respect to the voluntary sector: "If voluntary organizations took responsibility for large
areas of basic service provision, it is at least arguable that they would be
forced to accept the same preoccupation with equity which currently produces many of the 'bureaucratic' characteristics of statutory services.
They could well become enmeshed in much closer public accountability
which would inhibit risk-taking and responsiveness" (1985, p. 59). Thus,
the very characteristics of flexibility and experimentation that are thought
desirable may be possible only in fringe provision. Small shifts in the balance of provision may be able to take advantage of these characteristics,
but major shifts may have different effects. This complexity underlines
the importance of contextual evaluation of particular proposals.

To these features of reality that argue for a strategic perspective on the
mixed economy of social provision—and hence on privatization—can be
added four arguments drawn from analyses of the politics of provision.

First, the degree of consent to levels of social provision may be affected
by the form of that provision. Thus, Taylor-Gooby (1985) notes an "ambiguity" in British public opinion on social welfare: People appear to favor both public and private provision, finding characteristics in each that
are regarded as desirable. Higher levels of provision may therefore receive
consent in a mixed structure that they would be denied in a "pure" model
of either public or private provision. This is the argument underlying
Marc Bendick's analysis (Chapter 4) of the case for private delivery of
publicly financed social services in the United States.

A second argument is that the sets of interests accommodated during
the enactment and implementation of current social programs—and thus
the interests served by those programs—do not necessarily conform precisely to the benefit group identified in any specified set of social policy
aims. What was exigent to secure passage may no longer be required. In
such instances the withdrawal or restriction of certain elements of public
provision—privatization in the mechanical sense identified earlier—may
advance redistributive social aims.

A third, and related, argument is based on the multiple aims of many
social programs. Since few programs are aimed at only one target group
or seek to conform to only one criterion of impact or effectiveness, their
policy objectives are generally likely to require achieving a balance, or
tension, between competing aims. Adapting that balance to changed circumstances, or to a shift in the desired tension, may involve shifts in the
public/private boundary. To take the British NHS as an example one more
time, there is a tension, and thus a trade-off, between the competing aims
of universality and equity. Universality is sought both on ideological

grounds and as a vehicle to maintain widespread popular consent for the health service. Rendering this principle effective requires that any individual in Britain be able to obtain NHS treatment for most medical needs. Therefore, some NHS resources are devoted to treating the minor illnesses of middle income groups.

It is difficult to justify on equity grounds an allocation of resources that leaves chronic care services for the frail elderly or the handicapped significantly underfunded, while providing services without charge to remedy the minor illnesses of those who could without difficulty pay for treatment. That the justification is on universality rather than equity grounds does not reduce the conflict or tension between the two objectives.

At present, resources in the NHS are being shifted toward chronic care, in recognition both of the low quality of services in this area and of the pressures created by a changing demographic structure. Such resource shifts, while wholly necessary, will further increase pressure on other parts of the NHS, leading to longer queues for service and less comfortable conditions. Insofar as these parts of the service are used by those who could afford private health insurance or private health care charges (even if only for their less serious health care needs), this resource switch may constitute implicit privatization: privatization that comes about not only by open government decision to withdraw public services but also by reducing the quality of public provision to a group who have the capacity to make private provision for some of their needs. In this case, shifts to meet an equity objective may lead to privatization by social welfare erosion.

The existence of a tension between coexisting aims of policy illustrates the complexity of any attempt at *ex ante* evaluation. If a limited (or self-limiting) degree of privatization occurs without threatening the broad universality of the service, the equity gains may outweigh the loss of universality. But if the shift is sufficient to create a dynamic toward a transformation of provision into a clear two-tier model—private care for the affluent nonchronic ill, with a residual public service for the remainder—the short-term equity gains may be deemed inadequate. Evaluation, in other words, requires context.

This leads directly to the fourth and final argument from a political perspective. The implications and evaluation of any privatization, or of any shift in the public/private boundary, requires an analysis of power relations. If a proposal implies altering the distribution of the costs and benefits of provision (whether to consumers or to service producers), will the gains and losses be further shifted by the exercise of industrial, domestic, or class power? If a proposal implies placing new responsibilities on particular groups or sectors, will those responsibilities (or their costs) be shifted elsewhere? What price, trade-off, or quid pro quo will be required to secure a shift in the boundary or balance of provision? None of these questions has a general answer; none leads to eternal verities. Each can only be examined in the context of particular times, proposals, and circumstances.

The existence of a mixed economy and a mixed polity of social welfare implies that the location of the public/private boundary and the determination of the public/private balance is a strategic decision. The question of privatization (or socialization) is therefore a matter for strategic rather than instrumental or ideological analysis. But while strategic decisions may arise at any time, answering them—in other words, evaluating the likely outcome of any changes—can only be done in particular contexts. The analytic mode appropriate to the evaluation of privatization arguments should therefore be both strategic and contextual.

Operating within this mode, the next sections examine the forms that privatization may take and evaluate British experience since Mrs. Thatcher's conservative government first came to power in 1979.

Forms and Expressions
of Privatization in Britain

Setting the analysis of privatization within the mixed provision perspective outlined here allows a wide range of balance shifts to be viewed as privatization. Three major avenues may nevertheless be identified as routes for governments concerned to increase privatization in social welfare: transferring production to the private sector, enacting a private but regulated responsibility, and stimulating service consumers to greater use of and reliance on private provision. As the categories and examples will illustrate, these often involve opposite directions of change for state production, finance, and regulation: for example, less production may require more finance, and less finance may require more regulation.

TRANSFERRING PRODUCTION

Retaining public finance while transferring production to the private sector is the privatization strategy most favored by those who accept state responsibility for ensuring acceptable levels of social provision, but believe that provision through the market is more efficient and less distorting of resource allocation and preference expression. It is also the form most extensively implemented under the Conservative government in Britain, particularly in housing, health care, and social services.

The sale of more than half a million units of local authority housing (council houses) to their tenants has been one of the major political and social policy successes of the government—so successful indeed that the

Labour Party had to abandon its long-standing opposition to the principle of such sales. Although individual local authorities had previously sold some housing units—with varying degrees of encouragement or discouragement from central government—the Conservative Administration rapidly enacted a statutory "right to buy," accompanied by a very generous system of discounts (related to the duration of tenancy) for sitting tenants, and has actively pursued local authorities thought to be recalcitrant in facilitating tenant purchase.

In theory, such a policy could be significantly egalitarian and produce positive social effects. The "right to buy" and associated subsidies extend to many working-class families a choice that they clearly desire to have. A Labour Party member of Parliament and former director of the Child Poverty Action Group, Frank Field, has argued that it can provide an opportunity for significantly equalizing the distribution of wealth and power because of the importance of home ownership as a source of each.

Furthermore, the negative effects of sales on the aggregate availability of housing are slight in the short run, since houses are lost to reletting only at the point at which they would otherwise have been vacated by the family of the sitting tenant (Environment Committee, 1981). In the long run, any effects depend on whether the density of occupation of the sold units eventually changes from what it would have been in the public rented sector and on whether the tenant-purchasers would eventually have become owner-occupiers even without council house sales. They also depend on how the capital receipts from sales are used. Insofar as they are used to finance the construction of new housing units, any long-term effective loss of available dwellings is reduced. The relative income and cost changes from sales as compared to renting are obviously also important.

In practice, council house sales have been accompanied by the imposition of a sharp reduction in public sector house construction rates. The dwellings purchased have been, not surprisingly, the more "desirable" ones—those with gardens or in pleasant locations, houses rather than apartments, suburban rather than inner-city properties. Similarly, the purchasers have been the more affluent council tenants (Malpass and Murie, 1982; Kirwan, 1984).

The policy therefore seems to be effecting a reduction in the inequality of property holding between middle and lower income groups while increasing inequality within the lower income sector. It is reducing the possibility for an individual tenant of transferring to better quality accommodation within the public sector. Furthermore, by reducing the average housing quality and average income status of those in public rented housing (that is, those who do not buy), it increases the likelihood of council housing becoming (perceived as) a residual "problem-family" sector, rather than a universally available alternative tenure choice. Privatization in this context appears to be regressive in practice.

In the health service, attempts are being made to transfer production of many of the nonmedical aspects of provision—cleaning, laundry, catering—to the private sector. Health authorities are now being required actively to seek to subcontract services such as these to private firms. While the information in this case is officially expressed as instrumental—to increase production efficiency—the implementation has on occasion been ideological: The use of private options has been required even when the unit costs seemed higher. Although the process is at too early a stage to evaluate fully, there are signs that its main impact will not be a major increase in the use of private contract services so much as an increase in efficiency in the public sector. Faced with the possibility of outside competition, public sector working practices and restrictions are being relaxed and, on occasion, wages reduced, in order to secure contracts for the "in-house" providers.

The provision of social care—always an area of extensive nonpublic involvement—has seen three types of privatization of production: toward increased use of voluntary and nonprofit organizations, often directly financed by central government; toward private rather than public institutional care for the very elderly, with the costs of care being paid through the income support system; and toward private domestic rather than public institutional care for children. Information on the first of these is scattered and evaluation is only beginning (Webb and Wistow, 1985). But some effects and consequences of the other two are worth noting.

Public finance may be provided for the private care of the elderly through the Supplementary Benefit (SB) system (although the primary function of supplementary benefits is provision of means-tested income support). A government directive to SB regional administrative units to review and formalize the levels and scales of charges they were prepared to meet in respect of private care of the elderly significantly heightened both local authority and private awareness of these provisions. While the government was committed in a general way to expanding the use of private care, it was unprepared for and did not anticipate the consequences of this increased awareness (Challis, Day, and Klein, 1984).

Private suppliers both more actively sought SB-financed clients and—now aware of the scale of charges permissible in their locality—tended to raise their charges toward the maximum. Local authorities, facing severe fiscal pressures (not least because of strengthened central government controls on their permitted spending levels), saw an opportunity to shift costs from their budgets to the nationally financed SB system, transforming local government production and finance into central government financing of private production. Clients became customers, with a wider choice of provision, and suppliers were anxious to meet their needs—or those of their families or whoever made the choice of care institution.

The resulting happiness did not extend to central government. Faced with a budget item that had grown from relative insignificance to over one hundred million pounds, and was still increasing rapidly, the government withdrew from its unintended open-ended commitment to public finance for private care. It left the principle intact, but it regulated the permissible charges, enforcing significant cuts in the maximum payable and disrupting the developing market for provision in this area. The saga bears considerable similarities to that described by Derthick (1975) about U.S. federal government attempts to encourage the contracting out of social services to private agencies.

Institutional care of children is both relatively expensive and labor intensive, without being regarded as particularly appropriate or effective. Faced with pressure both on budgets and on staff levels, local authorities have increasingly sought and used foster care, with relatively generous allowances being provided as incentive and compensation to foster parents. In this instance, what was viewed as a desirable professional development appears to have been accelerated by political exigency, with beneficial social welfare outcomes.

These three examples (housing, health care, and social services) are conceptually analogous in that each is a form of privatization by transferring production out of the public sector. They differ, however, both in motivation and in the circumstances of their implementation, and lead to very different outcomes. With respect to transferring production, it appears that neither the fact nor the form of privatization allows the assumption of particular outcomes.

STIMULATED CONSUMER SWITCHING

A gradually lower quality of public service or a failure to raise service levels as private prosperity increased could be expected to lead to more people opting for private alternatives. The role of state services would diminish, not because of governments depriving clients of their entitlements to access, but because of consumers choosing to take their custom elsewhere. A degree of remarketization (as privatization is often termed in Europe) would be accomplished by attrition rather than assault (Ruggles and O'Higgins, 1987). Governments may pursue policies, consciously or otherwise, that will over time lead to a relative increase in the size and role of private provision. This may occur by policies of erosion, inadequacy, or incentive.

Erosion may consist either of reductions in the real value or quality of benefits or services, whether explicit or through failure to provide fully for inflation, or of restrictions on eligibility. In the case of income support it may simply reduce the standard of living of claimants or it may force greater reliance or claims on other sources of income (for example, family, friends, charities). It may be considered a form of privatization since it cuts state expenditure, reduces the extent of governmental acceptance of responsibility for income support and may lead people to make or increase private income security or social welfare arrangements out of fear of continued benefit or service erosion.

Even if the real value or extent of eligibility for a benefit or service is not eroded it may become less adequate compared to public expectations. This is particularly likely in a period of rising real incomes if public services do not improve correspondingly. If public provision leaves private wants unsatisfied it creates a vacuum that provides a potential market for private welfare. Privatization as a policy may, therefore, simply take the form of allowing any pressures for real increases in benefit values or service quality to be met only through private provision, thus decreasing the relative role of state services over time.

While erosion and inadequacy describe essentially negative or passive means of stimulating privatization, governments may also provide incentives for individuals to make alternative, nonpublic provision for themselves. Such incentives include remission of or exemption from contributions for public provision, or tax relief for the costs of purchasing private provision (such as mortgage tax relief). Given the similarity between tax expenditures and direct public spending, this type of incentive is clearly on a continuum with public finance subsidizing the purchase of private services.

These various ways of stimulating consumer switching can obviously overlap. In the United States, for example, the popularity of Individual Retirement Accounts (IRAs)—at least prior to 1986 tax-law changes—reflected both the tax break that they provided and the fears generated in recent years about both erosion and inadequacy in Social Security benefits in the future.

In practice, the Conservative government has avoided extending overt incentives (apart from a slight increase in the upper limit for mortgage tax relief) and has even restricted some forms of relief in pursuit of a desire for "tax simplification" though, as discussion later in this chapter indicates, incentives may be introduced in order to encourage people to build up private pensions. However, its general attitude toward government provision clearly encourages switching through fear of inadequacy, though what practical effect this has is unknown.

There was relatively little erosion in income security benefits during the first Conservative Administration—early cuts in some benefits were restored before the end of the first term of office. Recent increases in the child benefit, however, have been less than the rate of inflation, and there are indications that this benefit may suffer further erosion. In the service provision areas, charges at the point of use have increased significantly in real terms for prescription and dental charges, council house rents, and school meal prices. Although these may assist in maintaining the quality of services, they by definition reduce the net benefit (or consumer surplus at the point of use) of any given level of service to consumers.

As noted earlier, shifting priorities within a tight national budget have reduced service quality for particular treatment categories in the NHS. Geographical reallocations mean that this is also the case for particular regions, and it will be interesting to observe whether insured coverage rates for private health care change differently in the "loser" regions as compared to the "gainers." Erosions have also taken place in schooling provision in some local authorities. However, the high relative cost of private education in Britain would restrict the magnitude of any immediate reactions: Private school fees for children from middle income backgrounds are commonly paid out of savings funds specifically planned and provided for over a preceding period of years.

One of the relatively largest targets for financial erosion has been the university sector, which is largely publicly financed in Britain. This erosion has been accompanied by restrictions on student numbers in most universities. While forcing universities to search more actively for nongovernmental sources of finance, the major effect of this is a reduction in the number of students admitted to universities rather than much expansion in private provision, because the universities have generally sought to ration the reduced number of places by raising admission standards. Thus, people who are perfectly capable of acquiring good degrees are being denied university admission. Many of these may attend nonuniversity institutions such as polytechnics or colleges of higher education, or enter the labor market earlier. They may therefore "suffer" through having a less prestigious degree, or a job below their previous expectations. But the greater suffering will probably be by those denied admission at the bottom of the tertiary education hierarchy because of the "downward movement" of more highly qualified students, and by those who become unemployed because the jobs they might previously have obtained now go to those with better educational attainments who would earlier have gone to university or pursued some other tertiary sector option. These losers are in no position to generate an effective demand for alternative, nonpublic tertiary education provision to replace that being lost through erosion in the public sector.

REGULATED PRIVATE RESPONSIBILITY

If social provisions were simply eliminated, with individuals left to fend for themselves, one consequence would almost certainly be that public assistance or services would be required for those who failed to make such personal provision. Either because of a desire to avoid the fiscal, social, and equity implications of such "free-riding," or because of a more positive concern to ensure comprehensiveness of coverage even while reducing public finance or production, governments may privatize by either compulsory private insurance or mandated third-party coverage.

Motorists are generally required by law to be insured against certain risks, but the actual provision of that insurance is often left to private organizations. Such a strategy might be adopted with respect to income replacement benefits such as unemployment, sickness, and pensions, or to services such as health care. This could lead to individual insurance negotiations and contracts. But a more likely consequence in Britain would be the reemergence in Britain of a major trade union or friendly society role in providing such benefits, as was the case before the advent of social insurance. This possibility was indeed envisaged for unemployment benefits in a speculative policy document leaked during the first Thatcher government, but no changes took place during the second (1983–1987) Administration. More intensive consideration was given to transforming the NHS to an insurance-based service, but after a series of studies this possibility was publicly and unusually unequivocally rejected by the relevant Cabinet minister.

If a government's concern is not simply to divest itself of responsibility, but to lay a clear responsibility elsewhere, it may require third parties (usually employers) to organize or provide coverage. In such instances, governments are using their legislative and regulatory powers to ensure that such benefits are provided while avoiding provision or financial responsibility themselves. Mandating strategies can therefore seem particularly attractive ways of cutting public spending without affecting the level of assured provision available to individuals. Despite considerable European precedent, the only major example of this during the first Thatcher Administration (1979–1983) was a plan to mandate employers to provide sick pay for employees, in order to eliminate most of the national insurance benefit provision for sickness. This proposal and its fate merit a more detailed discussion as an illuminating case study of the theoretical possibilities and practical limitations of mandating strategies.

Sickness Benefits and Sick Pay

The Thatcher government's initial proposals would have required employers to pay sick pay at a flat rate for the first eight weeks of illness in any one year; as compensation, employers were offered a reduction of one-half of one percentage point in their national insurance contribution (payroll tax) liability. It was argued that this would compensate employers for their extra costs, allowing a projected reduction of public expenditure of 375 million pounds at the expense of a loss of 420 million pounds in national insurance contributions. The new statutory sick pay would, however, be liable to income tax and national insurance contributions, producing a revenue gain of about 200 million pounds, and the government expected a further saving of 30 million pounds on administrative costs. Overall, therefore, public spending would be cut by about 400 million pounds for a net revenue loss of only some 200 million pounds, so that the proposals met the aim of reducing both public spending and public borrowing. (For a fuller analysis, see O'Higgins, 1981.)

It also held apparent efficiency gains: Under the old system the majority of employees received, by virtue of their employment contracts, additional benefits from their employers during the early weeks of sickness. This meant, however, that there was a duplication of administrative effort, with a corresponding waste of real resources, in providing them with both sickness benefit and sick pay at this time. Mandating employer coverage for eight weeks would eliminate over 90 percent of claims for national insurance sickness benefit. It would also virtually eliminate a curious anomaly—a consequence of the absence of coordination between state and occupational provision—whereby about 10 percent of employees were entitled to full pay as well as state sickness benefit during the early stages of sickness. Since sickness benefit was nontaxable, the anomaly was not insignificant.

In theory, mandating of sick pay could also benefit claimants in two ways. First, the mandated benefit level could be fixed at either a more generous rate than national insurance sickness benefit or as proportion of usual earnings (which is how mandated sick pay operates in Germany, for example). Since the consequential extra costs would take the form of higher private expenditure by employers and (if the employers were compensated by reduced taxes) lower public revenue—that is, a smaller tax share in national income—the government could achieve its targets of cutting state spending and taxes while still increasing welfare benefits.

The second set of potential gains arose because of the existence of widespread occupational provision for sick pay at more generous rates than state benefits: More than 80 percent of full-time employees had some occupational provision in the mid-1970s, with about half receiving full pay (less state benefits). The distribution of this provision was, however, highly unequal: Almost all nonmanual, but only two-thirds of manual, workers were covered, and male employees had higher coverage than females. Among those with some coverage, nonmanual workers had more generous benefits and conditions. Mandatory occupational benefits could reduce this inequality either by setting a more generous lower limit for benefits or by generating trade union pressure for sick pay schemes to be set at more generous levels than required by the mandating law. Since many nonmanual schemes were already at the upper limit of generosity (full pay for extended periods of sickness) such pressure could have led over time to less inequality in occupational welfare.

These are the gains that are technically possible from the mandating version of a privatization strategy. The actual outcome in the sick pay case is then important as an illustration of the differences between the technical possibilities of privatization and the likely consequences, given the nature of the political pressures that promote privatization.

For claimants, the benefit levels proposed under statutory sick pay were intended to be broadly equivalent to those in the national insurance scheme. However, to avoid the necessity for employers to differentiate payments according to family status, there was to be a single level of benefit. The effect of this was to increase the gross amounts payable to single people and two-wage couples at the expense of single-wage couples and those with children. Furthermore, the low-paid were to receive not the statutory flat-rate amount but lesser amounts to ensure that their benefit entitlement did not approach their wages while in work. The opportunity to improve general benefit levels was not taken, therefore, and the structure of the benefit system was altered to the disadvantage of families and the low-paid.

For employers, however, the Conservative government made a number of concessions before the scheme became effective in April 1983. Employers' groups had objected strenuously to both the amount and the mode of compensation proposed, and in a series of attempts to meet these objections, the government announced five successive versions of the scheme, each offering more or different forms of compensation. The final, agreed, version compensates employers by allowing them to deduct actual payments of statutory sick pay from their national insurance contributions—a compensation mechanism earlier rejected by the government as having a major flaw. One effect of this concession was to reduce the number of civil service jobs saved by the changeover, since civil servants must now monitor employers' sick pay returns to prevent abuse of the scheme.

The amount of compensation was also significantly increased: In order to secure a cut of 400 million pounds in public spending the government offered compensation worth 585 million pounds to employers. This increase in compensation absorbed most of the revenue gains the government had expected from making sick pay taxable, so that the net gain to public finance was only 40 million pounds, compared to the 200 million pounds provided by the original proposals. The practical effect of this was that the taxation of statutory sick pay funded an income transfer from employees to employers!

The extent of employer satisfaction with the scheme as finally implemented is illustrated by the contrast between their vociferous original objections and the silence with which their representative organizations greeted a subsequent decision to extend the period of mandated coverage from 8 to 28 weeks beginning in April 1986.

The sick pay saga, therefore, suggests, not that privatization in income security is necessarily either inegalitarian or incompatible with social policy aims, but that in practice claimants' interests are unlikely to be a major consideration. It also suggests that the price of persuading others to take over social responsibilities may be high, particularly if the government is seen to be willing to subordinate cost or social policy considerations to an ideological commitment to privatization. A strikingly similar set of conclusions emerges from the analysis of the prospects for pensions in the next section.

Pensions and Privatization Prospects

The most significant failure of the first Thatcher government in its desire to cut social spending was income security. Real spending on this area grew by 25 percent, and from 25 to 30 percent of all government spending (O'Higgins, 1985). This was one of the major factors behind the establishment, after the re-election of the Conservative government in 1983, of a wide-ranging set of reviews of the structure, efficiency, and extent of income support provision.

Pensions were a major issue: They account for half of all income security spending, and serious fears had been expressed about the financial and equity implications of SERPS—the relatively new State Earnings-Related Pension Scheme (Hemming and Kay, 1982). SERPS was established under a Labour government in 1975 as a compromise conclusion to a political battle that had lasted almost two decades. It required that all employees belong to an earnings-related pension scheme (in addition to the basic flat-rate national insurance pension scheme), and set up SERPS. Those employees, however, whose employers registered them with an occupational pensions scheme providing benefits broadly equivalent to SERPS could be contracted out. The compromise was intended to protect the interests of clients while preserving scope for a private sector in pensions provision. (For a detailed discussion of this compromise, see O'Higgins, 1986.)

Because of the magnitude of pensions spending and these financial concerns, it was foreseeable that the abolition or radical restructuring of SERPS might be among the recommendations of the review process. As with sick pay, it should be noted that some forms of such privatization could be used to promote egalitarian aims. The 1975 compromise on earnings-related pensions offers significant benefits to those with higher incomes through state guarantees of the value of contracted-out pensions. These guarantees make the 1975 pension package both costly and only weakly redistributive, since those who are contracted out are the better-paid half of the workforce (Creedy, 1982, ch. 6; O'Higgins, 1986). The costs to the state could be reduced by shifting some of these indexing guarantee costs on to the occupational schemes; this in turn might lead to less generous occupational provision for those contracted out. Public spending savings are thus consistent with an increase in egalitarian impact by reducing the possibly unintended benefits being provided to the better-off. If some of these savings were redirected into more generous basic state pensions, or to supplementary provision only for those without significant occupational benefits, then this privatization could even improve the position of the elderly poor.

One of the review reports did indeed focus on SERPS, and identified four major defects: its costs, the fact that it was not targeted on those in need, its involving an unduly large role for the state, and its failure positively to encourage growth in occupational and personal provision (DHSS, 1985a). Two options for change were considered but rejected in the report. The possibility of abolishing SERPS without placing any additional obligations on individuals or employers to provide for pensions—the most libertarian form of privatization—was rejected because of a concern that, left to act freely, some people might take a short-term view that would eventually leave them dependent on means-tested supplementation by the state. The option of simply restricting the scope of SERPS by modifying benefit entitlements was rejected because it "would do nothing to encourage employers to set up schemes or people to make extra provision through personal pensions." This rejection came despite the fact that this option would have cut the long-run costs by half, and would "also make savings most from those with higher earnings and would best protect low earners with low pension expectations" (DHSS, 1985a, vol. 2, p. 5).

The report proposed a third option—abolition of SERPS, and its replacement with a requirement that employees should make a contribution of a minimum of 4 percent of earnings (of which at least 2 percent was to come from the employer) to a funded occupational or personal pension scheme. The fund would be used to buy an annuity for the employee at retirement, thus altering the nature of provision from a defined benefit to a defined contribution basis. Therefore, the more egalitarian possibility was explicitly rejected in favor of an ideological concern with the form of provision.

The consultation period allowed by the government, however, turned up widespread disagreement with the proposal to abolish SERPS. This was opposed not just by those groups primarily concerned with the elderly, or with the social security system but, crucially, by such bodies as the Confederation of British Industry and the National Association of Pension Funds. Among the concerns that they expressed were "the fear that the proposals . . . might lead to higher employment and administrative costs, and that the minimum pension contribution of four percent would be too low to secure an adequate pension on retirement." The Conservative government, despite its earlier comments, therefore issued revised proposals that fell back on the option of restricting SERPS, but with the addition of "realistic encouragement to extend occupational and personal pension coverage" (DHSS, 1985b, p. 12).

The proposed modifications—which are calculated to reduce the long-term cost of SERPS by almost a half—would reduce the value of SERPS pensions, limit the proportion that may be inherited by a spouse, and require contracted-out pension schemes to be responsible for an inflation adjustment of up to 3 percent each year. In addition, however, the proposals would allow occupational schemes the option of contracting out on the basis of a guaranteed minimum level of contributions, and would give to individual workers the right to choose to contract out to a personal pension, rather than remaining in the state scheme or contracting out to an occupational pension scheme. Such personal schemes would also be on a guaranteed minimum contribution basis, and the annuity purchased at retirement would also have to provide for inflation adjustments of up to 3 percent annually.

As an incentive to encourage further contracting out, the government proposed enhancing employer/employee contributions to a guaranteed minimum contribution scheme (whether occupational or personal) by adding an extra contribution of 2 percent of covered earnings, payable for the five years from 1988–1989 to 1992–1993, for all personal pensions and occupational schemes contracting out for the first time. The costs of this "would be found from within the National Insurance Fund" (DHSS, 1985b, p. 20)—in other words, they would be paid by contributors in general. As a further incentive to personal pensions, it was proposed that the administration of personal pensions should be simplified for employers by paying all contributions through the Department of Health and Social Security, which would operate as a clearinghouse. Thus, the administrative costs would fall on public funds rather than on the private sector.

The final outcome of the political and legislative process may be different again, but what is interesting for this analysis is the similarity of these sets of possibilities, pressures, and choices to those that emerged in the sick pay case. In each, egalitarian options existed but were ignored; in each, the original proposals were amended as a result of the opposition of employers' interests; in each, additional financial inducements, at the expense of taxpayers in general, were offered to secure a shift in the form of provision. While the amended proposals on SERPS contain some egalitarian aspects, they are primarily a witness to the government's focus on the form rather than the results of provision. In essence, a government committed to tax cuts is proposing to levy an additional tax on social security contributors in order to finance a growth in private income security, something that it is unwilling to do in the case of public income security. So, as with sick pay, in practice it is questionable whether the pressures for privatization will be concerned to advance social policy aims, however possible this is in theory.

Conclusions

This paper has argued that the analysis and evaluation of privatization should be carried out within the framework of the mixed political economy of social welfare. This implies allowing for the possibility of strategic shifts in the balance of provision within that political economy. The impact of such shifts is not determinate, but varies with the context in which such shifts are implemented. Privatization, as some examples showed, can improve social provision: Indeed, it would even be possible to combine privatization with increases in equality. If much privatization is inegalitarian in practice, this is the result not of any qualities inherent in all privatized provision structures, but of the political and social values that generate the pressure for privatization.

References

Challis, L., P. Day, and R. Klein. 1984. "Residential Care on Demand," *New Society*. April 5.

Creedy, J. 1982. *State Pensions in Britain*. Cambridge University Press.

Derthick, M. 1975. *Uncontrollable Spending for Social Service Grants*. Washington, D.C.: Brookings Institution.

Department of Health and Social Security. 1985a. *Reform of Social Security* (3 volumes). Cmnd: 9517–9519. London: Her Majesty's Stationery Office.

———. 1985b. *Reform of Social Security*. Cmnd: 9691. London: Her Majesty's Stationery Office.

Donnison, D. 1984. "The Progressive Potential of Privatisation." In LeGrand and Robinson, 1984.

Environment Committee. 1981. *The Second Report of the House of Commons Select Committee on the Environment for the 1980/81 Session: The Sale of Council Houses*. HC 366. London: Her Majesty's Stationery Office.

Hemming, R., and J. Kay. 1982. "The Cost of the State Earnings-related Pension Scheme," *Economic Journal* 92 (366): 320–340.

Judge, K., and M. Knapp. 1985. "Efficiency in the Production of Welfare: A Comparison of the Public and Private Sectors." In Klein and O'Higgins, 1985.

Kirwan, R. 1984. "The Demise of Public Housing?" In LeGrand and Robinson, 1984.

Klein, R. 1984. "Privatisation and the Welfare State." *Lloyds Bank Review* (January): 12–29.

Klein, R., and M. O'Higgins, eds. 1985. *The Future of Welfare*. Oxford: Blackwell.

LeGrand, J., and R. Robinson, eds. 1984. *Privatisation and the Welfare State*. London: Allen and Unwin.

Malpass, P., and A. Murie. 1982. *Housing Policy and Practice*. London: Macmillan.

Murray, C. 1984. *Losing Ground: American Social Policy 1950–1980*. New York: Basic Books.

O'Higgins, M. 1981. "Income During Initial Sickness: An Analysis and Evaluation of a New Strategy for Social Security." *Policy and Politics* 9 (2): 151–171.

———. 1984. "Privatisation and Social Security." *Political Quarterly* 55 (2): 129–139.

———. 1985. "The Public Spending Hydra." *New Society*. January 3. 171–173.

———. 1986. "Public-Private Interaction in Social Security Policy: A Comparative Study of Pensions Provision in Sweden, West Germany and the United Kingdom." In M. Rein and L. Rainwater, eds. *The Public-Private Interplay in Social Protection: A Comparative Study*. Armonk, New York: M. E. Sharpe.

Ruggles, P., and M. O'Higgins. 1987. "Retrenchment and the New Right: A Comparative Analysis of the Impacts of the Thatcher and Reagan Administrations." In M. Rein, G. Esping-Andersen, and L. Rainwater, eds. *Stagnation and Renewal in Social Policy: The Rise and Fall of Policy Regimes*. Armonk, New York: M. E. Sharpe.

Taylor-Gooby, P. 1985. "The Politics of Welfare." In Klein and O'Higgins, 1985.

Titmuss, R. 1963. "The Social Division of Welfare." *Essays on the Welfare State*. London: Allen and Unwin.

Walker, A. 1984. "The Political Economy of Privatisation." In LeGrand and Robinson, 1984.

Weale, A. 1985. "Why Are We Waiting? The Problem of Bureaucracy and Unresponsiveness in Public Services." In Klein and O'Higgins, 1985.

Webb, A. 1985. "Alternative Futures for Social Policy and State Welfare." In R. Berthoud, ed. *Challenges to Social Policy*. London: Gower.

Webb, A., and G. Wistow. 1985. *Planning and Scarcity: Essays on the Personal Social Services*. London: Allen and Unwin.

7

Governmental Responsibility and Privatization: Examples from Four Social Services

ARNOLD GURIN

In 1894, Amos Warner argued in favor of having states pay subsidies out of public funds to private charities, including those under religious auspices.[1] His arguments will not seem unfamiliar:

1. there is less stigma of pauperism in a private institution than in a public one;
2. the moral influence of a private institution is more wholesome;
3. private institutions are free from partisan politics and the spoils system; and
4. it is more economical to provide service through a private institution.

Views of the Governmental Role: A Backward Glance

The language may seem a bit quaint but the arguments, combining considerations of efficiency with moral exhortation, are not too different from those that animate contemporary discussion of the same issues.

Arlien Johnson, writing in 1931, quoted Warner's statement of thirty-seven years earlier in order to stress the changes that had taken place in the interval. No longer was it accepted, she said, that private institutions were superior to public. Indeed, she was able to point to exemplary public institutions that were widely regarded as superior in quality to any private institutions in their locality. She granted that some private institutions might be less costly than public ones, but found this to be true mostly in the case of religious institutions because of the large volume of contributed labor that they could muster.

The most important argument made by Arlien Johnson, however, was

[1] The views of Amos Warner are paraphrased from material quoted in Johnson (1931).

a political one. She was writing during a period when the public sector was growing in size and importance. New structures for the implementation of public social welfare programs were being formed and taking root in states throughout the country. Amos Warner's world was one where private welfare efforts were dominant. His mission was to harness public resources for the strengthening of that system and, consequently, to impede the expansion of public agencies in direct service functions. By the time of Arlien Johnson, the world was quite different. The center of gravity was shifting or had indeed already shifted to the public sector. She saw public subsidies not as an aid to the maintenance of the domination of private institutions but as "part of the evolution toward comprehensive and universal welfare services to be supplied by the state and local governments" (Johnson, 1931, p. 213). Going further, Johnson raised more basic questions as to whether such subsidies should be continued. She saw them as potential obstacles to the proper development of public services for the mentally ill, mentally defective, juvenile delinquents, dependent and neglected children, and other groups for whom state governments had responsibility. Massachusetts was cited as the state providing the best public care and one that, not coincidentally, had abolished subsidies to private institutions.

Pointing to the prevailing trends of that time, Arlien Johnson predicted that subsidies would be replaced by state and local public agencies that would "distribute services on a professional and expert basis." In a warning that has continuing relevance today, she stated, "This development presupposes, however, that the state will employ an adequate and well-qualified staff of workers, that it will insure tenure and advancement by means of a merit system and free from political interference, and that it will not only request but act upon the recommendations of its agents" (p. 219).

By the end of the 1930s the social welfare world had changed even more drastically. The long battle for social security had been won and there was firmly in place a system of social protection which, though incomplete, dealt with some of the major life hazards likely to affect most of the population. The universal problem of income maintenance in old age was provided for through a completely federal contributory insurance program, while other more selective income support needs were met through the states, with federal participation. The public welfare departments that were beginning to establish themselves ten years earlier became large bureaucracies concerned not only with their earlier social service functions but also with the distribution of massive economic aid. Although the service delivery systems included payments to the private sector, particularly for medical services and child care, the emphasis was overwhelmingly on the central role of government.

Leaders from the private sector played an important role in the establishment of the public services. Harry Hopkins, who moved from a traditional voluntary agency to become the major architect of the mass relief programs, first in New York state and then in the federal government, symbolized the trend. Down the line, professionals from the private sector brought to the public agencies the concepts and standards of work that had been the basis for Amos Warner's old argument that the private sector was superior. One of the characteristics of the period was a spirit of enthusiasm about government and its potential role in solving the severe social and economic problems that had affected so large a part of the population and had therefore become matters of universal concern. That mission attracted a cadre of young, talented, and committed workers who fulfilled the conditions that Johnson had set forth for an effective public service.

That the initial élan was not maintained may be attributed in part to the general tendency for the excitement of innovation to wear off as organizations grapple with the limitations of reality. There are, however, some specific elements in the public welfare story. One of them is the relationship between the social services and the means-tested income support programs. The state and local public welfare departments that developed during the New Deal combined both functions. The marriage proved to be an uneasy one. On the one hand, social services, instead of becoming the comprehensive, universal agencies that Arlien Johnson had envisaged, were deeply embedded in the means-tested assistance programs and thus shared in the growing public apathy or hostility toward those programs. On the other hand, through successive amendments to the Social Security Act during the 1950s and 1960s, the mission of the public social services was defined as helping to remove recipients from the assistance rolls, a task that was clearly beyond their capacities. Professionalization never took firm hold in the public welfare departments, except in specialized areas, notably child welfare. In addition, new public services, such as community mental health centers, grew up as separate categorical systems outside the welfare departments. By the 1960s it was clear that the public social services were fragmented rather than "comprehensive" and largely means-tested rather than "universal."

The next great watershed after the New Deal was the mid-1960s with the War on Poverty and the Great Society. That period embodied a curious paradox. It was a period of great government initiative and expansion—the greatest since the New Deal—but with some elements of anti-government rhetoric and activities. Some aspects of what we now call privatization also expanded in that period.

The programs of the Johnson Administration represented, in some respects, a continuation and filling out of the New Deal period but were, in other respects, discontinuous with it. The major thrust of the New Deal had been to create a new set of individual entitlements to be guaranteed and administered by government. The major omission in the New Deal legislation had been in the provision for health care. Under the Johnson Administration, that gap was filled, in part, by a compromise that rejected national health insurance but gave us Medicare and Medicaid instead. Another major entitlement program that began slowly in that period but grew rapidly during the 1970s was food stamps, which started as a selective, experimental anti-hunger program but became an important element in the halting, piecemeal efforts of the United States to approach some kind of guaranteed national income.

Important as these new entitlement programs were, they did not hold center stage in terms of the War on Poverty's rhetoric and public image. The latter were based on what became known, and much criticized, as a "service strategy." Underlying the new programs of that time was an analysis of poverty that stressed a variety of psychosocial, cultural, and political factors in addition to strictly economic issues of income or wealth. People caught in poverty, it was argued, suffered from a systemic lack of opportunities. To break out of the poverty cycle, it would be necessary to mobilize a combination of resources—educational, health, and economic. Perhaps above all, it would be necessary to help poverty populations overcome their political powerlessness through new forms of participation and control at the local community level.

The War on Poverty generated a number of concepts and undertook a number of interventions that reflected, either explicitly or implicitly, a vote of no confidence in governmental services as then being delivered. Its emphasis on local community development, for example, was an attempt to bypass the established federal-state grant-in-aid system in order to bring federal aid directly to the cities and targeted neighborhoods. "Maximum feasible participation" was an attempt to make both public and voluntary agencies more directly responsive to the needs and preferences of the people whom the programs were designed to help. The professional leadership of the social services was challenged as being unresponsive, and attempts were made to have more of the service delivery functions performed by people indigenous to the poverty areas. Finally, encouragement was given to the people in the neighborhoods and to both the professional and nonprofessional staffs of the new structures to serve as "advocates" in making the established agencies more responsive.

While maximum feasible participation now has a bad name, there is evidence that many elements of advocacy and participation have survived in different ways. The ongoing concern with "special interests" in the human services is one indication of the fact that some kinds of advocates are still at work and are making an impression. There has been a substantial growth of citizen participation of all sorts in a wide range of social service activities. The difference is that the participation is more specialized, linked to categorical agencies and programs rather than to the kinds of comprehensive planning and community action agencies that functioned during the War on Poverty period.

During the past twenty years, there has been a proliferation of self-help types of activities and organizations in regard to mental health and retardation, alcohol and drug abuse, all kinds of health conditions, and other service areas. This may be looked upon as one form of privatization, representing an alternative to services delivered directly by public agencies. There are on the scene today a large number of such groups and organizations that may have obtained their initial funding from Great Society federal programs but that have survived through many vicissitudes of shifting federal programs, learning to put together funding from a variety of both public and private sources. They are another strand, along with private for-profit organizations, in the pluralistic system (or nonsystem) of social services that we have today.

The 1960s, thus, were a period of great expansion in the role of government, especially the federal government, but also a period of expansion in privatization of various kinds, both nonprofit and for-profit, fueled largely by government funds.

One additional piece of the social service mosaic that emerged from this history was contributed by the various social service amendments to the Social Security Act that I mentioned earlier. Those amendments, which culminated eventually in Title XX, gave great impetus to the purchase of service as a major instrument for the delivery of public social services. Under the original open-ended provisions, states greatly increased their federal revenues by purchasing services from other state agencies, until Title XX was capped. Even under the cap, however, substantial funds flowed through this system to private providers—mostly nonprofit, but also proprietary—as in the case of homemaker services. That pattern continues despite the cuts in federal grants under the Reagan Administration's block grant program.

What conclusions can we draw from this review?

First, it is clear that the attitudes toward the social role of government have been both ambivalent and unstable over a considerable period of time. We have looked at a few points in time extending back almost a century. At the beginning of the period, a negative view seemed to prevail of the capacity of government to render services of good quality in a fair, competent manner. Later events proved the inadequacy of the free market and of the voluntary services to deal with major economic and social dislocations, making necessary a very substantial expansion of the role of government. That did not remove the ambivalence. The expansion did result in important structural changes that have persisted to our time; but reservations remain, leading to new debates on old issues and to some retrenchment in the extent and level of services.

What we now call privatization has always been part of this shifting scene. It is always a theoretical alternative, in any historical period, to try to meet needs through nongovernmental channels. This can take the form of simply forgoing government action, leaving it to the private sector—both profit and nonprofit—to meet the need; or of subsidizing nongovernmental entities to provide services, presumably without the negative features attributed to governmental operations.

Given this mixture of attitudes and pluralistic pattern of approaches, it was inevitable that the social services develop in a patchwork fashion rather than as a comprehensive and integrated system. By their nature, social services are extremely diverse—related as they are to different age groups with varying family constellations and to conditions that involve many different degrees and types of dependence. A governmentally financed service, whether provided directly or not, is one element—sometimes greater, sometimes smaller—in the total pattern of meeting a particular need, along with family and other informal support systems as well as formal agencies. Privatization is in that sense built into the social services.

The debatable questions are what form privatization should take and what the balance should be between private and governmental participation. Because of the diversity of the social services, no single answer will be appropriate to each. At most, it may be feasible to develop criteria or guidelines to help find an appropriate or optimum answer in a given case.

Current Issues in Social Services: Case Illustrations

In order to explore how this might be done, I shall turn next to a number of specific areas of social service, sketching the salient current issues in each and the prevailing relationships between public and private responsibilities in those fields. An effort will then be made to identify common elements as well as differences that may provide some guidance on the issues of privatization.

COMMUNITY MENTAL HEALTH SERVICES

The major issue facing the field of community mental health today is how to improve provisions for the chronically mentally ill outside institutions. That field is facing its own backlash in the form of challenges to the policies of deinstitutionalization that have dominated its thinking for the past quarter of a century. Most recently, the emergence of homelessness into public awareness has provided the basis for renewed criticisms of the mental health system—on the dubious assumption that homelessness is the result, primarily, of deinstitutionalization.

Although the overall census in mental hospitals decreased steadily over the past several decades, admissions have been rising (but lengths of stay are lower) and there are substantial increases in total volume of service in general hospitals (Kiesler et al., 1983). There is growing concern over the rising incidence of chronic mental illness among children and youth as well as the elderly and some retarded people.

Time has brought to the surface a host of serious deficiencies in the way mental health services are organized and financed. Despite all the years of deinstitutionalization, there has been relatively little shifting of resources from the state hospitals to community programs. The very substantial federal aid that went into community mental health centers created a new set of services in the communities; but these were not well articulated with state needs and were generally inadequate and inappropriate for the chronically ill deinstitutionalized population. No government agency has clear fiscal responsibility for that population. Medicare and Medicaid offer only very limited support for outpatient and community care. A recent review concludes, "the majority of patients now hospitalized for mental disorders could be efficaciously and cost-effectively treated elsewhere, if such programs were *reasonably funded, well organized, and easily available*" (Kiesler, 1983, p. 295; emphasis added).

State-funded community mental health programs make very extensive use of purchase of service contracting mechanisms. In Massachusetts, for many years, the state has contributed to "partnership clinics" (local nonprofit organizations covering a catchment area) by placing a number of state employees in such agencies. Contracts are also made with Community Mental Health Centers that were established with federal funding for a wide range of services. Many hundreds of smaller contracts are made with individual vendors, groups, and organizations (mostly nonprofit) for all kinds of services. The system is extraordinarily complex, requiring a great deal of staff time. A recent study in Massachusetts concludes that contracting did not reduce the overhead costs of the state agency because of the substantial increases in administrative costs that offset any reductions in costs of direct service (Schlesinger and Dorwart, 1984).

In addition to the burdens of administration, the contracting system has other defects. The expectations of competition, with beneficial results for both quality and costs, turn out to be largely illusory, because there is not a plethora of vendors to engage in competition. The expectation of innovation has also not been realized to any substantial extent. As contracting systems mature, there is a growing tendency for the field to be dominated by a few very large vendors that become as bureaucratized as the public agency. In addition, the clients require stability and continuity of care—a good reason for the public agency to favor large, well-established vendors.

The picture is not all bad. Contracting is particularly useful in starting new programs, like inpatient services for children, more quickly than is possible in the public sector, which is beset by many more constraints of personnel and budgetary controls. Some voluntary agencies have particularly skilled staff and professional expertise that are not as readily available in the public sector. But the public agency frequently has to struggle to make sure that the skills of the private agency are made available in proper measure to the population for whom its financing is mostly intended.

Networks of consumers and families are playing a growing role not only as advocates but as active parts of the service system, providing guidance and information to bring patients and services together. They are an important factor in the political environment in which the public agency works, as are the employee organizations and unions within the agency itself.

Most of the discussion about how to improve the system centers on the chronically mentally ill. What remains of federal support is targeted in that direction, and state departments of mental health are trying to give priority to the same population. One immediate result will probably be additional investment in state hospitals, at the expense of further investment in community programs. Some economists who have become interested in this area are proposing experimentation with new forms of financing.[2] To maximize independence and freedom of choice, they would change from the great reliance on either direct service by the state or on state funding of voluntary agencies to mechanisms such as vouchers or cash grants to families. Greater freedom of choice is also a reason for recent extensions of insurance coverage to provide reimbursement to psychologists and social workers as well as psychiatrists.

It seems doubtful, however, that the state mental health agencies will be able to shed much of their historic responsibility for the mentally ill. Regardless of whether the services are rendered directly or through vendor contracts, the state agencies are vulnerable and accountable for the defects in the functioning of mental health services that become visible to the public eye.

LONG TERM CARE

Long term care of the elderly and disabled is an area of great complexity and growing importance for many reasons, not the least of which is

---

[2] For a review of various options and proposals, see McGuire and Weisbrod (1981).

its growing demands on health and social service resources. In 1982, 32 percent of all Medicaid payments were made for nursing home care and an additional 12 percent for intermediate care facilities serving the retarded (Feinstein et al., 1984). At the same time, institutions or organized programs of any kind represent a small fraction of the total care being given. It is estimated that 70 percent of the elderly are cared for primarily by relatives, and the proportion is higher for disabled children and young adults (Callahan and Wallack, 1981). Some speak of a crisis in long term care due to the cumulative effects of demographic and social changes that are weakening the capacities of families to provide that level of service at the same time that the numbers of the elderly grow more rapidly than any other segment of the population.

Policy thinking in this field stresses the desirability of maximizing both the independence of the individual needing long term care and the participation of the families who have carried the brunt of the responsibility. While more services are needed, there is a concern to provide them in a way that will avoid a shift from informal to formal methods of care. Ways are being sought to provide relatively minor help to families that might give some relief from the burdens without removing the responsibility.

The defects in the present system are many and difficult. Perhaps the major problems are the generally low quality of institutional services (with some outstanding exceptions) and the lack of rationality in existing financial benefits, which have a heavy bias toward institutional care and offer disincentives to the maintenance of recipients in more independent and less costly settings.

Various proposals have been made to improve the situation, and many demonstrations are under way. Remedies lie in two directions—new financing mechanisms, and new types of organizational arrangements for delivering service. On the financing side, it has been pointed out that Medicaid (a program to meet the medical needs of the poor) has become the major resource to pay for long term care for the formerly affluent as well as the poor. This is because there is no adequate financial mechanism that the middle class can use for this purpose. Ways are being sought to create "risk pools" for insurance under both governmental and private auspices, and also to bolster various sources of retirement income. On the organizational side, proposals cover a wide range from case management to life care communities. The Social/Health Maintenance Organization project at Brandeis University is experimenting with a capitation system that will offer a full range of services, both home-based and institutional.[3]

It is clear that privatization of several varieties plays a critical role in

[3] For details of various proposals, see Callahan and Wallack (1981). An important possibility is the extension of Medicare coverage for long term care services both in nursing homes and at home. A recent proposal in that direction will be found in Blumenthal et al. (1986).

rendering long term care. Most fundamental is the role of informal helpers, mostly relatives, in maintaining old and/or disabled people in the community. This is one area where there might be broad agreement that the role of government should be indirect rather than direct—providing support in a way that will permit people to make their own choices.

The growth of the private nursing home industry as well as problems and scandals associated with that growth, have been publicized very widely. Government financing led, in this instance, to the expansion of services that had been in very short supply and for which there was a desperate need on the part of a rapidly growing segment of the population. Despite the abuses that have occurred, there is little doubt that there has been a substantial gain over the past twenty years in the availability of adequate nursing homes, both voluntary and proprietary. Many of the nonprofit institutions, although nonsectarian in their admission policies, are sponsored by religious groups upon whom they draw for volunteers and other forms of support. Even so, the financing is provided overwhelmingly by fees for service, including governmental funds as a major component.

Governmental funds have also spurred the expansion of home health and homemaker services. Private commercial firms entered this market only recently, responding to greatly increased demand and a very limited supply of services. The nonprofit voluntary agencies who had provided whatever services were available proved unable to respond adequately to the demand for a variety of organizational, financial, and also, to some extent, ideological reasons. Some of the hesitation was related to their definitions of quality, involving standards of training and supervision that were not compatible with rapid growth.

The issue of quality in home care services is difficult to evaluate. General experience indicates that it is very difficult for all agencies, regardless of auspices, to maintain a reliable, competent, and stable labor supply. That problem is not confined to home services but is true of nursing homes as well, and also of other fields of direct personal care. In some ways, the private for-profit agencies have an advantage. Because they tend to be larger than the typical voluntary agencies, they have a larger pool of workers and therefore the opportunity to organize them more rationally. They are also able to take advantage of economies of scale. Voluntary agency costs tend to be higher, reflecting to some extent a greater investment in supervision and training.

Government is already heavily involved financially and its costs are rising very rapidly. By being only a financial provider, leaving the delivery of services to the free market, it has provided support for services of low quality that sometimes reach the extreme of abusive exploitation of the people the support is supposed to help. The future would seem to call for a larger role for government, taking more responsibility for the effective use of its funds, but also for new forms of service delivery by private providers.

Youth Employment and Training

Youth employment and training programs lie at the intersection between the social services and the world of work. The relationship between welfare and work has been an extremely sensitive and problematic issue throughout the long history of social welfare, reflected in the deep-seated distinctions always made between the able-bodied poor and other more "worthy" people in need. Great ambivalence has always existed about providing income support to those able to work, and, except perhaps for a brief period of time during the Great Depression, there has been a widespread assumption that people who are able-bodied and do not work are in that situation because of some internal problems or faults.

Whatever views people may hold as to human behavior—and regardless of whether their approach to social welfare is punitive or supportive—there is a very broad consensus on the desirability of paid employment as the preferred method whereby those who are able to work should meet their economic needs. Some uncertainty remains about mothers of young children, but that is clouded by all the issues surrounding single parenthood and teenage pregnancy. Certainly, as far as youth are concerned (both male and female), the political spectrum from left to right is in broad agreement that schooling, training for work, and paid work represent the best foundation for personal adjustment as well as societal health. Youth unemployment is therefore perceived as a serious, indeed alarming, social problem.

Its dimensions are complex. To some extent, the volume of youth unemployment reflects the state of the economy. At the present time, under relatively favorable economic conditions, the teenage unemployment rate is estimated at less than 20 percent. That includes, however, young people who are still in school and who are seeking and available only for part-time work. This overall rate has been decreasing since the recession of 1980–1982.

The most alarming aspect of youth unemployment is not its overall incidence but the severity, persistence, and relative intractability of the problem among subgroups in the population. Despite overall improvement, teenage unemployment rates among minorities are growing (now estimated at 42 percent), so that the gap between social groups is increasing. Even within the minority population, there is a great deal of youth employment that is temporary and intermittent. The major concern of experts in this field is with smaller numbers of youth (estimated variously as 10 to 15 percent of all teenagers) who are permanently out of school and chronically out of work. One recent review states, "even within the black youth labor force, the labor market difficulties are increasingly the result of major problems facing a few rather than moderate problems facing the many." They are the problems of an "underclass that is extremely difficult to reach with public policies" (Hahn and Lerman, 1985).

Programs directed toward meeting the problems of youth unemployment are among the most embattled in the current period of retrenchment. They have been subject both to severe cutbacks in level of federal support and a high degree of privatization in various forms. The very large government program in this field, the Comprehensive Employment and Training Act (CETA), was attacked vigorously for alleged wastefulness, for serving too many who were not in need, and for failure to place youth in permanent jobs. It was replaced by a very much smaller program, the Job Training Partnership Act (JTPA). Unlike CETA, which provided training opportunities primarily in the public services and community-based nonprofit organizations, JTPA is oriented very strongly toward the private sector. It operates through local PICs (private industry councils) made up of representatives from the local business communities and it seeks placements primarily in the private sector, supplied for the most part by small businessmen.

If we accept the conclusion that youth unemployment is a selective problem, affecting a relatively small segment of the total population but affecting them very severely, with grave consequences for the future, then proper targeting of programs is a major issue. Evaluations of programs in this field agree on two major points: (1) that past programs have generally not been well targeted, and (2) that success is difficult to achieve and to demonstrate. The picture is not entirely bleak, however, and some evidence of successful programs does exist. The evidence indicates that to be successful the programs must bring together a combination of many elements, and that efforts of this kind tend to be expensive.

One of the most successful programs to date, the Youth Incentive Entitlement Pilot Project, was a demonstration project that combined the guarantee of a job with a set of requirements designed to keep trainees in school and in a training program that would provide enduring skills. Follow-up studies revealed that the program was not successful in reducing the eventual school dropout rates for this group of trainees but did help the trainees to obtain better job placements than would have been available to them ordinarily. The program was also able to report a high rate of response (55 percent) demonstrating that teenagers are motivated toward work if there is some assurance of being able to obtain a satisfactory job (Gueron, 1984).

Hahn and Lerman (1985), reviewing the evaluation studies that have been done in this field, conclude that work experience must be combined with basic skills training and support services if teenage youth are to be helped to improve their chances in the labor market. Such programs need to be carefully monitored and must demand standards of performance both at work and at school from the trainees. In other words, the crucial element for success with the teenagers who have the greatest needs and greatest problems is intensity. The Job Corps, considered by some to be the most successful program in this field, was also the most intensive, including a complete change of environment and a twenty-four-hour living situation.

Movement toward greater privatization in this field was the result of several factors. On one level, it was part of the general ideological preference in the current political climate for reliance on the private sector. More specifically, this change represented a deliberate shift away from public service jobs as the major area in which to seek opportunities for the most disadvantaged youth. CETA had been under attack from many different quarters for the way in which it had used public-sector positions. At one extreme, CETA was criticized for providing jobs of a synthetic, make-work character with no lasting value for the trainee. At the opposite extreme, CETA was accused of displacing workers from real jobs in the public sector.

The shift to the private sector has had the advantage of creating additional opportunities for some disadvantaged youth to find their way into better and more stable positions than were available to them previously. There are, however, limitations and drawbacks. To begin with, the placements in the private sector have been primarily in small businesses where opportunities for advancement are limited. An even greater shortcoming is that the current, much reduced programs, are directed to youth who are still in school and do not touch the hundreds of thousands of young people who drop out of school annually. There is also some indication that even among the population still in school a certain amount of "creaming" (picking the best applicants) is taking place in order to demonstrate successful placements.

Although data are not available to prove the point definitively, it thus appears that the move toward privatization has not improved and may indeed have affected adversely the targeting of youth employment and training programs toward the most disadvantaged. One aspect of this shift is the decline of the role of community-based nonprofit organizations in the total programs. Such organizations, which go back in many cases to the 1960s anti-poverty programs, were indigenous to disadvantaged urban neighborhoods and heavily involved with the most disadvantaged youth. The effects of cutbacks in federal funds have fallen disproportionately on this sector of the provider community.

Youth employment and training programs have never been an area in which service was provided directly by government agencies, except for the placement work of state employment services. Even when government expenditures were much higher than they are today, the service was delivered through contracts with private providers, both profit and nonprofit. Paradoxically, one effect of the current trend toward greater privatization may be the greater use of one public institution—the school system—as a training resource. That is coming about through alliances being formed between the PICs and the schools in an effort to improve the school systems while keeping more youth in school. Overall, however, there is nothing in the nature of this field that would argue for delivering the service through public rather than private agencies. On the contrary, since the goal of the program is to improve the chances of youth in the mainstream labor market, the stronger arguments would be in favor of private involvement.

Given all this, it is instructive to note that the only youth employment and training program administered by the federal (as opposed to local or state) government—the Job Corps—is also considered to have been the most successful. This is not to say that the federal government actually delivered the service. That was done, as elsewhere, by contracts with profit and nonprofit organizations. But the federal agency maintained a strong policy planning, program development, and monitoring function. It gave direction and technical assistance to the providers, collated their experience, and developed standards, guidelines, and materials for their use. The governmental role, and a centralized one at that, was a crucial element in the overall success of the program.

CHILD WELFARE

Public and private elements are mixed in a distinctive way in the field of child welfare. Public services in this field are based on the long-established role of the state to protect children and to serve in loco parentis when natural parents are unable or have failed to protect their children. Voluntary effort also has a long history, most of it representing the interests of different religious groups to provide care and protection to dependent or neglected children of their own faith. As the field developed during the course of this century, shifts have taken place in philosophy and practice, with consequent shifts in the roles of the respective sectors. But the constant element has been a continuing relationship between public and voluntary, nonprofit services—perhaps the most longstanding and continuous partnership among all the social services.

The major historical trend in child welfare has been from the public almshouses and private orphanages to foster care and adoption services, as well as income maintenance, homemakers, day care, and other services designed to strengthen the capacity of natural homes and to avoid substitute placement. In the early part of the century, foster homes were primarily the responsibility of the private, voluntary agencies. Noninstitutional child welfare services were a major element in the expansion and growing professionalization of the public welfare departments referred to at the beginning of this chapter.

Child welfare services occupy a central place in the history of the public social services. In the early period, they were the first and in many places the only noninstitutional social service provided by state governments. In many states in the middle west and western parts of the country that did not have a tradition of strong voluntary agencies, the child welfare services were the most professional and ubiquitous service available to families in trouble. They were also universal rather than means-tested. Divisions or bureaus of child welfare within the state governments had an identity of their own, were guided by standards of practice developed under the leadership of the U.S. Children's Bureau, and were dominated by professional social work personnel.

It had been an early hope that the child welfare services would provide the basis for developing a more comprehensive, universal public social service system, with a focus on service to the family, and encompassing all age groups. In an attempt to achieve greater integration, separate child welfare bureaus were absorbed into more comprehensive public welfare or social service or family service departments with a loss of separate identity and structure. As noted above, social services and income support programs were tied closely together for a time and then separated. Simultaneously, other services—particularly for the aged—have expanded, sometimes as part of public welfare departments, sometimes through separate structures.

Today, child welfare continues to be a core element in every public social service program. Recent years have witnessed expanded programs to deal with problems of child abuse and neglect. Here, the state exercises its legal protective functions under mandatory reporting systems that require expeditious investigation and resolution of all incidents. Because of the urgent nature of these incidents, there is a tendency for the protective service function to overwhelm other aspects of the child welfare program. The public departments are mandated, however, to provide supportive services to families in order to maximize the possibility of keeping children in their natural homes. Day-care services are a critical and growing part of these programs. Casework counseling and placements in foster homes, adoptive homes, and group homes for children or adolescents with special problems continue to be major responsibilities of the public departments.

Voluntary agencies continue to play a significant role as providers of service, but largely through contracts with the public agencies. There is a wide range of variation in the terms of these public-private relationships. At one extreme, in New York City, the voluntary agencies, each sponsored by a religious group, were for a long time the only providers, while the public agency financed virtually their total budgets but did not provide any direct services of its own. Eventually, growing needs for services, especially for minority groups, made this situation untenable and also raised civil rights issues around church-state relationships and racial discrimination. In other states with less of a history of voluntary agencies, the state role has always been dominant. In general, contracting in this field, as in other social services, expanded significantly during the 1970s.

Contracting was used as a way of coping with the rapidly growing volume of child abuse reports and investigations that were overwhelming the resources of many state agencies. In a study done in Massachusetts (Gurin, Friedman et al., 1980), it was found that more than 50 percent of total expenditures for protective service work were expended through contracts with voluntary agencies. Because of its legal position, the public agency was the recipient of complaints of child abuse, but it was in fact delegating a great deal of its responsibility both for assessment of the validity of the complaint and for follow-up intervention to voluntary agencies. The theoretical justification for doing so was the experience and competence of the agencies, their ability to attract professional staff, and the efficiencies involved in using an existing service. As a practical matter, general budgetary problems in the state prevented expansion of public payrolls, so that contracting was for some part of this period the only way to meet the need.

The Massachusetts study revealed some of the hazards and dilemmas involved in the contracting system. The public agency had developed criteria as to what types of cases to refer to the private agencies, but the pressures were such as to make implementation of the contract highly opportunistic, with the operating criterion becoming largely how to relieve staff pressure. The central dilemma was that the state remained legally responsible for children on whom reports were filed. It had the ultimate responsibility without having adequate control. Some cases that had been assigned to private agencies were, after a time, returned to state staff, because some of the voluntary agencies provided only counseling services; they did not do foster home or adoptive placement, nor did they work with the courts. The study also found that the private agencies were able to exercise some selectivity in which cases they would or would not accept. A system known as "open referrals" made it possible for the voluntary agencies to accept cases that came to them directly and to bill the state for services to those cases if they fell within the terms of the contract.

That limited the ability of the state to set its priorities on how to use the voluntary services.

On the other hand, there were instances where voluntary agencies provided highly specialized services that were very useful to the public agency and that were clearly beyond the capacity of the agency to organize efficiently on its own, such as specialized group care or highly skilled clinical services.

This sketch refers only to the protective services, where only voluntary nonprofit agencies are involved. On a much larger scale, public child welfare agencies also contract with day-care services, both nonprofit and for-profit, and, to a lesser extent, with homemaker services.[4] Each service has its own constellation of demand and supply problems, as well as problems of pricing that pose very specific issues for the management of the contracting relationship.

Issues in Governmental-Private Relationships

It is obvious from these brief sketches of a few of the social services that each is different and that generalizations are hazardous. Elements of both government responsibility and private involvement are present in all of them in varying degrees. No general guidelines for rational policy choice spring immediately out of the descriptions. At most, they suggest some issues and concerns that need to be considered in making such choices. The most fundamental issue is the definition of governmental responsibility.

1. In each of the fields described there is a growing problem of how to reach and deal effectively with that segment of the population whose needs are most critical, most chronic, least amenable thus far to intervention, and for whom intervention efforts are most expensive. This targeting issue points to a major role of government as the resource of last resort for the poorest and most vulnerable segments of the population—the chronically mentally ill, the elderly poor requiring custodial care at home or in institutions, the most alienated among unemployed youth, and children suffering neglect and abuse in disorganized families. While numbers in these population subgroups are not large, costs are high and positive results difficult to achieve. The incentives for private provision are therefore small. The problems are, however, troublesome and visible enough to require public attention.

There are many differences, both ideological and practical, as to how to define the groups that should fall into a governmental "safety net," what the level of governmental support should be in various fields, and

---

[4] See Chapter 9 for a detailed discussion of child care and privatization.

how services are to be delivered. A starting point does exist, however, in the form of a broad consensus, across a wide political spectrum, that government has a residual responsibility for vulnerable groups in the population whose basic needs are not being met through nongovernmental means, formal or informal.

2. Another point of consensus reflected in the social services described above is that existing programs, as they have worked out, have not been targeted sufficiently to those who are most clearly the responsibility of government. This, too, is an observation that cuts across the political spectrum. On the right, the criticism is based on a restrictive view of government that would limit its responsibility to those in most dire need. The criticism from the left is that governmental programs are not sufficiently redistributive and that when resources are restricted, those who are most in need or most difficult to reach effectively tend to be neglected. Both criticisms point toward a more selective (more targeted) approach to the use of government financing.

3. It is possible that a more selective approach to what government should pay for encourages privatization, in the sense that private means of financing would be expected to cover some needs that are now met by government. Long term care is a good example of this point. Here, efforts are being made to encourage private insurance to meet the need more adequately, in order to relieve the burden on Medicaid and to reserve public financing for those who cannot afford to purchase protection against the hazards of long term illness and disability through the private market.

Long term care is also an example, however, of one kind of limitation in the selective approach to governmental responsibility. It is not at all clear at this point that an adequate solution can be found in the private market. The alternative, equally or perhaps even more likely, is that it will become necessary to extend Medicare or to find a similar public and universal remedy that will create an adequate pool of income over the active lifetime of working populations to meet the high costs that a growing segment of the elderly population faces in seeking long term care either at home or in group facilities.

4. Greater selectivity in the use of government funds does not prescribe or preclude any particular form of service delivery. In actuality, most social services now involve a mix of private, voluntary, and public structures. This is not a new development but part of their historical pattern, although some new elements have entered into the picture more recently—as, for example, the entry of for-profit companies into the homemaker business. Theoretically, it is possible to reach judgments as to service delivery based on normative criteria of effectiveness and efficiency independently of the source of financing.

5. There is a growing recognition of the important role played by informal caretakers, and especially families, in the social service system. This level of informal support networks is the least explored of all the elements in the public-private relationship. Few studies are available of the costs borne by families of the chronically mentally ill or the disabled elderly, either financially or in other ways, but it is obvious that the financial contributions are very large and that the volume of service contributions is much more substantial than those provided by formal agencies (Perlman, 1983).

The relationship between governmental responsibility and that of families and other "natural" caretakers is looked at differently from different points in the political-ideological spectrum. A great deal of attention has been given, from the anti-government side, to the position that government support tends to undermine the family and to foster dependency. The other side of the argument is to seek the aid of government to alleviate some of the severe burden on families—as a way of preserving the positive contributions that they are able to make and to avoid less desirable and more costly care in formal institutions. The latter position leads to advocacy of a greater role for government in support of families through such measures as respite care, home care services, and income policies that might ease the financial burdens. That is an example of a view of government as supplementing and strengthening the private contribution as against substituting for it or leaving the field entirely to private effort.

6. Self-help and other indigenous organizations constitute the next level in a continuum ranging from informal to formal modes of social service delivery. These are prominent particularly in the fields of disability, mental retardation, and mental illness. They combine service functions and advocacy programs, thus linking the provision of care under one form of private effort with activities designed to obtain greater resources from government.

The strengths of this type of organization in the social service structure lie in their commitment to the particular group being served, and their understanding of and empathy with their needs. Since they rely heavily on volunteer effort, such organizations can also provide some services at less expense than more professional agencies. Self-help and local indigenous efforts of various types were a very popular mode of service delivery during the 1960s and received governmental support through the community action programs of that period. Although the impulse toward spontaneous voluntary activity continues to thrive, such efforts are not seen today as a major focus for governmental subsidy. On the contrary, they have been subject, along with the more formal agencies, to cutbacks in governmental expenditures and may even have lost out, relatively, in competition with other agents of service delivery, including the for-profit sector.

7. Formal social service agencies fall into three broad categories—governmental, voluntary nonprofit, and private for-profit. Most of the discussion on privatization in the social services revolves around the different responsibilities and functions of these three sectors and the relationships among them. In the case examples used in this chapter, all three sectors are involved. The most prevalent pattern in these fields, and one that has been growing since the 1970s, is the use of contracting as a mechanism used by governmental agencies to purchase services from nongovernmental providers. It is important to keep in mind that contracting represents, not a substitution of private for public responsibility, but a choice of a private (that is, nongovernmental) instrument to provide a publicly financed service.

There is now considerable literature on contracting. Much of it is based on strong ideological assumptions that are difficult to demonstrate empirically. A growing number of studies suggest the need to be skeptical and cautious in accepting any general conclusions as to the superiority of one sector or the other in regard to issues of equity, effectiveness, or efficiency. The major issues involved may be identified as (a) access, (b) quality, and (c) costs. Each of these will be discussed briefly.

ACCESS

For all social service agencies, there is a gap between the theoretical mandate to serve a specified population and the numbers actually being served. There are at least two reasons for this gap. One is the limitation of resources. The other involves various barriers that prevent access to the service, whether these are created by the provider or the potential client. The issue of access is essentially the question of who does or does not get served.

A major responsibility of government in the contracting relationship is to make sure, through financing and monitoring, that the people for whom its funds are designated do in fact obtain service from nongovernmental providers. That is not always easy to do and in some fields, like children's protective service, the government needs to provide a substantial part of the service itself. Both nonprofit and for-profit agencies have their limitations in dealing with the most problematic aspects of social service. In the case of the for-profit agencies, the issue is higher costs. In nonprofit agencies, the limitations stem from traditional practices and professional expectations. Examples cited above are the inability of the voluntary agencies to expand to meet the need for homemaker services and the limitations of some voluntary child-care agencies in dealing with cases that require court action.

On the other hand, governmental agencies have also had the problem of how to reach clients who may need service but who are not reached due to problems of communication, agency modes of behavior, or psychological or cultural barriers that exist between agency and client. Assuming that the resources are available and that there is a policy commitment to reach those in need, governmental agencies may be assisted in carrying out their mandate by using as their instruments organizations or groups (both formal and informal) that have some way of overcoming such barriers. That is the rationale for including indigenous, self-help, and similar resources in a contracting system.

QUALITY

The issue of quality has high priority in the thinking of social service practitioners and administrators and figures prominently in the debates regarding privatization. Unfortunately, there is considerable ambiguity as to how to define or measure quality. For the most part, quality tends to be defined in terms of inputs—like standards of professional staffing or size of caseloads—rather than in terms of service benefits. In some states and in some services, governmental agencies pay higher salaries than do the voluntary or private sector services. At the same time, voluntary agencies, though paying less, may offer more supervision and training.

In one of the few empirical studies done in this field, Willis (1984) compared homemaker services in two counties in Utah. In one, the county agency supplied the service directly; in the other, it purchased the service from a private provider. Recipients were asked to rate the adequacy and quality of the service on a series of questions. On half the questions, the recipients' perceptions were more favorable to the direct service; on one-fourth they were more favorable to the purchased service; and on one-fourth the two services were equal.

Staffing is a pervasive problem across all services and settings and is particularly difficult in regard to serving those segments of the population for whom government is likely to have responsibility. All agencies, whether public, voluntary, or private have to recruit, train, motivate, and supervise a staff that will have some stability and continuity and capacity to implement their policies. Without having real data as to what does or does not work, one can assume that the answer lies in some combination of personal and extra-personal incentives—not only salaries and working conditions, important as those are, but also some ideological and policy framework that can inspire a sense of commitment to the clients and thus provide a sense of satisfaction to staff in meeting their needs. At this point, it is not clear that any segment has an advantage in achieving this overriding objective, except perhaps for some small highly motivated groups that rely on a great deal of volunteer effort.

In the contracting relationship, government has responsibility for monitoring and quality control. In the Massachusetts study cited earlier (Gurin, Friedman et al., 1980), it was found that formal monitoring was limited almost entirely to fiscal controls and that where an effort was made by the agency to look at quality as well as expenditures, the agency was quickly overwhelmed by the volume of work. On the other hand, there was a less formal kind of quality control that did seem to be somewhat effective. This was the feedback obtained directly from clients and their relatives and advocates—not to the state offices, but to case managers in the field. Our conclusion was that, to be effective, monitoring in regard to quality issues should be decentralized to the service level, with opportunities provided for easy communication between clients and case managers or their equivalents.

Costs

A major argument in favor of contracting is that it will reduce costs. The evidence in regard to the social services is scanty but does not lend support to this contention. One of the few studies done rigorously enough to be able to compare public and private operations in the same field concluded that contracted services were slightly more costly if all the administrative costs of the governmental agency connected with the contracting process were taken into account (Pacific Consultants, 1979).

The Massachusetts study mentioned earlier (Gurin, Friedman et al., 1980) discussed in detail some of the complexities of cost analysis and pricing in the social services. Costs of service vary greatly among agencies. Some are related to volume of service and economies of scale, others to methods of staffing. In some instances, government must pay market rates to obtain the service. In others, it seems able, because of its large buying power, to obtain a better-than-market rate. Nonprofit agencies tended to complain that they were actually subsidizing the government agency. The problem of supply is a complicating factor in some fields where there are few providers. The theory that competition in the private market will help to reduce costs is not borne out in practice. In actuality, most of the funds are used to purchase services from a few large providers (Massachusetts Taxpayers Foundation, 1980).

The general conclusion of this analysis was that there is no single method of pricing that can achieve all the goals of the purchase of service system, but that a flexible and somewhat experimental approach would have to be followed in order to realize the potential fiscal benefits of purchasing. The public agency that is purchasing the service seeks the optimum balance among cost, availability of service, and quality. Since it is costly to monitor the financial experience of individual providers and to engage in individual negotiations with them, the tendency is to use fixed rates or rate schedules, at the risk of losses in supply, quality, or both. Competitive bidding is not always useful because of the difficulty of specifying the product in comparable terms, as well as the paucity of providers in some areas. Even the argument that nongovernmental providers are advantageous (since the government has to pay only the variable costs incurred for the services actually given rather than the fixed costs of maintaining the agency) is questionable. This is because the government needs an assurance of stability and continuity in the provider community in order to meet its obligations.

But the government does have market power and is in a position, under certain conditions, to obtain services at an advantageous cost. If both effectiveness and cost efficiency are to be optimized, it is required that contracting agencies be able to specify both the quantity of services they are seeking and the major qualitative elements that may involve differences in costs. The public agencies would then be in a position to make purposeful departures from uniform or average rates in order to achieve specific objectives, such as providing greater service to underserved areas or populations.

Political Implications

Broadly speaking, there are two levels of decision making in regard to governmental responsibility for the social services. The first is whether government will assume any financial responsibility for the particular problem, need, or service. The second is what form that financing will take. The preceding discussion has dealt mostly with the second-order decisions—that is, the use of nongovernmental channels of various kinds for the implementation of governmental financial commitments. We turn now to some comments on the prior question of whether or not government assumes a financial responsibility, and the place of privatization in that debate.

Whether government is to become involved in dealing with a particular problem is clearly a political question and is resolved through the political process. The current period is one in which the pendulum is over on the side of limiting the role of government and questioning the scope of its responsibility. The retreat from government responsibility that has been intensified since 1980 is directed at all three aspects of government involvement—financing, regulation, and service delivery. There are, however, some contradictory elements. The most obvious example is health care, where concern over cost containment has led to much more regulation rather than less and to significant departures from the fee-for-service private enterprise system of which this field was the prime example in the human services. There are also counteracting forces in the political process that have prevented the elimination of programs or mitigated the force of proposed cutbacks. Cutbacks, however, have been very substantial in many of the social services, including those delivered not by government but through public subsidies or contracts with the voluntary or private sector.

It is argued at several points in this book that privatization should be looked upon essentially as a political issue. The point is made forcefully by Starr (Chapter 1) that privatization cannot be considered on its merits in the present climate because it is an integral aspect of the political drive of the current Administration to reduce social welfare and to redistribute the benefits of society upward in the class structure. Bendick (Chapter 4) argues equally urgently a kind of "if you can't fight them, join them" position. His point is that opposition to privatization cannot win, that persistence in that battle may lose the war for social welfare, but that the espousal of privatization could have the effect of increasing the total quantity of public social welfare services. One of the reasons this would happen is because providers dependent on government funds would have a stake in the continuance of social programs, thus broadening the constituency in support of governmental financing.

I believe that both sides of this debate are overstated. The fact is that Bendick's proposition has been tested, since there does exist now a large body of providers in the pluralistic public/private system that characterizes the social services. There is no evidence that this has been a substantial factor protecting the services. With respect to Starr's argument, I see no reason to believe that an attack on privatization (in terms of service delivery, not financial responsibility) provides greater leverage in resisting the political backlash than direct engagement with the cutbacks themselves. It seems clear to me that the decisive issues are cost and financial responsibility rather than the form of service delivery. Privatization in the sense of how best to deliver social services and whether and how to use voluntary and for-profit providers can therefore be decided to a large extent on the basis of the merits of the case rather than on political grounds.

I have pointed out in the earlier examples of social services what some of these merits may be. Perhaps the most positive statement that can be made about privatization at the service delivery level is that it offers a range of options and therefore flexibility in meeting different kinds of human needs. The options range from vouchers that are exchangeable in the marketplace to contracting with large bureaucracies, both profit and nonprofit.

Some of these options have a particular appeal to analysts who are critical of government services for reasons that were characteristic of the 1960s rather than the 1980s. A case in point is the recent article by David Donnison (1984), who argues, like Bendick, for the support of privatization, but on different grounds. Donnison describes the "old system" (by which he means the structure of Britain's social services after World War II) as "centralized, professionalized, uniform, 'top-down' ... a functional, service oriented style of government." He calls for this "old system" to be modified or replaced by "systems that are more economically oriented, more area focused and more community-based." The goals of equity and efficiency, while still valid, are to be pursued through "community, democracy, enterprise, self-management, open government" (pp. 54–55). He proposes new kinds of subsidies and entitlements that would help both individuals and groups to create their own form of service. In short, he calls for a massive expansion of privatization, 1960s style. He also argues that this is politically feasible in the current conservative climate in the United Kingdom.

From an American perspective, I would question both the political feasibility and the social policy merits of this position. On the policy merits, it is important to remember that Britain has lived for forty years with the benefits of the Beveridge plan, which delivered many promised protections from the cradle to the grave. If changes of direction are to take place along the lines Donnison proposes, they will occur within a context where government continues to provide those basic protections. The United States, however, still lacks basic provisions for children and families in the spheres of both income and health. Our experience in the 1960s demonstrated that a decentralized, community-based strategy cannot make up for the absence of national, universal benefits in crucial areas.

In this social context, therefore, one needs to be concerned with maintaining and strengthening the role of government, in the social services and in the human services more generally. The major issues, as I have indicated, are those involving the nature and extent of financial responsibility. Experience in the management of health programs and in the contracting out of social services has demonstrated abundantly that government, if it is involved financially, cannot avoid being concerned about the organization and delivery of the services for which it is paying. The lack of attention to these matters has had large-scale negative consequences in the health services. Day-by-day experience in child abuse, mental health, and other difficult fields makes it clear that government cannot shed its policy responsibility even though it does not act as a direct deliverer of service.

The critical issue, then, is the capacity of government to perform well its roles in policy planning, financing, monitoring, and regulating. Obviously, it is difficult to build such a capacity in an atmosphere that denigrates government and that tries to deny that government should have such roles. The reality, in contrast with the rhetoric, is that the place of government in the social services will continue to be dominant. The great danger is that it will play its part with a diminishing capacity to do it well.

There are encouraging signs, here and there, that the tide may be beginning to turn once again. One might look at this time to the states, where favorable revenue experience (in some places) and creative administration have stimulated promising innovations in combining strong public policy initiatives with nongovernmental service delivery mechanisms. Several states, for example, are moving toward using Medicaid funds to purchase prepaid plans for Medicaid-eligible clients. Vouchers for day-care services are another example, as are employment and training projects for AFDC (Aid to Families with Dependent Children) recipients. These are examples of how privatization, properly employed, can help to answer an old problem—how to provide governmental assistance, selectively, for those most in need, without creating a two-tier system of services. One way is for government to provide the financial benefit but to make it possible for that benefit to be used in a nonselective general service system.

None of this can happen, however, without a reaffirmation of the positive role of government in dealing with human needs. As I noted at the beginning, there has always been ambivalence in regard to that matter in American history, but also an ebb and flow in the relative acceptance of the importance of government. In the inevitable move back from the negative attacks on government in recent years, it may contribute something to the process to focus sharply on the role of government as the major fiscal source of social protection and as the agent of social policy, leaving room for the creative use of various types of privatization in the delivery of service.

References

Blumenthal, David, et al. 1986. "The Future of Medicare." *New England Journal of Medicine*. March 13: 722–728.

Callahan, James J., and Stanley S. Wallack, eds. 1981. *Reforming the Long Term Care System*. Lexington, Mass.: Lexington Books.

Donnison, David. 1984. "The Progressive Potential of Privatisation." In Julian LeGrand and Ray Robinson. *Privatisation and the Welfare State*. London: Allen and Unwin.

Feinstein, Patrice Hirsh, Marian Gornick, and Jay N. Greenberg, eds. 1984. *Long-Term Care Financing and Delivery Systems: Exploring Some Alternatives. Conference Proceedings*. Washington, D.C.: U.S. Department of Health and Human Services, Health Care Financing Administration.

Gueron, Judith M. 1984. *Lessons from a Job Guarantee. The Youth Incentive*

Entitlement Pilot Projects. New York: Manpower Demonstration Research Corporation.

Gurin, Arnold, and Barry Friedman et al. 1980. *Contracting for Service as a Mechanism for the Delivery of Human Services: A Study of Contracting Practices in Three Human Service Agencies in Massachusetts.* Waltham, Mass.: Florence Heller Graduate School, Brandeis University.

Hahn, Andrew, and Robert Lerman. 1985. *What Works in Youth Employment Policy?* Washington, D.C.: National Planning Association. Report No. 215.

Johnson, Arlien. 1931. *Public Policy and Private Charities.* University of Chicago Press.

Kiesler, Charles A., et al. 1983. "Federal Mental Health Policymaking: An Assessment of Deinstitutionalization." *American Psychologist* 38 (December): 1292–1297.

McGuire, Thomas G., and Burton A. Weisbrod, eds. 1981. *Economics and Mental Health.* Mental Health Service Systems Reports. Series En No. 1. Washington, D.C.: U.S. Department of Health and Human Services.

Massachusetts Taxpayers Foundation. 1980. *Can State Government Gain Control?* Boston, Mass.

Pacific Consultants. 1979. *Title XX. Purchase of Service.* Berkeley, Ca. January.

Perlman, Robert, ed. 1983. *Family Home Care.* New York: Haworth Press.

Schlesinger, Mark, and Robert Dorwart. 1984. "Ownership and Mental Health Services." *New England Journal of Medicine* (October 11): 959–965.

Willis, David C. 1984. "Purchase of Social Services: Another Look." *Social Work* 29 (6): 516–520.

8

The Local Initiatives Support Corporation: A Private Initiative for a Public Problem

MITCHELL SVIRIDOFF

A strong belief exists in many quarters today that unless the welfare state is tempered and the role of the private sector is strengthened, poverty and dependency will increase, not diminish, and the role of government will grow increasingly intrusive and produce further unforeseen negative consequences. Time will tell whether these are valid propositions; there is little question that the first of them—the shrinkage of social welfare programs and an increased reliance on private initiative—is now being tested.

This is the story of a particular private initiative—an approach based on a combination of private, individual, and local initiatives—to tackle the problem of the breakdown of urban neighborhoods.

The Local Initiatives Support Corporation (LISC) is a national nonprofit lending and grant-making institution founded in 1980 to draw private-sector financial and technical resources into the development of deteriorated communities and neighborhoods. It invests these resources in projects of new construction and rehabilitation in housing, business, and industry that are being developed by community-based nonprofit organizations. It packages its support to bring local banks and other private-sector lenders into each investment and to assure that its own funds amount to a small proportion, currently about 10 percent, of total project costs contributed from all sources. LISC aims through such investments to help community development organizations improve local physical and economic conditions while also increasing their assets and incomes and strengthening their management and financial capabilities.

The Problem of Urban Neighborhoods:
A Brief History

Urban neighborhoods have been staging areas for immigrants entering the United States during the last 150 years. Except for those who quickly moved toward the American frontier, the urban neighborhood was the first contact with American culture, the first step in the assimilative process that enabled most to move up the mobility ladder. Those early immigrants had many of the same problems of adjustment that today's migrants have: language, culture, employment, education, housing, health, and social services. Nevertheless, the process seemed to work for them, though not without much pain.

Social intervention was limited but significant. For several decades beginning in the 1890s the settlement house, an idea borrowed from the English, was, in addition to the political machine, the primary support institution. These institutions were supplemented in various ways by *Landsmannschaft* organizations based on town or area of origin, churches and synagogues, the public schools and the trade unions. Of these, public schools were the major, if not the only, public support system. The public school assumed a teaching responsibility for children and adults alike. There was no social security or unemployment compensation, little public welfare, an insignificant amount of publicly assisted medical care, no food stamps, job programs, or subsidized housing.

On the other hand, unskilled and manufacturing jobs were relatively abundant. Though many people moved to outer parts of the cities as their economic circumstances improved, a large number of first- and second-generation immigrants stayed in their old neighborhoods and served as a stabilizing force even as new immigrants settled there.

Despite the disruption of the Great Depression of the 1930s most of the inner-city neighborhoods retained their viability due to a sizable enlargement of public intervention at that time. The post–World War II environment contributed to a remarkable period of economic growth and metropolitan expansion. The mobility achieved by second generation Americans during this golden age probably has no parallel in human history. Public programs of various sorts—the GI bill, FHA insurance, the federal highway trust fund—contributed to this era of affluence.

Meanwhile, a new group of Americans was arriving on the urban scene, seeking similar opportunities for the mobility that previous generations had enjoyed. Most were poor blacks whose new wave of migration was spurred first by the demand for labor during World War II, and intensified later by the technological revolution on the farm; then came the Puerto Ricans and other Hispanics, fleeing traditional rural poverty and attracted by contract labor operators and cheap air transportation. It was the American dream story playing itself out again in the most natural way. But, this time, for many the drama got stuck in the second act.

At least three critical factors caused this breakdown in the mobility patterns of the past. First, the flight to suburbia was an intense and sudden blow to central city economies and reduced investment and maintenance in old neighborhoods. Second, while the city was losing ground to suburbia, the industrial mix was also changing, requiring ever higher levels of education and technical skills. The new entrants in the urban labor force came from regions where they had not enjoyed adequate educational opportunity. They could not easily enter into the new growth occupations. Their problem was further compounded by something earlier immigrants did not have to contend with: the factor of race. Where the industrial revolution had facilitated the absorption of millions of immigrants, the postindustrial revolution of the past thirty years has been much less accommodating to the largely rural migrants who began arriving in the cities in the 1950s.

Among the many things that distinguish one migrant group from another is the height of the hurdle they must climb to get there. Some groups arrived in this country against obstacles whose effects might be best described as a Darwinian survival of the fittest experience: secret flights from oppressive regimes, extreme and prolonged deprivation, and the like. By the time these groups arrived, it was small wonder that they found the obstacles of urban poverty manageable by comparison. In hindsight, it is probably unfair to compare these sometimes superhuman achievers with groups of more ordinary folk whose barriers were lower and who have come less prepared to struggle confidently against adversity. This may be one reason why we still observe in some communities of immigrants and refugees a greater rate of success and absorption than in others. Nevertheless, it is certainly true that the current labor market is less hospitable in general to today's newcomers than it was fifty years ago, or even twenty.

It is no surprise therefore that there has developed in the cities a new and growing population for many of whom the traditional patterns of mobility and absorption do not work. The consequences of the breakdown in the system are now too well known to need repeating. Suffice it to emphasize at this point that while the city was losing its historical capacity to absorb new arrivals and provide mobility for them—a function it had performed brilliantly for earlier arrivals from across the sea—it acquired a new set of responsibilities and burdens that it was ill-equipped to manage. Little wonder that across the country the inner-city neighborhoods of the older cities began to sink into a state of economic and social crisis from which most have not yet recovered.

It's not that we haven't tried. Though various efforts cannot be neatly separated, for the last fifty years we have gone through a succession of federally initiated programs.

Public Housing

Public housing policy began in the 1930s. Its purpose was to enlarge the supply of standard affordable housing and to improve neighborhoods. While largely successful in the 1930s and 1940s, public housing began to show signs of stress from the 1950s forward. Upwardly mobile families were abandoning public housing and other old neighborhoods for the outer neighborhoods of the central cities and later for suburbia. Confused urban renewal policies in many cities converted public housing into a convenient dumping ground for the hard-to-relocate slum dwellers. The official demolition of Pruitt-Igoe in St. Louis in 1972 (a project that had earlier won a special award of merit) was, in a sense, an obituary for public housing as a means of combating slums. Along with public housing, stable working-class neighborhoods frequently became dumping grounds for the so-called "multiproblem family." It is ironic that the well-intentioned 1950s policy of urban renewal contributed unexpectedly to the demise of the 1930s policy of public housing, just as other well-intentioned policies such as federally underwritten mortgage insurance had sparked the growth of the suburbs while contributing to the decline of the city.

Urban Renewal

Urban renewal's purpose was clear from the start: to eradicate deteriorated areas through federally subsidized acquisitions combined with the use of the cities' power of eminent domain. With these tools, it was hoped that the cities could rebuild downtown economies, save declining neighborhoods, attract industry, hold the middle class, and bring back some of those who had long since fled. Urban renewal was not only well-intentioned, it left behind significant, though limited, evidence of success. Numerous downtown areas revived, at least partly, through urban renewal efforts. Renewal also greatly aided many federal housing programs and gave a start to today's emphasis on rehabilitation.

In addition, these efforts in the most distressed areas of the city inevitably displaced and relocated large numbers of poor blacks and Hispanics. Though some, in fact, improved their housing conditions, a significant number did not. The private housing market was not able to provide housing for the poor in safe and sanitary conditions at rentals they could afford. A subsidized housing supply could not be expanded rapidly enough to meet the demand. The consequent relocation of large numbers of the poor minority population only hastened the decline of both public housing and already degenerating neighborhoods. In time, urban renewal in many cities became widely known as "Negro Removal," a perception that contributed to the demise of urban renewal as the core of efforts to combat urban deterioration.

By the 1960s, the impact of the urban renewal program on minorities crystallized a new awareness of the social and human dimensions of urban poverty. Interest quickened in trying to find effective means to cope with this newly discovered, but deeply ingrained, social phenomenon: James Conant coined the term "social dynamite" in reference to out-of-school youth in his book, *Slums and Suburbs*; the Kennedy Administration, as one of its first acts, initiated a major experimental effort to deal with the problems of juvenile delinquency. Working with these government-sponsored experiments, the Ford Foundation organized a number of experimental social planning programs directed at inner-city poverty. Congress enacted the first job-training legislation as well as a set of social rehabilitative amendments to the Social Security Act. Michael Harrington's book on poverty, *The Other America*, suddenly became a best seller, read and recommended by President Kennedy.

"Maximium Feasible" Politics

A second major set of programs were developed during the 1960s, now commonly subsumed under the title, War on Poverty. During this period discontent among minorities and the poor and the stirrings of militancy came to a head. Martin Luther King and Malcolm X emerged as major national leaders overnight. In Chicago, Saul Alinsky laid the groundwork for community organizations across the country under the battle cry "Rub raw the sores of discontent."

The early 1960s were also a period of intense experimentation with social programs. The center of interest shifted from physical development to the schools, the job-training centers, the social agencies, the criminal justice and legal systems. High on the public agenda was the opening of the political system to wider participation by all sectors of the society, especially minorities.

After the election of Lyndon Johnson in 1964, there followed a rush of special legislation directed at the problem of poverty, especially urban poverty. The Great Society was officially launched. The Economic Opportunity Act, the Elementary and Secondary Aid to Education bill, Medicaid and Medicare, food stamps, civil rights legislation, and a monumental increase in appropriations for job training were among the dozens of new commitments undertaken in the mid-1960s.

In retrospect, it is easy to discern where the Great Society went wrong.

It was in the exaggerated expectations that accompanied each act of legislation and in the inadequate policy analysis that tended to accompany all efforts to advance new legislative agendas. It was in the lack of capacity at all levels of government to implement highly complex programs under self-induced political pressures for quick and easy solutions. It was too much, too fast, and too simplistic.

It was further complicated by the federal government's sponsorship of "maximum feasible participation." In many cities maximum feasible participation became an attack on city government and its political leadership, all in the name of opening up the political system. The problem was not that the political system did not need opening up. The harder issue was whether locally based political reform of this kind could be addressed by decree of the federal government. The inevitable consequence, the mobilization of an overwhelming political opposition, was neither widely understood nor foreseen.

Other factors coalesced to limit the potential effectiveness of the Great Society programs. During the recession, beginning in 1973 and stretching into the early 1980s, there was a significant decline in productivity and personal income for the first time since the 1940s. This spurred entry into the labor market of large numbers of women as families sought to make up lost income and alleviate inflationary pressures. This labor supply expansion combined with the accelerated changes in the skill demands of the labor market, the 1940s baby boom effect of doubling the supply of young workers, and a disproportionate growth in the number of minority, unskilled, and poorly educated young people. All these factors worked to overwhelm whatever progress these programs might otherwise have achieved.

In the declining days of the War on Poverty, a new effort was made by the government through the Model Cities program to regain its lost political initiative. Though Model Cities was again characterized at the federal level by comprehensive solutions and overblown goals, some new resources were provided for existing programs and for experimentation with new ones. It was, in a way, the transitional phase to what later was to become the Community Development Block Grant program—an important step in the direction of the New Federalism.

The dialectic of these years—growing federal intervention and eventual growing resistance to the costs and the authority of that intervention—had a profound effect on current U.S. public policy. Excessive expectations, an overly rapid effort at implementing programs involving huge sums of money, confused policies, and high political static all contributed to a public perception that these program strategies were confused, expensive, unproven, and poorly managed. The public mood, captured and magnified by President Reagan, was that the global solutions of the New

Deal and Great Society are inappropriate and ineffective for today's problems.

Private Initiatives

It was in this environment that private initiatives for urban development began to emerge. The first glimmering came in the closing days of the Carter Administration with UDAG (Urban Development Action Grants) on the physical side and PICs (Private Industry Councils) in labor force development. The UDAG program depended upon the leveraging of private-sector resources. PICs shifted the initiative in employment programs from the public- to the private-sector job market, and the direct management of these programs to councils controlled by the private sector. UDAG today appears vulnerable to the budget-cutting axe, but PICs have never been endangered and have emerged as the centerpiece of job-training programming.

The general disillusionment with centralized government solutions to local social and economic problems also produced a growing and lively interest in a variety of forms of decentralized, locally based community development efforts. As public support for Community Action Agencies declined in the latter part of the 1960s, a new type of community development program emerged, emphasizing economic and physical development along with community involvement. These new Community Development Corporations (CDCs), were largely free of the complicating political baggage of the community action programs. Some of these corporations sought to involve the private corporate sector. Perhaps the most impressive was the Bedford Stuyvesant Restoration Corporation in Brooklyn, which attracted large amounts of public and private money for housing and development. The Bed-Stuy corporation, among other things, managed to attract an IBM satellite factory that continues to this day as a major source of employment in the community. Another impressive example of private-sector involvement in Bed-Stuy was a commitment by several major insurance companies of a significant pool of mortgage money that helped Bed-Stuy in its housing revitalization efforts. Corporations also gave substantial financial, managerial, and technical assistance support, with several top corporate executives generously giving their time and talent to the day-to-day operation of the corporation.

Efforts to build on the Bed-Stuy experience were undertaken under special legislation in various parts of the country. In addition, the Ford Foundation through the late 1960s and 1970s provided more than $100 million in grant and investment support to a group of these development corporations in order to test their effectiveness in coping with the problems of declining urban and rural centers. Another type of locally based development organization that emerged at about the same time as the CDCs and like the CDCs, focused on specific solutions to specific community problems, was the Neighborhood Housing Service (NHS) Corporation. Spreading from city to city, NHS corporations defined for themselves a simple mission: the elimination of neighborhood blight through increased local bank financing, more effective code enforcement, improved city services, and below-market financing for those families and homes that could not afford conventional financing. These efforts provided the private financial community with an avenue for affirmative response to the attack being leveled against it by the so-called "anti-redlining" groups.

The anti-redlining movement, after decades of inertia, was in many cases successful. It was responsible for the passage of the Community Reinvestment Act, a powerful influence on federally regulated financial institutions. The noncontentious programmatic approach of the NHS corporations stood in refreshing contrast to the earlier redlining battles. Perhaps more importantly, as with the CDCs, the NHS emphasis on collaborative efforts with both government and the private sector has attracted significant local and national support. There are now several hundred Neighborhood Housing Services in operation across the country, including the outer boroughs of New York city. Like the CDCs, they are locally targeted, limited in objectives, and focused heavily on tapping private resources, talent, and experience.

By the late 1970s, a dozen or so major CDCs like the Bedford-Stuyvesant Restoration Corporation had proven themselves highly effective agents of neighborhood revitalization. Their philanthropic sponsors—notably the Ford Foundation—interested in finding ways to broaden and strengthen this promising invention, decided to test the notion of a free-standing, highly skilled intermediary that would seek out promising CDCs and enlist the help of the private and public sectors in providing investment resources to help them achieve higher levels of self-sufficiency. This led, in 1980, to the creation of LISC.

LISC

The Ford Foundation and six insurance, industrial, and banking institutions were the founders of LISC, starting it off with capital of $9,350,000. Since 1980 this intermediary has attracted funds from more than 350 corporations and foundations, has generated more than $100,000,000 dollars and has invested in more than 500 projects in hundreds of cities across the country, including the South Bronx and several neighborhoods in Brooklyn.

LISC operates through a nationwide network of twenty-six local areas of concentration, each of which draws on its own pool of funds comprising contributions from local corporations and foundations and a matching amount from LISC's general capital fund, which in turn is provided by major national corporate and foundation donors. Representatives of the local donors sit on advisory committees in each area and work with a LISC program officer to select projects and organizations for investment subject to final approval by LISC's national board of directors.

All areas of concentration are formed by explicit decision of LISC's board of directors to allocate from national funds an amount that must be matched dollar-for-dollar by local donors. The board's decision is based on an assessment of the proposed area's development potential and the availability of sufficient national funds. The process usually begins with approaches by possible local donors and community development leaders. LISC then explores the proposed area's development potential. It looks for two critical conditions: (1) a high level of interest by local banks, corporations, and foundations in funding the revitalization of deteriorated areas and (2) demonstrated capacity on the part of local community organizations to develop and manage socially beneficial housing and commercial/industrial projects.

Within each area of concentration the selection of community organizations to receive project support reflects a fundamental LISC policy. This is to support groups that already have some physical and economic development experience and are ready to take on progressively larger and more demanding projects. To demonstrate this capacity, a community organization should have such characteristics as strong leadership, community support, good ties with local government, experience in program management, and the potential to increase its local public and private sector backing. The groups that can benefit by LISC support may vary considerably in their strengths among such characteristics. Selection for support depends on comparative judgments by LISC within the area of concentration. In all cases it places its loans and grants to serve the following objectives:

to help build strong and lasting ties between community organizations and the local and national private sector;
to help community development organizations increase and safeguard their incomes and real assets;
to encourage and support local organizations in achieving the business discipline they need to raise and invest their own funds most effectively.

LISC supports three main types of neighborhood physical and economic development projects: housing, commercial, and industrial. The range of projects within each of the three types is broad. Housing projects can be for new construction, as with the Hispanic Housing Development Corporation's Linden Place Townhouses in Chicago; rehabilitation, as in Pittsburgh's Manchester Citizens Corporation's acquisition and resale of more than one hundred units in its historic district; rural, as in the Cabrillo Economic Development Corporation's provision of farmworker housing in Saticoy, California; or high-density urban, as with SEBCO Development's $17-million, 385-unit project now completed and occupied in the South Bronx. Commercial development projects range from support of small businesses to development of shopping centers like the one opened in March 1986 in the Liberty City area of Miami by the Tacolcy Economic Development Corporation. Industrial development can focus on a small operation like the "R2B2" bottle and can recycling business of the South Bronx 2000 Local Development Corporation; on industrial parks like that of the UDI Commercial Development corporation in Durham, North Carolina; or on "incubator" buildings, converted factories that, like one operated by the Industrial Council of Northwest Chicago and one near completion in the South Bronx, provide technical assistance and low rent to launch small local commercial and manufacturing enterprises.

Housing has predominated cumulatively over the last four years among LISC investments, with 170 projects and almost $18 million in loan and grant investment. Next comes commercial development, with 100 projects and $8 million. Industrial development has accounted for 45 projects and $3.7 million. During LISC's first two years of operation, nearly 60 percent of the program actions approved were in support of housing projects or housing-related capacity development efforts. During the third and fourth years, there was a decline of about 10 percent in these projects, and a corresponding increase in program actions in support of commercial and industrial projects, primarily those involving real estate.

This shift resulted partly from LISC's intention to broaden its range and partly from a change in the priorities of many community organizations. When the Community Development Corporations sprang up in the 1960s, they gave highest priority to the need for decent living conditions for their low-income constituents; government responded by offering below-market funds for new and rehab housing. Since then, and especially in the 1980s, these subsidies, along with government funding for social service programs, have declined sharply. Community-based organizations, already motivated to strengthen the neighborhood economic base as a complement to their housing programs, have moved toward commercial and industrial development since 1981, all the more urgently in the hope that these will also make up for lost grant income.

LISC's relative increase in support to commercial and industrial projects reflects primarily an increase in projects involving real estate development, like the industrial parks, shopping centers, and "incubator" buildings I have described. LISC experience makes it clear that such projects benefit strongly from the presence of an experienced private co-venturer. When they have such support, they appear to be the least risky, best collateralized kinds of enterprise investments for community development, as well as the most fruitful in terms of income for CDC sponsors, and jobs and services for the community.

By intention and as it actually happened, LISC's development has been open-ended, an evolution rather than the fulfillment of a carefully wrought plan. In a sense, LISC is the confluence of two streams of private-sector initiative for urban redevelopment. One of these is the nationwide movement to form and operate nonprofit community development corporations that are led by and represent the residents of deteriorated neighborhoods. The other is the increasing interest of banking, business, and industrial corporations in investing some of their resources in the rebuilding of the urban communities that surround them and from which they draw both customers and workers.

The donors that provided $9,350,000 to launch LISC represented both streams. The Ford Foundation, which started the process with a grant of $4,750,000, had for most of the preceding two decades contributed through its nationwide grant and PRI (Program-Related Investments) programs to the evolution of the forms, methods, and programs of CDCs. The six major insurance, industrial, charitable, and banking institutions that provided additional loans and grants totaling $4,600,000 had long been national leaders in corporate social investment.

The founders of LISC were relying on the Ford Foundation's experience in long-term support during the 1960s and 1970s for a dozen large CDCs like the Watts Labor Community Action Committee in Los Angeles and the Bedford-Stuyvesant Restoration Corporation in Brooklyn. Such CDCs had proved to be powerful vehicles with which to draw new private and public resources into neighborhood revitalization that served the needs of low-income people. The Foundation's experience suggested that there was a "second generation" of U.S. community development groups ready to follow the model of the first.

A nationwide survey confirmed this view, indicating that more than 200 of such groups met at least minimum criteria for plans, leadership, and experience. It was the founders' cautious estimate that LISC could find in its first year twenty CDCs and projects around the nation that would be ready for the funding and technical assistance its charter provided for, and perhaps eighty more after five years. LISC began, therefore, as a national program, managed from a single office, with support from a few national funders.

What happened in the next two years surprised everyone concerned.

LISC found 133 significant "bankable" projects and CDCs within two years. Moreover, it found clusters of these in several areas where there were corporations and foundations eager to raise money to form "local LISCs." The Ford Foundation agreed to supplement LISC's national resources with additional matching funds in these areas. As LISC committed its dollar-for-dollar match to those pools, each became the nucleus of an area of concentration.

By late 1981 the areas of concentration had become the central mechanism of LISC's operation. The Ford Foundation continued to encourage this development. Its additional grants since 1980 have totalled more than $20 million and have enabled LISC to create new areas of concentration, expand existing ones, and carry on the program and administrative work thus generated. Other national donors, both founding and new, have also helped with several millions of dollars of further grants and loans.

From all sources—local and national—LISC's original $9,350,000 for ongoing program actions and operations had by June 1984 grown to more than $70,000,000, with grants, loans, and commitments from 252 corporations and foundations. What had been conceived at first as an exploratory effort to support a limited number of CDCs and projects across the nation had reached 272 of them in 93 communities after four years. The donors, like LISC's staff, have been well aware that it is inevitable that some projects will be disappointing; fortunately these have been rare.

This growth is not merely quantitative. It has come in a form—the national network of areas of concentration—that unites the initiatives of local CDCs and their corporate funders with the growing interest of national corporations and foundations in social investment.

A picture of operations in some of the older LISC areas of concentration over the last five years will serve to illustrate how the basic LISC concept can evolve and produce increasingly sophisticated forms of private-sector community participation that respond to local needs and ideas and offer models for other areas.

Cleveland–LISC

Since 1981, in response to a challenge by the Cleveland Foundation, twenty of Cleveland's largest corporations and foundations have raised more than $900,000 for LISC. With the LISC national match, these funds generated a pool of nearly $2 million for the Cleveland–LISC area of concentration. Recognizing that traditional sources of government funds were decreasing, these organizations—among them the Cleveland Foundation, Standard Oil of Ohio, the Gund Foundation, TRW, Cleveland

Clearinghouse, and Ohio Bell—saw the need for an organization that could provide a wide range of financing arrangements to neighborhood-based community development organizations. Since then, LISC has placed $1,550,155 in loans, grants, and guarantees to support twenty-three projects developed by eleven neighborhood-based organizations.

The majority of Cleveland–LISC projects have been housing related. The city's stock of run-down or abandoned wood-frame, single-family, detached housing, a legacy of disinvestment and outmigration, has compelled the attention of neighborhood-based community organizations. They have responded with housing rehabilitation projects that have improved the lives of low-income residents and helped the organizations themselves to develop strong managerial skills. The organizations are now exercising these skills in projects of increasing scale and even greater impact on their communities.

The Famicos Foundation is an example of such growth. It began in 1969 staffed by volunteers who wanted to improve housing conditions in the riot-torn Hough area of Cleveland. Within a few years Famicos had evolved into a program that by 1983 had acquired more than 250 run-down or abandoned homes at low cost and rehabilitated them to sell with no down payment to low-income families. One of LISC's first Cleveland actions was a $44,000 grant to help Famicos improve administrative and fiscal controls. With tightened management and increasing experience, Famicos has since put together a plan to build a 606-unit, $13-million garden apartment complex—"Lexington Village"—in Hough. The 183-unit Phase I of this ambitious project has attracted a private developer as co-venturer, the support of Cleveland's foundations, corporations, and city government, and a $400,000 loan from LISC.

Comprehensive city-wide efforts in Cleveland have produced the Cleveland Housing Network (CHN), a coalition of seven housing development organizations stimulated by the example of Famicos, which is one of the members. CHN is actively working to expand the scale of single- and two-family housing rehabilitation in Cleveland, providing training to member organizations, and centralizing their fund-raising and coordinating their projects. In 1982 LISC made a $200,000 loan to CHN to rehabilitate forty-four units of housing. Recently, CHN and the Enterprise Social Investment Corporation, a subsidiary of the Enterprise Foundation, formed the Cleveland Housing Partnership. This entity seeks to increase the housing rehab output of network members by attracting corporate financing through the sale of limited partnership interests. LISC will probably provide bridge financing for these syndication proceeds.

In addition to these housing development projects, LISC has provided financing for several revolving loan funds used for housing rehabilitation.

LISC also supported test litigation that made it possible for CDCs to become receiver-developers of tax-delinquent and abandoned housing.

LISC funding in Cleveland is increasingly being used for economic development projects as neighborhood organizations try to complement their housing work by upgrading adjacent commercial areas. Among such projects are a marketing survey for a neighborhood arcade, a revolving loan fund for small business capital improvements, renovation of a building to house a consumer food coop, legal services related to the development of an inner-city industrial park, and working capital and equipment for a neighborhood-based recycling center.

Now capable of implementing projects of scale, local CDCs continue to need below-market financing as they address themselves to the urban decay around them. The LISC–Cleveland Advisory Committee, composed of the original corporate and foundation funders of LISC–Cleveland, recognizes the need. The committee has begun fund-raising for a second round of LISC program activity. The goal is to raise $666,000 from Cleveland corporations and foundations. These funds will be supplemented by $500,000 from LISC–national to provide Cleveland with a pool of funds that can be used to finance challenging development projects by Cleveland neighborhood organizations.

South Bronx–LISC

The South Bronx–LISC program was organized in 1980 with support from thirteen local corporations and foundations. (These were the Vincent Astor Foundation, Bankers Trust Company, CBS, Charles H. Revson Foundation, Chase Manhattan Bank, Chemical Bank, Metropolitan Life Foundation, Morgan Guaranty Trust Company of New York, the New York Community Trust, New York Life Foundation, New York Telephone Company, R. H. Macy & Company, Inc., and Time Incorporated.) To date, sixteen of such private funders have provided more than $1.9 million in support. These funds, together with the LISC–national match, have created an investment pool of approximately $3.5 million specifically earmarked for South Bronx community development organizations. This pool has helped fund projects whose total costs are more than $50 million dollars.

The investment strategy undertaken by South Bronx–LISC reflects both organizational needs and market realities. During the first year of operation 72 percent of all LISC actions were grants; most were small and targeted on program development as the seed capital for future projects.

For example, the Banana Kelly Community Improvement Association (BK) used about $130,000 in grants from LISC to help develop its Beck Street project. With these funds, including a $41,000 recoverable grant that has been repaid in full, BK was able successfully to package a $3.2-million development plan for ten adjacent buildings along Beck Street containing eighty-five units. Today BK manages more than 350 units of low-income housing, and its total annual revenues from operations exceed $550,000. This record has helped the group develop traditional banking relationships with Chemical Bank and Citibank, both of which actively seek business from Banana Kelly. Banana Kelly is now in the process of renovating a $5.0-million, sixty-five-unit Section 8 rent subsidy project along Kelly Street and is negotiating with the city for the development of six multifamily buildings along Fox Street.

LISC grants also helped the Northwest Bronx Community and Clergy Coalition to establish its own entity, BUILD. Earlier, the coalition had assisted in the development of rehabilitation loan packages for forty-one buildings with 2,637 units totaling $16.3 million in its neighborhood. With a $15,000 LISC grant, BUILD was able to secure the legal and accounting support that made possible the acquisition and rehabilitation of 168 units in four buildings in the Northwest Bronx. This $3-million project enjoys the financial backing of the Aetna Corporation and a $125,000 loan from LISC. BUILD recently syndicated this project for approximately $900,000, $220,000 of which will flow to BUILD. BUILD continues to evaluate new development opportunities in its neighborhood and is now discussing with the city the rehabilitation of an additional eighty units in its neighborhood.

Although a disproportionate number of early LISC South Bronx actions were grants, half of the dollar amount was for recoverable actions, mostly loans. A majority of the early loan dollars went for housing. A stable residential section is vital to the well-being of any community. BUILD's large-scale developments adhere to that principle. So also did LISC's provision of a vital $250,000 to the South East Bronx Community Organization (SEBCO) at a time when its entire financing for a 385-unit Section 8 project appeared vulnerable. Though only a small piece in this $17-million project, the loan enabled SEBCO to take an equity position and thus was an essential part of the development process.

When LISC began its South Bronx program, the prevailing perception throughout the private and public sectors was that little could be done in a community so devastated by urban blight. LISC and its community development corporation partners and the government-funded South Bronx Development Organization (SBDO) have changed that perception considerably, as two of their jointly sponsored projects show: Charlotte Gardens (also sponsored by Mid-Bronx Desperadoes, a CDC) and the 190 Willow Avenue Incubator Project.

Despite promises by the Carter and Reagan administrations and the city of New York to promote new housing in the Bronx, by 1981 the residents of the Bronx had yet to see any. Both the federal government and the city doubted that an economically viable project could be built in the South Bronx. But SBDO and Mid-Bronx Desperadoes thought otherwise. Their plan was essentially speculative—to build single-family manufactured homes on a new subdivision along Charlotte Street, a national symbol of urban devastation. At first, LISC was the only organization to give financial backing to that vision. With grant and loan support totaling approximately $250,000, LISC financed the construction of two model homes. Since then, ninety homes with a purchase price of approximately $60,000 have been pre-sold to families, mostly members of minority groups, with a median income over $30,000. LISC's original $250,000 has leveraged more than $7 million for the one project. A waiting list of two thousand families now exists for future developments; 20 percent of the applicants were from outside the Bronx. A demographic and income profile of the ninety homebuyers under contract reveals some very interesting statistics. Median family income is $33,000, with minimum liquid assets of $9,000. Ninety percent of these homebuyers currently reside in the Bronx, with 65 percent of them already residing in the South Bronx. The risks that SBDO and LISC took with Charlotte Gardens seem to be paying off programmatically: many levels of government are now responding to the housing crisis in the South Bronx.

LISC, together with the Port Authority and with SBDO, also developed the Willow Avenue Incubator, the first such industrial facility in New York City. LISC assistance totaling $150,000 in grants and loans has leveraged approximately $600,000 in private and public financing for this project. The speculative nature of incubator facilities makes them very difficult to finance in the private sector. This project was no exception. Despite such reservations on the part of the private sector, the project is now meeting its objectives. With 90 percent of the building renovated, 66 percent of the space is already leased, ahead of plans and expectations. This momentum has been an important factor in the Port Authority's decision to develop a much larger, second Bronx incubator facility at its Bathgate industrial site.

The South Bronx–LISC program continues to respond to the development needs of community groups as these needs have changed over the last few years. Whereas many groups requested and received grant support from 1980–1982 to strengthen their development abilities, the majority of requests now received and approved are to provide loans to implement actual development projects. In the last two years, approximately 80 percent of all funds approved in the South Bronx have been in the form of loans and other recoverables. Two years ago these actions accounted for only 44 percent of all funds committed in the Bronx. While a direct correlation cannot be drawn between early grant

activity and current loan activity, it is clear that the experience and so-
phistication that these groups gained earlier in the development process
have been of great assistance to them in implementing their current projects.

LISC experience in the South Bronx is a classic illustration of the proposition that economic development in a troubled urban area is best stimulated by a program that leads to community stability. In this case such
stability was the product of carefully designed, community-based housing
programs; in effect, housing in these circumstances becomes economic
development.

Boston–LISC

Boston was one of the first cities to set up a LISC area of concentration.
In 1981, the Permanent Charity fund, the city's largest foundation, spear-
headed a campaign to elicit the necessary support from local corporations
and foundations. Within several months, the program had received sufficient commitments to begin operations.

In its first three years, the Boston–LISC program has received almost
$1.5 million from fifteen local corporations and foundations, including
four commercial banks, two insurance companies, Gillette, Polaroid, the
Boston Globe, Boston Edison, and Boston Gas Company. With matching
funds provided by the national LISC donors, the Boston program has to
date invested $2.4 million in loans and grants in neighborhood develop-
ment projects sponsored by seventeen different community-based organizations.

In Boston, approximately 75 percent of the LISC funds committed have
been in the form of loans. Of this amount, close to $700,000 has already
been repaid to LISC, with a default rate of less than one-half of 1 percent
of outstanding principal. The projects supported with LISC dollars in
Boston are split evenly between housing and economic development.
Among the housing projects are a 190-unit complex of newly constructed
units for low-income families and two 50-plus-unit rehabilitation projects. The economic development projects have included renovations of
office buildings in three distressed neighborhood commercial districts, financing for a community-owned real estate management company, and
support for a broad-based program of technical assistance to CDCs involved in commercial development. Collectively, these LISC-funded projects have leveraged more than $30 million in private and public funds.

The first recipient of LISC program support in Boston was Inquilinos
Boricuas en Accion (IBA), a housing organization operating in the Hispanic community of the city's South End. A LISC loan of $250,000
helped IBA to complete the financing for a $12-million federally subsi-

dized housing and commercial development. This project has been completed, is fully occupied, and has repaid its LISC loan in its entirety. LISC's loan provided a relatively small, yet crucial, piece of the front-end financing without which the project could not have gone forward.

Following IBA, LISC funded two large rehabilitation projects, one involving fifty-nine units and the other fifty-four. Each of these projects, one in Cambridge and the other in Jamaica Plain, has completed construction and is fully occupied. Each marked a significant expansion in the level of output and development capability of the sponsoring community groups. Both groups, like IBA before them, have moved on to other large-scale housing initiatives in their respective neighborhoods.

While LISC's first several projects in Boston were housing-related, an increasing proportion of the more recent commitments have been aimed toward economic development. These changing proportions show not only LISC's intensified effort to balance its development portfolio, but also a change in the priorities of some community-based groups. Organizations whose previous activities were almost exclusively in housing are trying to build complementary strength in the neighborhood economic base.

Two such examples can be found in separate commercial districts within the Dorchester neighborhood. Each of these districts has experienced all the classic stages of inner-city deterioration since the end of World War II: exodus of the white middle class to the suburbs, influx of increasing numbers of lower-income minority families, shrinking retail market, abandonment in surrounding residential areas, and, finally, disinvestment and deterioration of the neighborhood commercial center.

In more recent years, with the active involvement of neighborhood-based development groups in these areas, significant inroads have been made in reviving the housing stock surrounding these commercial districts. Building on this momentum, these community groups have begun targeting key commercial properties for rehabilitation in an effort to expand the revitalization that has begun in housing. LISC has funded three such projects to date with loans totaling $650,000. Each is an important commercial anchor parcel in its neighborhood; their success is likely to stimulate additional development in these areas.

While Boston–LISC continues to support projects undertaken by individual community groups in the city, on a different level, several prominent bankers have taken an important step in the evolution of public/private efforts to support local community development. They have worked to create the Boston Housing Partnership, a coalition of private and public sector resources aimed at improving housing opportunities for lower income residents. The partnership's first project, two years in the making and about to get underway, is a $30-million program to rehabilitate more than 700 housing units throughout the city. These projects are being developed by ten CDCs and are to be constructed with a complex array of federal, state, city, foundation, and bank financing.

In its objectives, its reliance on community-based organizations, and its emphasis on substantive public/private partnership, the Boston Housing Partnership closely parallels LISC and is a natural extension of LISC's pilot activities in Boston over the past three years. Because the purposes and methodologies of LISC and the partnership are so similar, LISC has embraced the partnership as the locally initiated embodiment of its program in Boston, at least as far as housing is concerned. LISC has committed a substantial portion of its housing funds to the partnership and fully expects to look increasingly to it for leadership in future housing activities. In this sense, the housing component of the Boston–LISC program has now been successfully institutionalized on the local level.

CHICAGO–LISC

Chicago became one of the first LISC Areas of Concentration because it gave early evidence of the soundness of the assumption on which LISC was launched: that the private sector can invest substantial capital in physical and economic development of blighted neighborhoods with acceptable risk and significant social return. In the year after it started in 1980, LISC found worthwhile loan and grant opportunities nationwide in numbers that far exceeded expectation. These turned out to be clustered primarily in a few areas in the Northeast, Midwest, and California.

Among those areas, Chicago proved especially well endowed not only with community organizations experienced in developing and managing socially beneficial housing and commercial enterprises, but with banks, foundations, and industrial and business corporations that wanted to help fund them. As a result, during the first year of its national operations, LISC was able to support eight projects in Chicago with loans and grants totaling $1,328,500.

This strong early momentum in Chicago led a group of potential local investors and donors to take a further initiative. They offered to raise $1 million locally and asked LISC to match it dollar for dollar to create a special LISC pool in Chicago.

The local investors, sixteen in all, included the Chicago Community Trust, the John D. and Catherine T. MacArthur Foundation, Illinois Bell, Beatrice Foods, Inland Steel, Quaker Oats, and Borg-Warner. In addition, two Chicago-based corporations, International Harvester and Continental Illinois Bank, had been major founding donors to the national LISC fund. Since its formation, Chicago–LISC has placed more than a score of loans and grants totaling more than $2.3 million. Thus, together with the cluster of earlier projects under its national programs, LISC had approved program actions of more than $3.6 million in Chicago by December 1984.

From the beginning, Chicago–LISC operations have benefited from the depth of interest of local private-sector funding in community revitalization and the resourcefulness and capacity for growth of an unusually large number of community-based development groups. Among these is People's Consumer Cooperative (PCC), which started fifty years ago as a food-buying club of black residents of Chicago's South Side. PCC has in recent years built 610 apartment units for the elderly, is now building a nearby 190-unit townhouse and rental complex and, with LISC help, is assembling adjacent land for a 464-unit complex for families and the elderly. The organization has accomplished this growth by using early Illinois Housing Development Authority (IHDA) loans and then entering joint ventures with private developers.

The Hispanic Housing Development Corporation on the Northwest Side has also used the progression from IHDA support to joint venturing. LISC helped in the process with a 4 percent, five-year capital loan of $135,000 that permitted Hispanic to hire key staff, including a property manager and accountant. As a result, Hispanic is now an active housing developer, with a downtown office, co-ownership of twelve rehabbed apartment buildings, and substantial regular income from management fees and syndication proceeds.

On the commercial and industrial side, Chicago–LISC has helped Pyramidwest Development Corporation (a community-based for-profit group that has also done extensive LISC-supported work in housing) promote the growth of its own bank in Lawndale. Pyramidwest wanted to deploy some of the bank's resources into commercial reinvestment in its housing area. It sought LISC support for a new office building to give the bank the additional space it needed and to create rentable space for other business tenants. The Chicago–LISC program officer and national LISC staff opened discussions with the Prudential Insurance Company that eventually led to concessional rate loans of $250,000 by LISC and of $1,250,000 by Prudential as a long-term co-lender. These added up to the first major new investment in the Lawndale area in many years.

The North River Commission has pioneered in commercial development in the multi-ethnic area near the North Shore Channel of the Chicago river. It originated a "facade-rebate" plan, now adopted by the city, to reimburse businesses for part of the costs of refurbishing the fronts of their stores and offices. With LISC help this group is planning to develop a $3.7-million, 50,000-square-foot retail and office building in the heart of its target area.

Two recent developments in Chicago–LISC exemplify the strong local initiative that LISC's programs have helped reinforce. One is that a new local fund-raising campaign is gathering a capital base of $10 million with which LISC can become an independent, separately incorporated entity. Such a capital base would permit Chicago–LISC to cover operating costs out of interest income, establish a larger loan reserve, and assist some $100 million–$150 million worth of promising revitalization projects. The drive to achieve this capital base has been sparked by a $2.5-million challenge grant from the MacArthur Foundation.

Another city-wide initiative that, like that of the Boston Housing Partnership, promotes the institutionalization of LISC in Chicago, is Community Equity Assistance (CEA). Despite development of a number of successful housing projects by major CDCs, Chicago–LISC has found that many well-run CDCs have often been unable to use syndication because their projects are too small or are poorly structured and because the CDCs cannot find equity investors. Community Equity Assistance, a non-profit corporation, will help CDCs structure and market equity syndications of rental housing rehabilitation projects.

CEA will play a very active role in project planning, financing, and development. To overcome the problem of scale, CEA (or a related entity) will assemble perhaps several projects into a package large enough to syndicate on a cost-effective basis. For example, an initial effort involves about 450 units to be developed by six CDCs at a total cost of $11 million. For each proposed project, CEA will prepare a complete financial feasibility analysis. If a project appears to be feasible, CEA will help prepare the syndication offerings and related documents, with a view to uniformity and standardization among projects. CEA will also provide certain guarantees to investors, such as completion of rehabilitation and payment of debt service. With these elements in place, CEA can market limited partner shares on an ongoing basis and develop a large pool of interested investors. Shares at $500,000 each are now being offered, and several have already been subscribed. CEA expects to raise $5 million this year by this means among major Chicago-based business corporations. LISC's Chicago office estimates an immediate market of at least $1 million in equity investments, and an annual market exceeding $3 million.

In addition to syndication proceeds, expected sources of financing include:

> tax-exempt lower floater bonds, the proceeds of which would be used for first mortgages;
> a credit facility that will guarantee payment on the bonds should interest rates rise;
> Community Development Block Grant and housing development grant funds from the city;
> possible short-term bridge financing from LISC;
> a possible limited guarantee on the bonds, to be provided by LISC.

Summing Up and Looking into the Future

As LISC has developed its network of areas of concentration, its approach to projects and investments in all twenty-six areas has developed certain patterns. These are perhaps best described in the words of a group of analysts that have observed LISC from the outside: the four faculty and research staff members of Harvard's Kennedy School of Government who are conducting an independent, three-year evaluation of LISC's programs and performance. In a preliminary report resulting from their first year's research and observation (Vidal, 1986), these evaluators noted that, as a nontraditional approach to neighborhood revitalization, LISC can be perceived in three distinct but related ways:

1. As a social banker channeling capital to community development projects and requiring that recipients exercise financial discipline in all their operations. As a banker, LISC tries to protect its own solvency and preserve its future usefulness, but it is equally interested in the financial health of the organizations it helps and in the larger social and economic effects of its investments.

2. As a result-oriented philanthropist, spending its resources to promote long-term social and economic change. At the same time, LISC insists on financial discipline so that projects are planned and carried out effectively and aided organizations become more self-sufficient and increase their chances for future service to their communities.

3. As a social experiment that could offer a model for widespread change in society's approach to economically and socially distressed areas. As an experiment, LISC provides some experience with a new social policy and, if successful, might increase the use of this model of community revitalization by attracting more funds for itself, encouraging replications of itself, and persuading some existing banks and philanthropic organizations to become more LISC-like.

LISC's ultimate objective, the evaluators observed, is to use the combined effects of the economic enterprises LISC supports and the community institutions it helps to create, to produce economically and socially strong communities to replace poverty, isolation, and dependence. The mechanisms are both economic and social. Successful economic activity and institutions will attract more economic activity and institutions. These, in turn, will increase the incomes of community residents and the wealth of the community at large, thus helping to build a stronger and more stable community. This, in turn, will attract more funds from sources other than LISC. The whole set of effects can be described as the "community effects" of LISC's activities.

The evaluators point out that LISC offers the hypothesis that this method for revitalizing neighborhoods would be superior to many others designed to achieve the same social results. In essence, LISC is pursuing the social objectives of reducing economic and social inequalities through economic development targeted on particular parts of the social environment—poor communities whose economic and social aspirations can be formed into successful economic activity. This approach provides a significant and arguably superior add-on to the traditional main alternative ways of alleviating poverty: income redistribution through welfare programs and the "trickle-down" of economic growth.

On the one hand, welfare programs often reduce poverty at the expense of increased social dependence and make little contribution to community revitalization and stability. Welfare programs not only miss opportunities for local economic development, but actively suppress some of the economic incentives and social attitudes that could stimulate economic activity. On the other hand, the "trickle-down effect" of general economic growth is unreliable for such communities; there is no guarantee that the weak neighborhoods that are the focus of LISC's efforts will participate in the benefits of a general economic growth. Indeed, because they are so unstable, many of these communities continue to deteriorate even during periods of general growth.

LISC hopes that if this machinery can be made to work for any of the communities in which it is now operating, then the operation will be expanded, certainly through a simple increase in LISC's own operations, but also by the appearance of other intermediaries in collaboration with LISC or operating in cities or neighborhoods where LISC is not now operating. Similarly, the funds for such expansions could come from two different sources. One source would be traditional philanthropies that decide to spend their funds on LISC, or LISC-like operations, rather than their current activities. In effect, charitable funds would be donated to LISC or other intermediaries. A second source would be the attraction of wholly new funds, especially social investment funds from corporations, as well as public funds, even if only from local and state sources.

To the evaluators' measured words I would add an assessment of the activities of LISC and intermediaries like it. My assessment uses a different type of vocabulary, but may be as illuminating.

It was once taboo in liberal circles to speak of the underclass phenomenon because to do so implied that the victims, and not society, were to blame for their condition. We appear to be past that stage of doctrinaire blindness, and it is now generally recognized that this is a condition that can no longer be ignored or easily explained away. These are the boats that apparently won't rise with John Kennedy's "rising tide"; few in this underclass have responded well to the multiplicity of interventionist strategies devised over the past several decades. Seemingly intractable, the underclass persists—characterized by alienation, instability, dependency, anger, escapism, and destructiveness. These are conditions that a city ignores at its peril. Not only do they blight the lives of their immediate victims, but their spread threatens blue-collar and working-poor neighbors and the larger community as well. The growth of these conditions undermines the voluntary social contract that reinforces community stability and tranquility.

Where does this leave us? What can we do? If the marketplace and the passage of time don't work with this population, if economic growth alleviates the condition only slightly, and if the expansion of the welfare state tends to increase a condition of dependency and makes matters worse, what policies, strategies, and programs are available to us?

The work of LISC and other intermediaries brings me to define an "antibody" strategy: a plan of identifying and strengthening positive antibodies wherever they can be found in neighborhoods, antibodies that can serve as the beginnings—however scattered and incremental they may appear—of an effective urban neighborhood strategy, neighborhood by neighborhood.

What constitutes an effective antibody and where do they come from? They are generally gifted individuals in poor, blighted areas who become focal points of leadership, energy, creativity, endurance, and entrepreneurship. They usually assume leadership naturally and remain in place for a period of time, eventually establishing an organization or institution to which other talented and motivated people can rally.

Nearly every community has such people and organizations, at least in potential. One need only visit the less inviting neighborhoods of Pittsburgh or Cleveland or the Bronx to see that such antibodies—both people and institutions—are still around, even in a less expansionist time. But you must visit such places to find them; they do not typically rise to media celebrity as they did in the 1960s or 1970s. In many places you will find them only in the background. Most often, they are simply the gifted achievers who might otherwise have gone into more traditional avenues of achievement and instead, usually for personal reasons, have chosen to succeed closer to home.

A strategy that builds on antibodies is necessarily different from the governmental interventions of the past. It is characterized by many more local partnerships of city government, the corporate sector, foundations, and community organizations, sometimes built around agendas and projects too idiosyncratic to suit national programs.

But the individual projects—and even the agendas that surround them—are not the only point of these strategies. They may not even be the most important point. What makes local antibodies effective is that, besides building houses or managing local services, they offer a rallying point for responsible elements of the community to gather. It almost doesn't matter—except to the community itself—what projects they choose. They operate housing and commercial development programs, street patrols, and school-improvement programs; they manage deteriorated dwellings and organize programs for teenage unwed mothers; they provide work-oriented alternatives to welfare or head-start programs. They use whatever government resources are available for such projects, but they consistently resist dependence on purely public resources.

Some would say that these microstrategies for social and economic development still add up to the zero-sum game, or that they are merely apologetic responses to a new, more conservative national mood. To such critics, the minority CDC that screens tenants carefully for its housing project, that patrols its hallways and sidewalks to repel loiterers, drug dealers, and hustlers, is simply pushing the problem people into someone else's neighborhood, or into depopulated urban wastelands.

But the new incrementalists see more than "push-out" here; they see conditions that promote "stay-in" and "come-back-in." As the perimeters of reclaimed neighborhoods expand, and as the climate of positive action, self-help, and cooperation improves, so also do the prospects for families that otherwise teeter between survival and disintegration. Decent housing, revived services, work opportunities, positive peer pressure, and an atmosphere of self-respect, self-control and hope—all these help to hold marginal families together, to hold them on the favored side of these perimeters, and even to draw them back across.

This kind of talk disturbs those who still think—as many of us thought twenty years ago—that small, incremental solutions are too timid for a society with such great problems. And I certainly don't mean to minimize the problems. But if we have learned anything after twenty years of honest experimentation with massive and uniform public policy, it is that no model can be crammed into every situation or community without unwanted and dangerous side effects.

On the other hand, there is vastly more potential in local leadership and community enterprise than has been tapped and supported up to now. Multidimensional community development works for large sectors of the troubled population, at least on the scale we have tried so far. Furthermore, it is something we now know we can do. It widens the area of urban civilization, but does not seal its frontiers. It is often painfully slow, but it can speed up if we can continue to expand the cadre of competent practitioners and intermediaries in the field, and if we can deploy enough resources—both private and public.

We don't know yet how much of their resources the public and the private sectors can or are willing to allocate to this kind of neighborhood development. We don't know how much further public policy will go in creating inducements for this kind of private-sector investment, but we do know there is plenty of room for an increase in both. If these resources can be expanded to the next order of magnitude (from the current hundreds of millions of dollars to billions), this strategy may turn out to be the least costly way to achieve self-sustaining revival of our troubled urban neighborhoods.

Despite my cautious "if's" and "may's" let me venture at least a guess about the prospects for reaching that next level of magnitude in a climate in which the direction of most change is toward less, not more. Given the instability of current domestic policy any prediction here is a high-stake gamble; but if I had to take a stand somewhere among the bulls and the bears, I would plant myself bravely in the middle.

I believe it is at least possible that the current retrenchment in domestic national policy has begun to lose steam, and that the future of federal activity in housing and community development is somewhat less bleak than many people believe. More importantly, there are signs of commitment at the state and local levels, where the stakes in local development are highest, that still offer limited hope for the antibodies of the next generation. In addition, large potential gains may well come from the corporate and philanthropic sectors, whish are still discovering opportunities and benefits in this area, especially in the field of social investment.

I want to be careful not to overstate the case. Local development is ripe for far more growth and refinement than will be possible in the current climate. Some of the potential community leaders of the next generation will find less opportunity in their own neighborhoods than their predecessors did, and these will move on to other fields. But the hardiest will remain, and many of them will succeed. And when the climate changes and the pendulum swings again toward a more active and expansive federal policy, if we play our cards right, the local public and private sectors will already have laid the groundwork for a revival of the inner-city neighborhood as the first step in the mobility process for all immigrants, both domestic and foreign.

References

Alinsky, Saul. 1946. *Reveille for Radicals*. University of Chicago Press.
———. 1971. *Rules for Radicals*. New York: Random House.
Conant, James B. 1961. *Slums and Suburbs*. New York: McGraw Hill.
Harrington, Michael. 1962. *The Other America: Poverty in the United States*. New York: Penguin Books.

LISC (Local Initiatives Support Corporation). 1987. *Report of Progress, 1986.* New York.

Vidal, Avis C., et al. 1986. *Stimulating Community Development: An Assessment of Local Initiatives Support Corporation.* Cambridge, Mass.: State, Local, and Intergovernmental Center, J.F.K. School of Government, Harvard University.

9

Child Care and Privatization under Reagan

SHEILA B. KAMERMAN AND ALFRED J. KAHN

The need for day care for the children of working parents has greatly increased over the past 20 years and is expected to continue into the 1990s. More married women are entering the work force than ever before and more are remaining at work during their child-rearing years. For many single parents with small children, child care services enabling the parent to work are a necessity . . .

At present the Federal Government is shifting away from giving direct support and subsidies to day care centers and toward an emphasis on tax credits for parents and tax incentives for employers. This trend is likely to continue.
U.S. DEPARTMENT OF LABOR, 1982

Child care is essential for working parents to meet their responsibilities. In order to help families have flexibility and to be able to determine the setting and type of care for their children, we are working to encourage greater private sector involvement in child care, we have supported modifications to the dependent care deduction and we have proposed that nonprofit dependent care facilities be classified as tax-exempt organizations . . . The President's Private Sector Task Force has been actively involved in promoting employer supported day care.
JO ANN GASPER, Deputy Assistant Secretary, Office of Human Development Services, DHHS (U.S. House of Representatives, 1984a, pp. 98–99)

Child-care services are acknowledged by Jo Ann Gasper, the official spokesperson for the Reagan Administration on child policy, to be of "immediate concern to families." She reminds us, also, that "women work for economic reasons. Two paychecks are frequently necessary to support a family. In addition, the number of working single parent families has increased. Child care is essential for such working parents" (U.S. House of Representatives, 1984a, p. 98).

There is no general disagreement with the Administration about the importance of child-care services, at the very least as a service for the children of working parents, or about the high and still rising rate of labor force participation among women with young children. Where there is disagreement is about: who should pay for this service, how, and how much; how the service should be delivered and by whom; whether, how, and by whom the service should be regulated; and finally, whether the existing supply of services is sufficient to meet consumer demand.

Child-care services in many ways constitute the prototypical illustration of "privatization" as an explicit policy of the Reagan Administration. The child-care industry has always been a "mixed economy," in that privately funded and operated programs have always coexisted with totally public programs. The Reagan Administration set out to change this by: reducing direct federal expenditures for child-care services; stressing a policy of subsidizing demand rather than supply and creating an incentive for parents/consumers to purchase care in the open market; encouraging private-sector providers to produce and deliver services; eliminating the federal role in setting minimum standards for federally funded child care; and stressing the value of informal rather than formal care. We address two questions: How effective has the Administration been in carrying out its policies? What have been the consequences?

The Reagan Legislative Changes

There are two major ways for government to subsidize child care. One is to provide financing for those who provide the care—supply subsidies. The other is to provide financial assistance to those who use the care—demand subsidies. In addition, government can develop and monitor standards for the subsidized care.

In 1980, federal expenditures for child care were $2.8 billion.[1] Supply subsidies accounted for roughly $1.6 billion, about 60 percent of the total. The largest single item was Social Security Title XX funds, amounting

[1] The estimates that follow are compiled from a variety of sources. For expenditure data and trends in child care at the end of the 1970s, see Kamerman and Kahn, 1981, pp. 185–190. Relevant studies of the supply of day care (preschool programs were not surveyed) include Abt Associates 1979, 1980; also see Blank, 1983, 1984; Duval et al., 1982.

to $600 million.[2] This is the social services title of the Social Security Act under which child-care providers meeting specified standards received funds to provide care for children of low-income families. The next largest item was Head Start (about $0.8 billion), implemented as a part-day compensatory program for income-eligible children, but beginning by 1980 to serve working parents' needs through all-day programs as well (10–15 percent of participating children).[3] The only other major supply program was the Child Care Food Program, with expenditures of $239 billion going to finance day-care center lunch programs.[4]

Demand subsidies accounted for almost $1.2 billion, about 40 percent of the total. The largest of these was the Dependent Care Tax Credit (about $1 billion).[5] This credit amounted to 20 percent of child-care expenses up to a maximum of $2,000 for one dependent, and $4,000 for two or more. The other two demand subsidies were for welfare-eligible mothers: $0.12 billion in child-care disregards (credit in budget computation for child-care costs), for working mothers on the Aid to Families with Dependent Children (AFDC) program, and a little less for mothers in job training or placements under the Work Incentive (WIN) program.[6]

Finally, a set of federal day-care regulations were to become effective on July 1, 1981. These had been developed through a research and public information and reaction process over the previous decade. Because of the long anticipation process, according to an Office of Human Development Services report (U.S. Department of Health and Human Services, 1982), most providers were already in compliance with the proposed federal standards.

Since most federal reporting requirements were dropped as part of the Reagan initiatives, available data to estimate federal child-care expenditures under Reagan are incomplete. Nevertheless, the general picture is clear. There is no doubt that the child-care picture had changed substantially by 1986. According to the best estimates we have, federal expenditures on child care in fiscal 1986, including the Dependent Care Tax Credit, were $5.5 billion—increased only by the expanded tax credit. Di-

---

[2] Federal funds estimates are from data supplied by Patricia Devine Hawkins of the Administration for Children, Youth, and Families, Department of Health and Human Services; additional expenditure data are cited in U.S. House of Representatives, 1984a, 1984b. State add-ons are estimated at $929 million in 1980 dollars. The 1980–1985 adjustment for inflation is 31 percent, according to Congressional Budget Office personal communications. Fiscal year 1986 began in October 1985.

[3] U.S. House of Representatives, 1984a, and Blank, 1983.

[4] Blank, 1983.

[5] Congressional Budget Office, 1981.

[6] Duval et al., 1982.

TABLE 9.1 Federal Expenditures for Child Care, Fiscal Years 1980 and 1986

	Expenditure in Millions of Dollars	
Programs	1980	1986
Title XX (SSBG)	$ 600[a]	$ 387[a]
Head Start	766[b]	1,040
AFDC Disregard (Title IV–A)	120[c]	35
Child Care Food Program	239[a]	501[a]
Title IV–C (WIN)	115[d]	0
ARC (Appalachian Regional Commission) Child Dev.	11[b]	1
Employer-Provided Child Care	0	110[e]
Dependent Care Tax Credit	956[a]	3,410[a]
Total	$2,807	$5,484
Total without Tax Credit	$1,851	$2,074[f]

[a] ACYF estimate provided by Patricia Divine-Hawkins. A recent Department of Labor report re-estimates this total as $660 million for 1986. If correct, this increase would still not change the conclusion that supply subsidies did not keep up with inflation between 1980 and 1986 and that the real increase was in tax credits (U.S. Department of Labor, 1988).

[b] Testimony, Jo Ann Gasper, Deputy Assistant Secretary for Social Services, *Child Care: Beginning A National Initiative* (Washington, D.C.: Government Printing Office, 1984).

[c] E. Duval et al., "AFDC: Characteristics of Recipients in 1979," *Social Security Bulletin* 45 (4): 4–19.

[d] Congressional Budget Office (CBO).

[e] CBO, based on Joint Tax Committee estimates.

[f] Since the inflation rate was 31 percent between 1980 and 1985, according to CBO, this total would have had to be $2,425 to sustain the 1980 direct expenditure level.

NOTE: State and local education and social service expenditure not included in table.

SOURCE: Reprinted from *Child Care: Facing the Hard Choices,* by Alfred J. Kahn and Sheila B. Kamerman (Dover, Mass.: Auburn House; 1987), p. 19, by permission of the publisher.

rect budgetary supply subsidies were down by $350 million in constant dollars.

The distribution between supply and demand subsidies thus had changed considerably. Currently the demand subsidy constitutes almost two-thirds of the total. Supply subsidies accounted for under $2.1 billion in 1986. The major reason for this was the Omnibus Budget Reconciliation Act (OBRA) of 1981. This cut Title XX funds by one-fifth, and amended Title XX to create the Social Services Block Grant, which states could allocate as they chose and for which there was no state matching requirement. Head Start was not cut, increasing slightly in real terms to about $1.0 billion in 1986. The child-care food programs (also under OBRA) were cut initially from $0.24 billion but then raised to $0.5 billion.[7]

Demand subsidies, in contrast, increased absolutely and became a much larger proportion of the total. The major increase was in the Dependent Care Tax Credit—to $3.4 billion in 1986 (almost triple the 1980 total in real terms).[8] This was the result of 1982 tax legislation, which increased the credit to 30 percent for taxpayers with incomes of $10,000 or less and permitted the credit to be taken even by those who did not itemize their deductions. The percentage credit was then reduced by one point for each $2,000 of income up to $28,000. The maximum expenditure for one dependent was raised to $2,400 and for two or more to $4,800. (The actual tax credit is now $480 for one child and $960 for two or more.) The child-care disregard for working mothers on AFDC was continued, but a reduction in the maximum expenditures allowed, coupled with a lower percentage of working AFDC recipients, led to a decline in this expenditure to $0.35 billion.

The Reagan Administration also added a new demand subsidy, financed through the tax system—employer-sponsored child care. This is estimated to have amounted to $0.1 billion in 1986.[9] The Internal Revenue Code now explicitly excludes from an employee's gross income any payments by an employer for dependent care assistance, if the assistance is provided under a plan that meets certain conditions (Section 129 of the Internal Revenue Code).

Another related subsidy provided through the tax system is a salary reduction plan: the employee and the employer agree that the employer will lower the taxable income to the employee and set aside the difference, between that amount and what would have been the employee's salary, for spending on child care (or certain other benefits, such as medical care). In effect, the employee spends pretax, "cheaper" dollars for child care and the employer has a lower wage base on which to pay Social Security and unemployment insurance taxes. Both sides benefit.

Finally, under the OBRA amendments, the OBRA changes canceled the proposed federal day-care regulations and left in place the "applicable standards" of state and local laws.

Assessment of the impact of the Reagan Administration's efforts to pri-

---

[7] Blank, 1983, 1984; Blank and Wilkins, 1985.

[8] Congressional Budget Office, 1983, Table A–1.

[9] Congressional Budget Office, 1983, Table A–1.

vatize child-care services is complicated by two factors. First, as noted, the reporting requirements previously imposed on the states were eliminated, as was the publication of regular reports by the federal government on social services expenditures, users, and services.[10] Added to this is the absence of any recent consumer or supply survey regarding the number of child-care places available and the numbers of children in different types of services. Estimating effects, therefore, is hampered by data limitations.

Second, labor force participation of women, particularly married women with young children, has continued to increase rapidly. For example, labor force participation of married women with children under age 6 increased from 45 percent in 1980 to 54 percent in 1986; most of these mothers worked full time. Half of all children under age 6 had working mothers in 1986. The proportion of young children in working families increased from 42 percent to 51 percent in two-parent, husband-and-wife families. This trend increases the demand for child care, other things being equal, and makes it more difficult to disentangle the effects of the privatization initiative from the effects of the demographic pressures.

These data limitations notwithstanding, the work of the Children's Defense Fund, combined with continuing research by ourselves and others, makes it possible to identify at least the direction of effects in several areas. We focus our discussion on five facets of the child-care market that are expected to be influenced by the privatization initiative: consumer choice and sovereignty, supply of and types of services, equity, quality of care, and efficiency.

Consumer Choice and Sovereignty

The emphasis by the Reagan Administration on increasing the relative importance of demand subsidies was deliberate. Permitting parental

---

[10] The Office of Human Development Services last published *Social Services U.S.A.: 1977–1978* in 1980. This report, published quarterly from 1976, with three annual summaries, included statistical tables, summaries, and analyses of services under the Social Security Act, Titles XX, IVB, and IVA/C for the fifty states and the District of Columbia. Day-care services were given special attention. Data were provided on the total expenditure under Title XX for day care, and the amounts spent for direct provision, purchase of services from other public agencies, and purchase from private agencies. According to the last issue of this report, $709 million of Title XX federal funds were spent in FY 1978 and 580,000 children were served. Similar data are provided for child-care funded through Titles IVB, IVA (AFDC), and IVC (WIN). No such data are now available. The best source for subsequent child-care expenditures data are *estimates* from the Children's Defense Fund's annual survey of the states. However, states classify their child-care expenditures in different ways now and many no longer distinguish between federal and state funds.

choice and responding to parent/consumer preferences was a major goal of those favoring privatization of child-care services, and demand strategies were thought of as the primary way to reach this goal.

Did this new emphasis on demand strategies in fact result in a wider range of child-care options for parents? For those with incomes high enough to take advantage of the Dependent Care Tax Credit, the answer is certainly yes. Increased subsidization occurred under Reagan and the subsidy could go for a wider variety of care.

There are no data on how parents spend this subsidy, but it can be spent on far more varied forms of child care than can a grant given directly to child-care providers. Thus, family day care, in-home care, and various forms of out-of-home group care (centers, nursery schools, prekindergartens, kindergartens) all qualify under the credit as child-care providers for children under age 6, as do summer camps and various after-school activities for school-aged children.

Equally certain, those who can take advantage of the increased flexibility under the credit are not the poorest families. Of the 4.6-million families claiming the Dependent Care Tax Credit in 1981, largely for child care, the majority of families (64 percent) were above the median income level. Only 7 percent had incomes below $10,000. There were widespread complaints that the credit did not benefit lower-income families and provided only limited support to lower-middle-income families.

Nonetheless, child-care advocates lobbied successfully in 1983 to get the federal Dependent Care Tax Credit added to the short income tax form (1040A), so that it might better serve low- and moderate-income taxpayers. This objective was achieved. In 1983, there were 6.4-million families claiming the dependent care credit—an increase of 1.4-million claims from the 1982 total. Those with adjusted gross income under $20,000 represented one-half the increase. Forty-nine percent of the $2.1 billion in tax benefits claimed through the credit for 1983 went to taxpayers with adjusted gross incomes under $25,000; 22 percent went to those with adjusted gross incomes under $15,000.

For families with income too low to benefit from the Dependent Care Tax Credit, the total funds available to subsidize child care were smaller. For them too, however, the range of child care for which the subsidies could be used increased. This development was due to two factors, both related to the conversion of Title XX funds to social services block grants to the states.

The first factor is that several states, faced with a curtailment of funds, reduced the proportion of these funds spent on child-care providers and turned instead to use of the AFDC disregard. As noted, this has the effect of providing working AFDC mothers with funds (up to a maximum of

$160 per child per month after the OBRA changes) to pay for child care of their choice.

The second factor was that several states responded to the freeze in Title XX by altering their day-care financing from direct public delivery (publicly operated programs) and direct purchase of service contracts with providers, to purchasing care on a per-child basis or other types of vendor/voucher programs.

Thus, for example, in a three-county area of Florida (and later through much of the state) all block grant child-care funds have been channeled into one agency that determines eligibility, rates providers, sets maximum reimbursement rates, and pays for individual "slots" or places, once parents choose the provider. It is not the provider who is given a grant under this system. The payment follows the child. Parents choose a program from a list of approved (licensed) providers and if the parents qualify, the provider is reimbursed by the county. (The working parent may pay the provider a partial fee.) Similarly, the California Alternative Payment Program, with state funds subsidizing a vendor/voucher program, has made it possible for public child-care dollars to be used to pay for family day care for the first time, and to expand the supply and variety of infant-care services, a service in very short supply earlier.

Other states have designed their own vendor/voucher programs, but the major strategy is the same: to have the public dollars follow the child to whichever provider the parent prefers, usually limited only to the choice of a licensed caregiver, but obviously limited also to one whose fee is covered by what the parent can pay plus what the agency will reimburse. Typical programs may involve:

giving the consumer authorization to purchase child care and paying or reimbursing the provider either through a public agency or a special private agency given funds to pay for care or given control over how they are spent;
giving the consumer a "voucher" to purchase the service directly;
using the AFDC disregard to permit the consumer to pay cash for the service.

One result of this shift from supply to demand subsidies has been a significant increase in the mix of services available generally, and in the diversity of services used by those in receipt of public subsidies in particular. The heads of several proprietary chains have indicated that the child-care tax credit was a special boon to their companies since it provided an indirect public subsidy to providers that would never have qualified for Title XX funds under proposed standards or been eligible under child-care policies in many states. Consumers who qualified for Title XX child care under the earlier system could enroll their children only in specific centers.

Clearly, the diversity of services available has increased. For many parents, this means that they have a wider range of options in choosing child care. For middle-class parents in particular, the range of choices is greater and they are assured of at least some modest subsidy regardless of the type of care used.

It may be worth noting here that part of the diversity comes from the growth in public preschool programs, a recent development that has occurred on the state and local levels in response to factors other than the Administration's policies. Further development of such public-school-based programs clearly would expand access to group programs. Some minority groups and organizations object to this development as less responsive to children's and their parents' needs than the more traditional social welfare day care and Head Start systems are said to be (National Black Child Development Institute, 1986). In this sense, they are against public provision of the type stipulated in the 1980s, preferring the more traditional systems that stimulated the entry of community organizations into the child-care service delivery field. This is a type of privatization. For that reason, such groups could be said to be implicitly in favor of the Reagan thrust (U.S. Department of Labor, 1984). We doubt it. A different kind of privatization is stimulated by the move toward demand subsidies.

But for low-income parents the picture is mixed. Some among those who qualify for Title XX funds now are able to place their children in a center of their choice. Most directly subsidized centers under the prior pattern tended to be in low-income neighborhoods and were therefore attended largely by minority children. Parents may now have more opportunity to choose an integrated center, if they wish, or they may be able to choose family day care, if they prefer.

At the same time, however, for many low-income families, the shift to a demand subsidy and the simultaneous decline in Title XX funds means a reduction in available options. Their problem is the far more restricted eligibility for Title XX child care and the lower eligibility levels set by states coping with inadequate budgets. States allow block grant child-care support only to women actually working or in training (and often restrict the time period for the latter, sometimes for the former). Since a good number of states now give help only to the very poorest, in most places more than 90 percent of the eligibles for state-subsidized child care (not counting protective services cases, refugee programs, and limited programs for the handicapped) are employed single mothers with very low salaries.

Some states do not have sliding fee scales and drop a mother as soon as a small salary increase puts her income above the threshold. Parents who once preferred center care or preschool programs now find themselves in a situation where they may no longer qualify for any subsidized care at all, and thus are left to use whatever care they can themselves afford, often poor quality, informal family day care. Even for those who still qualify, the prevailing reimbursement rate may not permit their child's enrollment in a high-quality program. The $160 per month maximum under the AFDC work expense child-care allowance will certainly not pay for decent quality group care in almost any state; and AFDC parents are clearly not in a position to supplement that amount further. Many use underground, unregulated family day care.

The Supply

Economists tell us that if consumers have greater purchasing power there is an increase in effective demand and the market will respond by expanding supply. Economists tell us, also, that if regulations are reduced, the numbers of providers as well as the numbers of services available will increase (Rose-Ackerman, 1983, 1986; Young and Nelson, 1973; Robins and Wiener, 1978). These expectations are repeated by those who favor privatization. The Reagan Administration expanded consumer (demand) subsidies and essentially eliminated federal regulations. Did the supply of child-care services increase as a consequence?

According to the Children's Defense Fund, twenty-four states were serving fewer children in 1985 than in 1981 (Blank and Wilkins, 1985); despite the increase in female labor force participation rates, seven more states were serving the same number of children; only seventeen states had increased the number of children served. These reports by the states may not tell the full story since the statistics only cover the social welfare (that is, income-tested) stream.

At the same time, it should be noted, at least half the states have been paying growing attention to public kindergarten and preschool programs for four-year-olds. States such as Delaware, Florida, and Kentucky have mandated availability of kindergarten for all five-year-olds. Some places, like New York City, North Carolina, and Tennessee, have moved toward full-day kindergarten (six or six-and-a-half hours), comparable to a full school day. And some states—including South Carolina, Texas, Vermont, and several districts in Pennsylvania—have established part-day programs for four-year-olds. There is a parallel increase in schools providing before- and after-school programs, too, but here we are focusing only on care for children under age 6.[11]

---

[11] Seligson et al., 1983, is a major source of information on these services; also, U.S. Bureau of the Census, 1987.

The large proprietary child-care chains have grown substantially during these years, either by expanding internally or by purchasing other chain operations. Thus, for example, at the end of 1980, Kinder-Care—the largest commercial child-care service chain—was operating about 510 centers serving 53,000 children. By 1986 it was operating 1,050 centers serving more than 100,000 children.[12] Children's World—the third-largest chain and one of those described by others in the industry as a "high quality child care operation"—was operating eighty-four centers in seven states in 1980; by 1986 the company was operating 248 centers in a dozen states.[13]

An "experiment" in moving toward demand subsidies began earlier, in the late 1970s, in California.[14] This Alternative Payment Program, as it is called, was conceived initially as a cost-effective method of increasing the supply of child-care services in the state and expanding the variety of program sponsors offering subsidized care. A major impetus in supporting the initiative was a desire to increase the supply of infant care. California data suggest the device has been effective, in particular in providing a direct public subsidy for family day care for the first time for working parents and in increasing the numbers of providers who now offer infant care.

Nationally, there also is a significant volume of activity involving regulated and unregulated family care funded by social services block grants, sliding fees, and various other kinds of vender/voucher programs. There is no way to estimate the effect this activity has had on supply.

Finally, in advancing a policy of encouraging private-sector initiatives, the Reagan Administration created various incentives for employers to sponsor child-care services for their employees. A 1978 national survey, updated in 1981, found nineteen day-care centers sponsored by industry at or near the workplace, seven sponsored by labor unions, fourteen by government agencies, and seventy-five by hospitals. In addition, 200 centers were sponsored by the military (Perry, 1980; Women's Bureau, 1981). Another survey shortly thereafter identified 415 civilian employers as sponsoring some forms of child-care services. This highly publicized study found that about half of these employers were hospitals—a result of the special problems these institutions had experienced in the late 1970s in hiring and retaining nurses. The union-operated services had

[12] See testimony by Gail Schmitt, district manager, Kinder-Care Learning Center, in U.S. House of Representatives, 1984b, pp. 72–75; 1980 data from Argus Research Report, 1980; and 1985 data from Kinder-Care press release of 1987.

[13] Robert Benson, then president of Children's World, personal communication, interview notes; Children's Defense Fund reported 187 centers for 1985 (Blank and Wilkins, 1985).

[14] See Kahn and Kamerman, 1987.

declined to four. Although about 200 nonhospital private employers offered some form of child-care-related service, only forty-three were on- or near-site service programs and seventy-five involved only modest financial contributions (Burud, Aschbacher, and McCroskey, 1984).

Dr. Dana Friedman (1985), a researcher at The Conference Board (a nonprofit, national business research organization) and recognized expert on employer-sponsored child care, estimated recently that about 3,000 out of the more than 6 million employers in the country offer some form of child-care sponsorship. Once again, hospitals dominate the on-site providers, of which there are only 550: 400 hospitals and 150 others. The major types of child-care help offered by these employers are:

paying for information and referral services for their employees (500);
obtaining discounts, in particular from large commercial chains, for employees using the chains' services (300);
setting up flexible spending accounts or salary reduction plans that include child-care coverage, often with no financial contributions from the employer but using employees' pretax dollars (80).

Although the increase in the expressed interest on the part of employers has been substantial over the last five years, the numbers of employers involved is still minuscule; and the actual increase in the total number of employer-provided child-care slots in licensed group facilities is practically zero. Unless something very different occurs in the future, employers are neither going to establish new centers for their employees' children nor contract for new centers to be established. Nor are they likely to subsidize a significant part of the costs of providing, or purchasing, such a service. Employers' contributions to the child-care scene will be limited largely to providing information and referral services to their employees to help them locate services, facilitating employees' obtaining a modest discount from for-profit service providers, or facilitating employees' use of pretax dollars to pay for care.

On balance, has the overall supply of child-care services increased? Probably. Certainly the total number of day-care centers of all sorts has doubled, but because definitions have changed, comparisons are uncertain. Have the Reagan Administration policies, rather than the demographic pressures, led to this increase? It is unclear.

Eliminating federal regulations undoubtedly led some large commercial chains to expand into states with standards that are low enough to ensure the operator a profit (and in the case of high-quality operators, high enough to let them be competitive). Increased use of demand subsidies also may have led to some growth in supply. But it may have had the main effect of making family day care more visible in some places (a good thing but not necessarily leading to an increase in the numbers providing such care) or of leading to some shifting around in the market (as when children were moved from centers to family day care because their families lost eligibility for Title XX services) or both, rather than any real growth.

The rise in female labor force participation rates of married women with very young children has certainly increased the use of child care and the pressure for more services while the social service funding streams failed to grow and even the tax credits did not offer adequate resources. This is one of several factors in the growing move toward public school involvement in creating preschools for the three-to-four-year-olds, and full-day kindergarten for the five-year-olds.[15] This is a development suggesting clearly that the existing supply of services for three-to-five-year-olds is either inadequate, or not of the quality or type parents prefer, or not at a price they can afford. In any case, this state-level expansion of public school–based programs, largely financed by state and local funds, is a development that has emerged independent of any explicit Reagan Administration policy; nor has it been acknowledged by the Administration as important or worth encouraging.

To conclude this section, we note that a Reagan Administration child-care spokeswoman insisted as late as 1987 that there was no evidence indicating a shortage of places, because there is an unknown and indeterminate amount of informal care available that is as good as or better than professional care.

Equity and the Distributional Impact

Those who object to the decline in publicly operated and publicly sponsored nonprofit programs, and the concomitant growth in the private for-profit delivery system, argue that these developments have left middle- and upper-income families better off and low- and moderate-income families worse off. Are they correct?

As noted earlier, direct federal funding for child-care services has declined over the past five years, when one adjusts expenditures to take account of inflation. The "decline" effect is greater in the light of increased demand. According to the Children's Defense Fund, the leading child advocacy organization in the country, controlling for inflation, Title XX child-care dollars (both federal and state) are now about 75 percent of

[15] Obviously, other important factors in this development have been the increased concern with the quality of education generally, state interest in a more skilled labor force for economic development, optimism about the impact of early schooling on deprived youngsters, and the growing conviction that early childhood education pays off generally in the primary and secondary school years. For a discussion of the developments concerning school-based programs, see Kahn and Kamerman, 1987.

what they would have been in 1982 if OBRA had not been passed and if Title XX had not been turned into a block grant program. Head Start funding has been increased modestly, as has child-care food money.

At the same time, however, tax benefits for child care have exploded: from less than $1 billion in 1980 to $1.2 billion in 1982 and more than $3.4 billion in 1986. Tax subsidies for employer-sponsored child care increase this still more.

The total federal expenditure on child care increased during these years, but it would have declined except for expenditures through the tax system. Almost all the real growth is through these indirect subsidies and many such subsidies are not available to the working poor. Some of this has occurred because the Administration wanted to reduce direct federal social expenditures and some because it has favored lower taxes.

Families that qualify for Title XX child-care services are likely to have very low or quite moderate incomes. Even generous income eligibility criteria—60 percent of median income, for example (far higher than in many states today)—would limit receipt of these services to families with incomes under $14,500 in 1981 and not very much higher in 1985. Indeed, in some states, a single parent earning $10 a week more than minimum wage would not qualify for Title XX child care. Moreover, as indicated, more than 90 percent of the families who do qualify are single-parent, mother-only families, overwhelmingly low income. (And Head Start is required to serve definitionally poor families: 90 percent of the children enrolled must be from families with income below the poverty level.) Finally, the $160 per child per month cap imposed on demand subsidy under the AFDC child-care disregard is lower than the prevailing fees for group care throughout the country.

The large commercial chains estimate they have a 20 percent vacancy rate in their centers. This is not because parents have enough child care; it is because low-income parents cannot afford the fees these chains claim they must charge to survive. Similarly, there are reports of nonprofit centers closing. The reasons given are similar: inadequate direct public financing, the inability of low- and moderate-income parents to afford the fees, and the inability to stay in business charging the fees that these and other families in their communities can pay. Providers—whether in Texas or North Carolina, New York or California—talk about the gap between what their costs are and what the parents in their communities can afford.

Still another supply problem has emerged from this move toward the market by encouraging demand rather than supply subsidies. Most private, for-profit providers—the large commercial chains, for example—will not locate their services in low-income neighborhoods. Time and again senior executives of these firms explain their marketing strategies by stressing careful selection of sites. A major highway, a location between a middle-class residential area and a commercial area, a community with high female labor force participation rates, and husband-and-wife families with two earners and incomes more than 50 percent above median family income—these are what they seek.

One Texas child-care agency director pointed out to us that Texas has continued to provide both supply and demand subsidies because the state and the cities recognize that private providers will not enter low-income or minority communities. If these communities are to be served, a public—or publicly subsidized—center must be established; otherwise families living there will have no options at all.

Demand subsidies in child care, as in other fields, assume that an adequate supply of services will be forthcoming. The issue is, of course, at what price and for whom. The shift to a policy of indirect expenditure from one of direct expenditure has occurred at the expense of those who benefited most from the direct expenditure—the lower-income families. The decline in direct funding (supply subsidies) has led to fewer low-income children being served within the organized service system—and in some instances to the unavailability of formal services for them—while service options and subsidies have increased for the middle-income groups.

Quality of Care

As noted, a major change implemented by the Reagan Administration was elimination of the Federal Interagency Day Care Requirements (FIDCR), subsequently referred to as the Health, Education and Welfare Day Care Requirements. These minimum standards for federally funded child-care programs were established in 1980 after more than a decade of debate and research, and were due to be implemented on October 1, 1981. Before that date, OBRA 1981 was passed and Title XX became social service block grants, in effect eliminating federal standards along with all other requirements imposed by Title XX.

Most states at that time were said to be already in compliance or close to it in 1980, and many private providers who received no federal funds were upgrading their standards nevertheless, because the FIDCR were emerging as the preferred norm.[16] What has happened to the quality of care, compared to the standards being observed in 1980?

By 1984, according to a survey of states conducted by the Children's Defense Fund, thirty-three states had lowered their child-care standards for what had been Title XX programs (Blank, 1984). At the same time,

[16] U.S. Department of Health and Human Services, 1982. There is some debate about the accuracy of the state reports, but this is not relevant to the present discussion.

many states had reduced the numbers of their inspectors or inspections of service programs, or both, and followed a far less rigorous approach to enforcement than previously. And some states changed their policy of licensing family day-care homes to one of requiring only that providers register and list themselves as meeting standards.

Beginning in 1984, a rash of incidents of sexual abuse of children was reported to have occurred in child-care centers around the country, many documented, others unsubstantiated. Documented reports and allegations continue. It has been suggested by critics of the current policy that the decline in monitoring and the lowering of standards are directly responsible. Evidence is not available to substantiate or refute that claim.

Some supporters of current policy criticize state licensing and registration requirements as failing to achieve their basic objective (to ensure minimum health and safety standards for children) and artificially restricting supply. One report critical of regulation states that it leads instead to an increase in the costs of service by "driving providers underground and limiting the number of children who can benefit," and further that "Unnecessary regulations are stifling the supply of day care at a time when the need has never been greater and shows every sign of continuing to surge" (Lehrmann and Pace, 1985, p. 1).

When the issue of supply of adequate quality is raised, such critics of regulation increasingly stress consumer/parent assessment of quality as the preferred approach. How is this working?

Beginning in the 1970s, but increasing in the 1980s, a few states—and many organizations—established child-care information and referral services.[17] These services offer parents information about all types of child care, including fees, available space, and so forth. In addition, almost all issue or publish guidelines for parents to help them choose among the diversity of programs available. They identify the characteristics associated with good quality and offer help to parents trying to decide which program is best for their child. Some do this briefly; others do it in more detail, including the offer of extensive counseling.

Although parents seem more aware than formerly of the importance to their child of a good experience, it is not known how many parents can and do assess differential quality correctly as a consequence of the educational or counseling resource expansion.

As part of the ongoing debate about what is happening to the quality of child-care services, some have expressed concern about the growth since 1980 in the numbers and percentage of for-profit child-care providers, in particular, the large commercial child-care chains. They are convinced that proprietary child care lends itself to the same types of

---

[17] For a good history of this development, see Levine, 1982.

scandals as have been documented in proprietary nursing homes, and that making a profit out of child care will inevitably lead to cost cutting and a decline in quality.

The current estimate is that about half the licensed day care centers (those licensed under health and welfare regulations, not education) in the states are under for-profit auspices (compared to less than one-quarter in 1981). How does the quality of care they offer compare with that given by the nonprofit agencies?

Our own very limited assessment of the for-profit and nonprofit services reveals no consistent pattern. Good quality programs are as likely to be found among the for-profits as among the nonprofits, and vice versa. The for-profits do not include the model, experimental programs with very high staff/child ratios and highly trained and well-paid professional staff; but apart from these special programs, which are very few in any case, the whole gamut is covered. Thus, visiting Children's World centers in Colorado and Palo Alto Preschools in Arizona, we found well-equipped, well-staffed programs, with happy, healthy, and spontaneous youngsters, much interchange between children and staff, and a generally positive atmosphere. We also saw both for-profit and nonprofit programs in several regions of the country with sparse equipment, limited space, few and untrained staff, and children sitting around watching TV in darkened rooms.

There has been no comprehensive and rigorous research comparing the quality of programs under for-profit and nonprofit auspices, so the issue remains unsettled and important. One statewide study in Connecticut is near completion and preliminary findings have been made available (Newton and Kagan, 1985). This study found no differences between nonprofit and for-profit centers in average group size. Systematic differences along other dimensions were found, however. Nonprofit centers have higher staff/child ratios (they have more volunteers). The nonprofits also have more special equipment, rank higher on caregivers' behavior in relation to children (and caregiver/child interactions), have more racially and ethnically diverse child groups, and serve more low-income children. On the other hand, for-profit centers offer more hours of service per week than the nonprofits and tend to be open for a greater part of the calendar year.

Finally, in assessing the differences between the proprietaries and the public—or publicly subsidized nonprofit—centers, we note a few unresolved issues: In many communities around the country, the for-profits are fighting against the growth of public (free) preschool programs, accusing them of constituting "unfair competition" and "stealing our bread and butter business—the 3- and 4-year-olds—just as they have already

taken over the 5-year-olds."[18] They consider it unfair for public policy to
have left them a service vacuum to fill and now to threaten their large
capital investments and livelihoods by creating school-based, tax-financed competition. These same providers reject the notion of concentrating their service on the younger group—those under three—because,
they say, infant and toddler care is only viable at present because it is
subsidized by the higher-than-cost fees they charge for the three- and
four-year-olds.

On Balance? There appears to be some decline in the quality of the
services available to low-income families. Poor parents are often limited
in what they can obtain; and much of this is of poorer quality than in the
early 1980s. There seems to be a very wide range in the quality of care
available to and used by parents who purchase care in the marketplace.
Some affluent parents use excellent care and some use poor quality care.
Whether parents are unable to judge quality differentials—or are unwilling to pay for such care even if they can afford it and can identify it—is
unclear. Whether the auspice is profit-making does not seem to correlate
with the quality of care provided. In any case, parents do not typically
ask whether a center is operated for profit or not. But the very existence
of such a wide range suggests to some that leaving the issue of quality
control entirely up to the consumer may not necessarily provide effective
quality assurance.

Efficiency

The conventional wisdom is that the private sector is more efficient
than the public. A repeated statement by those encouraging privatization
of child-care services has been that substituting demand for supply subsidies and permitting parents to buy what they want in the market, substituting private providers for public, and eliminating regulations, would
inexorably lead to an increased supply of services, and at lower cost. We
have already dealt with the issue of supply. Here we turn to the question
of cost. Is child-care provided by the private sector cheaper than that provided by government? Obviously, for this question to make sense, it must
be considered in the context of service quality. A cheaper service of lower
quality is a different service. Once again, we do not have the data to answer this question definitively. We can shed substantial light on it, however, by considering the experience of North Carolina, about which there
is considerable information.

---

[18] Interviewee from a proprietary child-care chain who did not wish to be cited. News-
papers were full of such statements early in 1985, when a proposal to establish a program
for four-year-olds in the school system was being debated in North Carolina. See *The News
and Observer*, Raleigh, N.C., February, 1985.

North Carolina is one of the leading states in the quantity of child-care services available. It had a county-operated day-care system in the 1970s that included a large number of high-quality centers serving poor children. As the demand for care increased, more families qualified for subsidized care. As the state picked up more Title XX funds, the county governments purchased slots in the private sector for children for whom there were not spaces in the county-operated centers. These slots, however, were reimbursed at far lower levels than the cost of care in the public centers. As the costs in the public centers continued to rise, the disparity increased. Since the public centers were considered to be the highest quality centers in the state, there was growing resentment expressed by parents whose income was quite modest but not low enough to quality for Title XX care in the public centers, and by parents whose children, even though covered by Title XX, were enrolled in the private centers.

In the late 1970s the state legislature set up a study commission to analyze and review the costs of day care in the state. The commission criticized the county operations and recommended that the state fund the counties only at the same level per child-care place as the counties were reimbursing the private providers.

The main impact of the commission's report and the subsequent follow-up activities was that, almost throughout the state, the counties gave over their public centers to nonprofit organizations to operate. (This and similar processes elsewhere led to the virtual disappearance of publicly operated child care in the U.S. outside the educational system.) In effect, by 1981 almost the whole child-care delivery system in North Carolina had become privatized in this sense. In Mecklenburg County the United Way set up a task force to review the recommendations of the commission and to assess how the county should proceed. The task force's analysis made it clear that the county would be getting substantially less money from the state and would have to fund the centers themselves if they were to be operated. Therefore, the United Way recommended the establishment of a new agency to handle all public and private child-care dollars for the county. State child-care funds to Mecklenburg now get channeled directly to this agency—which then handles information and referral services, eligibility determination, and purchases care from a range of providers. Four different levels of standards applied to child care in North Carolina until 1985; and the prevailing standards for staff/child ratios for infant care, for example, were among the lowest in the country. Since the agency is not permitted to provide evaluations of specific centers to parents asking for referrals, the agency copes with the differential quality by explaining to parents the differences between the various levels of licensing standards and indicating what level applies to a particular child-care service.

Clearly, in North Carolina the private-sector programs are being operated at lower cost than the public programs were; the quality is lower, too. Privatizing the delivery of child care may have led to lower costs per child, but at a cost in quality that many would question: lower staff/child ratios, larger groups, larger centers, less equipment, lower caregiver salaries.

This experience is almost certainly shared by other states. It should be noted here that the increase in the proportion of proprietary centers through the demand-subsidy initiative could very well be exacerbating the downward trend in quality. Even the best of the for-profit chains, for example, will not locate in states with high minimum standards because of the costs imposed. They cannot meet the competition with regard to fees. Also even the best of the proprietary chains define a minimum facility size as 100–150 children; this is viewed as too large by many as an environment for the very young. A smaller facility is not viewed as feasible economically, even though 50–75 children is often cited as a desirable standard.

On balance? Per-child costs for publicly subsidized care have been reduced as a consequence of increased private delivery and decreased public provision. But there has been a concomitant decline in quality (with unknown consequences for children) and a probable decline in caregivers' real salaries—as a consequence of the static minimum wage over the last several years. Several executives among the leading for-profit chains acknowledge that their programs clearly "cream," that is, serve an affluent, relatively problem-free group of youngsters. That indeed is why a lower staff/child ratio can be satisfactory. With a more representative group of children, some needing more intensive care and attention, a higher staff/child ratio and therefore a more expensive service would be necessary for the same effective quality.

The Case For or Against Privatizing Child-Care Services

The child-care service industry is a mixed economy. Service programs can be located on a continuum from the completely private to the completely public, with most somewhere in the middle. For example:

Private Funding and Private Delivery	Private Funding and Public Delivery	Public Funding and Private Delivery	Public Funding and Public Delivery

And there are various models for monitoring and regulating services under both public and private auspices.

Historically, the industry has always been a mixture. In the past the largest components were the private nonprofit providers and the informal caregivers (domestic servants and mothers). Over the last two decades domestic servants have declined in numbers and importance, nonprofit providers have declined as a proportion of providers, and for-profit providers have increased significantly. At the same time, demand has increased many times over as mothers increasingly join the labor force.

THE EFFECTS

The Reagan Administration announced at the outset a policy of privatization to include a decrease in federal funding, an elimination of federal regulation, and encouragement and incentives for greater private-sector financing and delivery.

In the first half of the 1980s, federal direct funding for child care did decrease in real terms, federal indirect funding (tax benefits) increased, state funding increased in some states, stayed the same in others, and declined in the majority. Private philanthropic funding and private employer financing increased modestly but still constitutes an insignificant amount overall.[19]

There has been some increase in the supply of services available, but it is unclear how much of this, if any, is attributable to the Administration's policies of shifting from supply to demand subsidies and decreasing federal regulation. Some growth has occurred, clearly, in public school-based programs. This development is due to demographic and social pressures, probably intensified by federal program cutbacks. Interestingly, the growth in public preschools is not acknowledged by the Reagan Administration, suggesting that such a consequence was not expected. It is certainly not consistent with any concept of privatization.

There has been a significant increase in diversity and therefore in the options available to some consumers. At the same time, the reduction in direct federal spending has curtailed the options of low-income families, in particular, those preferring preschool programs.

More children, especially middle- and upper-income children, are receiving at least some public subsidy for child care—more than in 1980— but the poor are receiving considerably less than before.

There is some evidence of a decline in the quality of care available to low- and modest-income children; it is unclear what has happened to the quality of care provided those for whom costs and fees are not an issue.

There is some evidence that private programs operate more efficiently

[19] Despite the Administration's policies, little in the way of new "private" philanthropic funds have been contributed to support child care. United Way–reported allocations for child-care services are modest at best (2.4 percent of total allocations in 1981 and 2.8 percent in 1985). Although these have increased by a little more than 15 percent between 1981 and 1985, the base is so small to begin with that clearly the effort cannot be viewed as significant. (Data provided by Eleanor Brilliant from her work-in-progress on United Way.) Employers' financial contributions have been even more modest.

in the sense of lower cost; but there is some concomitant evidence that these lower costs carry with them lower quality care for children and (what may exacerbate quality problems) lower wages for caregivers.

There does appear to be a larger constituency for publicly subsidized child care than in 1980. Is this due to the privatization initiative? It is difficult to sort out the effects of broadening the base of participation through the child-care subsidy versus pressure from the continued and dramatic growth in labor force participation rates among married women with children under age 6—almost 20 percent between 1980 and 1985. Indeed, one could argue that the growth in the middle-class constituency for child care is not due to the Reagan Administration's stress on privatization but rather to increased need through enormous growth in the labor force participation of mothers. It is also not clear that these mothers typically prefer privatized delivery—given the increased attention on the state level to preschools, all-day kindergartens, and after-school programs.

On Balance?

Privatizing the delivery of child-care services in the 1980s through increased demand subsidies has meant more public subsidy for family day-care homes, expansion of proprietary programs and services, and lower, less consistent, and less enforced minimum standards of care. For many it also has meant greater choice; for some, options were curtailed.

Privatizing the regulation of child-care services has led to a decline in standards and enforcement and a greater stress on parent/consumer monitoring. What evidence there is, suggests that quality may have declined as a consequence.

Privatizing the financing of child care has meant reduced subsidies for low-income children, higher subsidies for middle- and upper-income children, and a failure to maintain the previous level of public support, given the growth in need/demand for care for children under age 6. For the Reagan Administration, privatizing child care has been first and foremost an ideological statement—an integral part of the Administration's overall philosophy. Second, it has been an experiment in "load-shedding," in reducing the social role and responsibility of the federal government. Third, it has been part of a larger effort at reorienting federal social policy, from concern for the poor to concern with middle- and upper-income families.

For many of us, as ideology, the policy is suspect. For all of us concerned about children, the load-shedding aspects are dangerous. And for those concerned with trends in social policy, the reduction of resources to the poor is anathema. Ultimately, society must confront the issue of responsibility for children, child rearing, and child care. What should the government role be? It is only in that context that we can fruitfully explore the financing and delivery mix that best meets the overall public purpose.

References

Abt Associates. 1979. *The National Day Care Study.* 5 vols. Cambridge, Mass.: Abt Associates.

———. 1980. *National Day Care Home Study.* Cambridge, Mass.: Abt Associates.

Belsky, J., and L. Steinberg. 1978. "The Effects of Day Care: A Critical Review." *Child Development* 49: 928–949.

Berrueta-Clement, John R., et al. 1984. *Changed Lives: The Effects of the Perry Preschool Programs on Youths through Age 19.* Ypsilanti, Mich.: High/Scope Press.

Blank, Helen. 1983. *Children and Federal Child Care Cuts.* Washington, D.C.: Children's Defense Fund.

———. 1984. *Child Care: The State's Response.* Washington, D.C.: Children's Defense Fund.

Blank, Helen, and Amy Wilkins. 1985. *Child Care: Whose Priority?* Washington, D.C.: Children's Defense Fund.

Burud, Sandra L., Pamela R. Aschbacher, and Jacqueline McCroskey. 1984. *Employer-Supported Child Care.* Boston, Mass.: Auburn House.

Clarke-Stewart, Alison. 1982. *Day Care.* Cambridge, Mass.: Harvard University Press.

Congressional Budget Office. 1981. *Tax Expenditures: Current Issues and Five-Year Budget Projections for Fiscal Years 1982–1986.* Washington, D.C.: Congressional Budget Office.

Congressional Budget Office. 1983. *Tax Expenditures: Current Issues and Five-Year Budget Projections for Fiscal Years 1984–1988.* Washington, D.C.: Congressional Budget Office.

Duval, E., et al. 1982. "AFDC: Characteristics of Recipients in 1979." *Social Security Bulletin* 45 (4): 4–19.

Friedman, Dana. 1985. *Corporate Financial Assistance for Child Care.* New York: Conference Board.

Harrell, Adele. 1983a. *Preliminary Report: The Effect of the Head Start Program on Children's Cognitive Development.* Washington, D.C.: Government Printing Office.

———. 1983b. *A Review of Head Start Research Since 1970.* Washington, D.C.: Government Printing Office.

"How's Business? A Status Report on For-Profit Child Care." 1986. *Child Care Information Exchange, No. 52* (November): 26.

Kahn, Alfred J., and Sheila B. Kamerman. 1987. *Child Care: Facing the Hard Choices.* Boston: Auburn House.

Kamerman, Sheila B., and Alfred J. Kahn. 1981. *Child Care, Family Benefits, and Working Parents.* New York: Columbia University Press.

Lehrmann, Karen, and Jana Pace. 1985. *Day Care Regulation: Serving Children or Bureaucrats?* Policy Analysis No. 59. Washington, D.C.: Cato Institute. September.

Levine, James A. 1982. "The Prospects and Dilemmas of Child Care Information." In Edward F. Zigler and Edmund W. Gordon, eds. *Day Care: Scientific and Policy Issues.* Boston, Mass.: Auburn House.

Lindner, Ellen W., et al. 1983. *When Churches Mind the Children.* Ypsilanti, Mich.: High/Scope Press.

McKey, R. H., et al. 1985. *The Impact of Head Start on Children, Families, and Communities.* Washington, D.C.: CSR, Inc.

National Black Child Development Institute. 1986. *Child Care in the Public Schools: Incubation for Inequality?* Washington, D.C.: National Black Child Development Institute.

Nelson, John R., Jr., 1982. "The Federal Interagency Day Care Requirements." In Cheryl D. Hayes, ed. *Making Policies for Children: A Study of the Federal Process.* Washington, D.C.: National Academy Press.

Newton, James W., and Sharon L. Kagan. 1985. *Survey on Profit and Quality Child Care: Progress Report.* New Haven, Conn.: Bush Center in Child Development and Social Policy.

Perry, Katherine S. 1980. *Child Care Centers Sponsored by Employers and Labor Unions in the United States.* Washington, D.C.: U.S. Department of Labor.

Robins, Philip K., and Samuel Wiener. 1978. *Child Care and Public Policy.* Lexington, Mass.: Lexington Books.

Rose-Ackerman, Susan. 1983. "Unintended Consequences: Regulating the Quality of Subsidized Day Care." *Journal of Policy Analysis and Management* 3 (1): 14–30.

———. 1986. "Altruistic Nonprofit Firms in Competitive Markets: The Case of Day Care Centers in the United States." *Journal of Consumer Policy* (9): 291–310.

Seligson, Michelle, and Andrea Genser, Ellen Gannett, and Wendy Gray. 1983. *School-Age Child Care: A Policy Report.* Wellesley, Mass.: Wellesley College Center for Research on Women.

U.S. Bureau of the Census. 1986. *School Enrollment—Social and Economic Characteristics of Students: October, 1982.* Current Population Reports. Series P–20, no. 408. Washington, D.C.: Government Printing Office.

———. 1987. *Who's Minding the Kids?* Current Population Reports. Series P–70, no. 9: 8–9. Washington, D.C.: Government Printing Office.

———. 1988. *School Enrollment—Social and Economic Characteristics of Students: October, 1985 and 1984.* Current Population Reports. Series P–20, no. 426. Washington, D.C.: Government Printing Office.

U.S. Department of Health and Human Services. 1982. *Report to Congress: Summary Report of the Assessment of Current State Practices in Title XX Funded Day Care Programs.* DHHS Publication No. OHDS–81–30331. Washington, D.C.: U.S. Department of Health and Human Services.

U.S. Department of Labor. 1981. *Employees and Child Care: Establishing Services at the Work Place.* Washington, D.C.: Women's Bureau.

————. 1982. *Federal Legislation on Day Care*. Washington, D.C.: Office of the Secretary, Women's Bureau.

————. 1988. *Child Care: A Workforce Issue*. Washington, D.C.: Government Printing Office.

U.S. House of Representatives. 1984a. *Child Care: Beginning a National Initiative*. Hearings of Select Committee on Children, Youth, and Families. Washington, D.C.: Government Printing Office.

U.S. House of Representatives. 1984b. *Exploring Private and Public Sector Approaches*. Hearings of Select Committee on Children, Youth, and Families. Washington, D.C.: Government Printing Office.

U.S. House of Representatives. 1984c. *Families and Child Care: Improving the Options*. Hearings of Select Committee on Children, Youth, and Families. Washington, D.C.: Government Printing Office.

Young, Dennis, and Richard Nelson, eds. 1973. *Public Policy for Day Care of Young Children*. Lexington, Mass.: Lexington Books.

Continuing the Discussion and Taking a Stand

We began with an attempt to define, to describe, and to explain, but the public policy mission also is to assess and recommend. The exploration must face the normative and the prescriptive. Here, estimations of current context, of fundamental value systems, and of political goals define the divisions.

The Arguments For and Against

The results are in one sense at least paradoxical. On the one hand, our authors, for the most part, are not unsympathetic to the idea of privatization. They either accept some of it as inevitable in a complex, mixed economy—or believe some of it is inevitable for historical reasons—or they acknowledge the idea that it may at times claim advantages of greater efficiency and flexibility. The reader in this context will recall the variations on one or another of these themes by Starr, Bendick, Rein, Gurin, Rose, O'Higgins, Sviridoff, and Kamerman–Kahn. On the other hand, despite a readiness to be open on the issue and empirical, a call for caution and even resistance to privatization is also to a greater or lesser degree sounded in Starr, Bendick, Gurin, and Kamerman–Kahn. They either see a need for aggressively defending a role for public services or for ensuring that the potential advantages of privatization in fact are realized because privatization is carried out correctly and not indiscriminately. Why such an outcome?

The fact is that a review of available experience makes it difficult to justify extreme advocacy of privatization—aggressive measures to decrease governmental finance, production, and regulation with regard to social programs—and engenders suspicion as to the motives of the all-out campaigns.

The pro-privatization case begins with the economy-efficiency argument: nonprofit and for-profit agencies are said to be more cost effective and less wasteful than government. To this is added the responsiveness and access claims—nongovernmental agencies will better meet needs in a sympathetic and flexible fashion—to which some will add: agencies in the marketplace offer more scope for innovation and specialization. Privatization also may improve management and evaluation. As all the specific areas examined in Part II of this book, as well as Starr's essay in Part I, make clear, these arguments as stated either are far too global to be tested or do not hold up against fact and experience. It is not that there is no evidence at all—but it runs both ways, apparently varying with field, time, context, and scale. Governmental, for-profit, and nonprofit programs come in too many variations in different fields for any simplistic pattern to prevail. Size is probably an important variable. The large nonprofit agency or the large for-profit may be more like the large governmental unit than like the small voluntary neighborhood program. Major differences are claimed between the for-profits and the nonprofits—at least in some domains—yet the evidence suggests, as the child-care case illustrates, the differences are modest at best, and probably as great within sectors as across. Indeed, we would argue that the evidence suggests that as more public dollars flow into for-profit as well as nonprofit organizations, for the same purposes, the distinctions between the two are inevitably blurred.

In view of all this, Gurin would differentiate by field of service and time, assuming the importance of privatization but being sure to maintain government as well. Bendick would protect government's financial contributions, but emphasize privatized production. Sviridoff is enthusiastic about the particular privatization he has helped develop, as appropriate to its problem and time. O'Higgins would go beyond the ideological or the narrowly instrumental in choosing increased privatization, but sees much opportunity in "contextual evaluation of particular proposals." For example, governments might give priority to deprived groups in some of its own programs, while creating a supply for other consumers by mandating provision by employers or offering tax relief to those who might buy service in the marketplace.

These would appear to be sensible, modest conclusions. Why, then, the larger reservations? Why a strong anti-privatization tone in several essays despite such perfectly reasonable advice? None of our authors opposes markets or voluntarism. In an era when even Eastern Europe is attracted to markets or market-like mechanisms, there are here no advocates of government monopolies.

Something else is going on. In assessing these policies, our authors note that apart from the efficiency-economy-choice arguments, which are not proven by the evidence, the other major arguments for large-scale aggressive privatization come from the libertarians at the far right: there is too much government and it endangers freedom; government programs may be well intentioned but they cause harm; a free market eventually creates better results for everyone (or for all those who act responsibly); to the extent that we need charity, it is most sensitively and effectively administered by local programs with whom recipients share close cultural-ethnic-religious ties. Such positions may not be sustainable empirically. They seem to ignore the reality that, however valuable the informal and the personal, these are not the same as or substitutes for the formal benefits, services, and programs on which modern community life also depends. One can favor attention to the church, neighborhood associations, and mutual aid while also believing in a strong public sector and adequate government social security. Nonetheless, these viewpoints—offering the informal as an alternative to major welfare state institutions, tap important streams in the ethic and become a potent political force. They become especially powerful if their supporters are added to those who are converted to large-scale privatization for strategic reasons.

The most telling part of the anti-privatization case points to two of privatization's radical manifestations:

1. As Bendick notes, at its extreme, privatization becomes load-shedding, a device to diminish federal *financial* commitments to basic social policy. Behind the screen of encouragement to "mediating structures" and "private sector initiatives," according to this argument, there is a decrease of funding on a scale that makes any replacement impossible; there is also a withdrawal of federal data collection and reporting, as seen in the child-care field. There is even a giving up of capacity for government to operate in some areas. Soon it lacks yardsticks and alternatives, and can be at the mercy of contract agencies, unable to enforce expectations.

2. In its rhetoric and its practical implications, privatization thus goes from mere load-shedding to a basic attack on the modern mixed-economy state and its system of protections and social provision. It is not merely an attempt to save money but an effort to *redefine government*.

Those who fear privatization because of its radical wing, dominant in the Reagan–Thatcher era, note that even where there is merit in some of the claims, resistance is the best policy—lest guards be dropped in the face of reasonableness and the more extreme policies sweep in.

The anti-privatization, pro-government argument is most completely presented in Chapter 1. Starr sees privatization in its political meaning as the most serious attempt at a conservative alternative—as described above—growing out of the countermovement versus the welfare and regulatory state. For this reason, he says, while favoring some of the specific proposals of the privatizers, he opposes privatization as ideology. The decision is political and the rationale for opposition direct and open. In his view, those who would look at privatization as a technical issue or problem in public administration are missing the point.

The anti-privatization case has another component, relevant to proposals to privatize prisons and other correction facilities as well as programs that "protect" or control subjects or deprive them of freedom. We, as a society, have developed important doctrine and procedures with regard to due process and infringement on liberties. It is dangerous for democratic government to delegate these.

The final case against privatization is made in the name of the solidaristic and egalitarian objective of social welfare programs. Only central government can ensure national uniformity, protect all groups, and adequately finance what needs to be done. It has taken the United States a long time to understand this and translate it into institutional responses. Privatization is an attack on societal responsibility. Perhaps it need not be in the abstract, but it is in the current political context. Nor is it the case that the public wants government to do nothing or to do uniformly less; there are specific objectives, programs, and governmental roles that do receive endorsement. Load-shedding privatization is not so subtle.

We conclude that the public discussion of privatization today involves three streams.

The first is an instrumental discussion concerning the use of the private sector(s) as a policy instrument or strategy to achieve any of the several goals mentioned earlier—greater efficiency, increased choice, enhanced consumer responsiveness. Here the issue is the specificity of the analysis and the extent to which there is evidence in support of one or another choice, from case to case. The private sector may have a useful role to play but it will vary by function, and it will vary depending on the issue or problem.

The second is a pragmatic debate about feasibility of implementation, the possibility of winning political acceptance of a given program, access of consumers to the bureaucratic and policy-determination machinery, and so forth. These could be as relevant as the efficiency issues in leading planners, strategists, advocates, and politicians to making their choices.

The third is an ideological debate between those who are convinced of the importance of a strong social role for the federal government, and those who are equally convinced of the value of minimalist government, and wish to diminish the role of government as it has evolved since the New Deal. Here, the debate is political, and of fundamental importance to the future of social policy in the United States.

Although the ideological question and the practical-applied issues are (or can be) debated as separate matters, increasingly they are not independent. As long as the federal government continues to finance social programs, one can avoid an ideological confrontation. Those favoring a strong governmental role can join with those favoring a strong private sector role, by selecting out those policy issues and problems in which the private sectors could be effective. Our own assessment of the situation today, however, is that policy strategies cannot be addressed unless the ideological issues are confronted directly.

Certainly, among those who oppose a social role for government on ideological grounds, the choice of policy strategies is resolved in advance. As a result, the debate about the analytic task tends to be carried on largely by those whose ideological positions are either liberal or centrist.

Thus, in one important sense, the debate about privatization is a political battleground rather than a search for an optimum or a satisfactory policy, or an effective tool. The analysts and the more moderate proponents of privatization may insist—as we do—that privatization is never pure, often appropriate, and certainly not new. The welfare state reality is a blending of sectors and interdependency, a "mixed economy of welfare." Those on the radical right would agree. But they would use the argument to diminish the social role of government on principle and, as they are able to do so, in almost all areas, except for the areas in which they are convinced of the correctness of government control and when they are in political control of government (for example, eliminating legal abortion, requiring school prayer, or regulating hospitals to keep a lid on Medicare costs).

The Obsolescence of Minimalist Government

Inevitably, therefore, the battleground on which the privatization issue is confronted has to do with one's view of the role of government.

Whatever the words, the dreams, and the impulses in the political arena, few serious observers believe that a modern, complex, interdependent, industrial society can live with a minimalist government in the pre–New Deal sense. There are social, technological, international, and economic realities that have superseded ideology and political party in the United States on this matter, just as they supersede East–West differences in the requirement for certain social service responses to social change, whatever the words used to describe such services.

The welfare state and its costs belong to both political parties, because the fundamental process goes beyond narrow ideology. The greatest rate of growth in U.S. social expenditures in modern time came with presidents Nixon and Ford in the 1970s.

All sectors have developed a stake in big and strong government. That is the nature of modern society, though of course many key actors do not use the term "welfare" for important domestic programs.

For example, industry counts upon the public sector in major ways for the presence of a needed infrastructure. We need only remember the relationship between the federal road program and the automobile industry, the importance of air terminals and control towers for airlines, the role of subsidies and harbor work in supporting the merchant marine. To all of this we could add the importance of various types of investment credits and other tax incentives.

The agriculture story also involves investment credits and tax incentives. Furthermore, we need hardly be reminded of the long history of direct intervention: parity and payments for nonproduction of certain grains and other agricultural produce; the public provision for responsive credit institutions; subsidies to dairy and tobacco producers; the importance of the fruit fly monitoring by government for California, Texas, and Florida agriculture; the role of labor force policy and immigration policy in ensuring a cheap guest-worker labor supply as needed; the role of water policy and grazing land policy.

To the above illustrations, hardly complete, we might add the place of strategic oil and energy policy in protecting American industry and consumers. Could the marketplace have avoided a national banking disaster if the anti-government Reagan Administration had not intervened in the Continental Illinois National Bank and Trust Company crisis in 1984, or without the federal and state insurance systems that rescued many overextended savings and loan associations between 1985 and 1988?

How, without a strong government program, are we to be protected against such externalities as pollution? Where, without government investment, will there be consumer protection in the fields of food and drugs, tires, home appliances, clothing, and product safety—or against cars that are "lemons"? There is enough history to tell us that the mythical "free" market does not protect here. The 1986–1987 liability insurance crisis called for a governmental solution. Moreover, a public health agency can mobilize societal action the way the market cannot, whether for finding the cause of Legionnaire's disease, searching for the nature and etiology of AIDS, or deciding what to do in the face of evidence that over-the-counter drug packages have been tampered with. Would we have a modern and thriving building industry without government permission for deductibility of mortgage interest and real estate taxes, thus ensuring flow of investment capital? Or without building standards to protect investor, builder, buyer, or renter? In capital markets, we can note the role of the Federal Reserve Board in regulating the money supply, thus shaping the cost of credit and ensuring some protection for industry. What marketplace variables exceed federal fiscal and monetary policy in their influence on equity markets?

Leaving the federal level for a moment, we can note how states have been scrambling with tax incentives, infrastructure, and advertisements about the quality of their human capital and their physical amenities as they compete at home and abroad for new industries. We can also note how now, once again, states are investing in upgrading their educational systems because of the belief that it will pay off economically. Nor, despite announced intent, was President Reagan able to abolish the Department of Education. The society saw it as more than consumption; it was useful investment.

Let us return to the federal level and discuss provision for retirement. Despite a media hysteria phase a few years ago, no one today seriously discusses retirement income without noting the basic universal foundation assured by social security. Nor will second-tier, employer-provided private pensions, or private personal pensions (IRAs and Keogh plans) survive without extensive and costly tax subsidies.

And despite the limited coverage available under unemployment insurance, clearly only this public social insurance benefit offered protection at the time of the major recession in 1982–1983. Indeed, what was underscored at that time was the inadequacy of private-sector provision when millions of unemployed and their families were forced to do without health care as they tried to cope with the loss of job-connected health benefit coverage. New public laws were needed to add protection.

A final illustration suggests that people variously located on the political spectrum do know that government cannot really leave social services to the free market—if only because the market can inflate costs and that is not helpful to government budget making. We refer of course to medical care, originally the small-enterprise-dominated branch of the social sector. It is useful to review Paul Starr's award-winning study, *The Transformation of American Medicine* (1982) for its insights into how the free market provided a variety of vehicles for use of the medical profession in organizing a privileged and prosperous monopoly against which consumers were and are helpless.

This is not the time or place to discuss changes that are occurring as big business enters the hospital field and doctors and medical societies no longer retain their full powers. Nor need we here explicate the medical inflation and its control. What is relevant is the readiness of the present so-called "anti-government," anti–welfare state national administration—with all of its free market ideology—to respond by proposing greater regulation (as well as more co-insurance, deductibles, and fringe-benefit taxation).

The main strategies are the hospital prepayment, the diagnostic related groups, the health maintenance organization (HMO), and the preferred provider organization (PPO) to control costs. The mechanisms come out of the marketplace but the regulatory policies come from the government. The only debate is about whether all of this can succeed without setting similar procedures for private health insurance and fully private patients. Clearly there are certain basic responsibilities that are government's in assuring every citizen a minimum standard of living as a matter of right. These responsibilities may be allocated to different levels of government, but they are governmental nevertheless.

While there are those who would dismantle those components in our welfare state of which they disapprove, or significantly diminish government, their arguments are ideological and their capacity to ignore realities heroic. Modern societies require large, if sensitive, governments. None of the major domestic problems and challenges experienced in industrialized societies can be adequately solved by active efforts to decrease the potency of the federal government. The critical issue here is what is an alternative rallying cry for the advocates of a strong social role for government? How can these groups recapture the national agenda?

Beyond the Ideological Battleground

But privatization is something more than an ideological battleground. As this book has demonstrated, privatization is also a policy tool. As part of the repertoire of public administration it is not new, cannot be pure, is not just one uniform phenomenon, and should not and cannot be dismissed as such. While it is necessary to note how unreal it is to advance the private sector as a substitute for federal financing of social provision, one should recall that privatization may be an effective instrument with regard to the production or delivery of certain publicly funded benefits and services. It is worth stressing again, however, that the specifics depend on the nature of the benefit/service to be provided and often require a significant governmental role in regulating or monitoring the "production" process and the extent to which the service(s) produced meet(s) some predefined standard.

The governmental role of regulator remains an important one, especially if the role of the private sector increases. Indeed, there is a potentially more important use of the governmental regulatory function that can substitute for such other major functions as financing and production. Many other countries have gone much further than we have in employing this role. Thus, national legislation can be used to require—to mandate—that employers establish certain social security or educational policies, for example, or provide certain health insurance or pension benefits, in lieu of government taking on the task itself as a direct responsibility (or employer mandates may involve a supplementary, second tier of social protection).

Consideration of all of this leads us to conclude that it is doubtful whether public policy will get very far by approaching the major domestic problems confronting the society as essentially or critically questions about privatization. Far more than privatization is at stake in these matters. These are best thought of as fundamental, substantive policy questions in the public arena. For many things, the policy simply must be developed at the national level. Others belong to state and locality. But they are public policy issues and should be carefully explored in all their ramifications.

In short, if the goal is to analyze policies or programs and the choice of action strategies, we must begin with problems, issues, needs, goals, objectives—not with tools or ideological heat. And all policy processes must attend to realities and to preferences, to real-world constraints on political and administrative feasibility, and to fundamental values. Within such processes it must be understood that privatization is only one policy tool, not even a new one, and it is certainly not a magic potion or an all-ailment nostrum. It is misleading to pretend that privatization could be the central organizing variable for a modern industrial mixed-economy society. To the extent that it is offered as such, the medicine men should be challenged. To the degree that it belongs and fits well in a particular mix, ideology should not block it.

We urge, then, that the debate turn to the core social issues of today and every day: work, income, family, medical care, housing, education, and all the rest, and face them as issues. We need such confrontation, not a campaign for "privatization" or, for that matter, for "free markets." The nonprofit and the for-profit sectors are part of the picture and will remain. But preferably they will be in roles and relationships, and with accountability and monitoring, determined by the particular question and the preferred strategy. The privatization slogan should be avoided when obviously advanced as an alternative to analysis, as a substitute for debate. The privatization tool should not be forbidden, discarded, underplayed: nor should it be employed indiscriminately.

Nor would we propose to ignore questions of governmental responsiveness and efficiency, raised by privatization advocates. Adjustment and reform are permanent agenda items for government in a pluralistic democracy. The pathologies of large bureaucracy are always frightening and must remain spotlighted, while constantly dealt with. Devolution and reformed federalism are legitimate strategies, constantly reshaped. The recruitment by government of for-profit businesses and nonprofit agencies to share in its work is inevitable and essential but, again, with controls and protections specified and with constant adaptation to task and time.

Our purpose should be to shape a responsive society that helps people—all people—satisfy their needs and protect their rights. Changes in polity, economy, and international relationships generate constant adjustments and adaptations. Our national judgment could be impaired if one of many possible components of planned action—privatization—were to be treated as though it were a golden calf.

References

Paul Starr. 1982. *The Transformation of American Medicine*. New York: Basic Books.

NOTES ON CONTRIBUTORS

MARC BENDICK, JR. is co-principal at Bendick and Eagan Economic Consultants, Inc., Washington, D.C. He is an economist and has published extensively on employment, human resource development, and evaluation of programs serving low-income populations.

EVELYN BRODKIN, assistant professor at the School of Social Service Administration, University of Chicago, was previously affiliated with the political science department at Stony Brook. Her current work is focused on the politics of dependency. She is the author of *The False Promise of Administrative Reform* (Temple).

ARNOLD GURIN, professor emeritus and former dean at the Florence Heller School of Brandeis University, is a researcher, teacher, and consultant in the fields of social planning, social services, and social policy. He has published extensively in journals and texts in these fields.

SHEILA B. KAMERMAN and ALFRED J. KAHN are professors of social policy and social planning at the Columbia University School of Social Work. They are co-directors of the Cross-National Studies Program. Their research focuses on United States and comparative social policy, child policy, social services, child care, income maintenance, and family benefits. Among their sixteen joint books are: *The Responsive Workplace: Employers and a Changing Labor Force* (Columbia), *Child Care: Facing the Hard Choices* (Auburn), *Income Transfers for Families with Children: An Eight-Country Study* (Temple), and *Child Care, Family Benefits, and Working Parents* (Columbia).

MICHAEL O'HIGGINS is a managing consultant in the London offices of Price Waterhouse Management Consultants and (during 1987–88) a principal administrator in the Social Affairs Division of the Organisation for Economic Co-operation and Development in Paris. Previously, he was a reader in social policy at the University of Bath in England. He is co-editor of *The Future of Welfare* (Blackwell) and of *Poverty, Inequality and the Distribution of Income* (Wheatsheaf). He has written widely on social policy, public expenditures, and income distribution.

MARTIN REIN, professor of social policy and urban studies at the Massachusetts Institute of Technology, is the author of numerous books in the fields of social policy and income transfers. These include: *Income Packaging in the Welfare State* (Sharpe); (with L. Rainwater and A. Schwartz), *Public and Private Interplay in Social Protection* (Sharpe); (with G. Esping-Andersen and L. Rainwater) *Stagnation and Renewal* (Sharpe).

RICHARD ROSE is director of the Center for the Study of Social Policy at the University of Strathclyde, Glasgow. He is author and editor of more than thirty-five books on comparative social public policy and government. These include: *Understanding Big Government* (Sage), *Do Parties Make a Difference?* (Macmillan), and (co-edited with Rei Shiratori) *The Welfare State East and West* (Oxford).

PAUL STARR is professor of sociology at Princeton University. His books include the 1984 Pulitzer Prize winner, *The Social Transformation of American Medicine* (Basic Books) and (co-edited with William Alonso) *The Politics of Numbers* (Russell Sage). He is currently working on a book on the development and future of public institutions.

MITCHELL SVIRIDOFF is professor of urban policy and co-director of the Community Development Research Center at the Graduate School of Management and Urban Professions, New School for Social Research, New York. He is the former president of the Local Initiatives Support Corporation and former vice-president for national affairs of the Ford Foundation.

DENNIS YOUNG is director of the Mandel Center for Non-Profit Organizations and Mandel Professor of Non-Profit Management at Case Western Reserve University, Cleveland. His books include (with Michael O'Neill) *Educating Managers of Non-Profit Organizations* (Praeger), *Handbook of Management for Non-Profit Organizations* (Haworth), *If Not For Profit, for What?* (Lexington).

INDEX

Abramson, Alan, 105, 114
Abt Associates, 236n
Administration for Children, Youth, and Families, 237n, Table 9.1
adoption services, 192
AFDC. *See* Aid to Families with Dependent Children
"agenda setting," 143
Ahlbrandt, Roger S., Jr., 30
Aid to Families with Dependent Children (AFDC) program, 64, 91, 237, 239, 241, 244, 248, Table 9.1
Alber, J., 90
Alchian, Armen, 28
de Alessi, Louis, 28
Alinsky, Saul, 211
Allardt, Erik, 75
allocation function of government, 124
Alternative Payment Program, 245
American Enterprise Institute, 92, 115
amateur proprietor, 61
"antibody" strategy, 230–31
anti-government attitudes, 101
anti-poverty programs, 191. *See also* poverty, War on Poverty
Ariès, Philippe, 19
Aschbacher, Pamela R., 246

baby boom, 212
Bailar, John, III, 144n
Bailey, Robert W., 43
Banana Kelly (BK) Community Improvement Association, 220–21
Bardach, Eugene, 147n
barter, 76–77
Basic Education Opportunity Grants, 113
Bathgate, 222
Bator, Francis M., 125
battleground of privatization, 143–49
Baumol, William J., 33
Bays, Carson W., 60, 65–66
Bedford-Stuyvesant Restoration Corporation, 213, 217
behavioral theories, 133

Bendick, Marc, Jr., 104, 104n, 106nn, 109–10, 109n, 112–13, 117, 117n, 134, 162, 202, 262–63
Bennett, John T., 30
Berger, Peter L., 34, 115, 130, 138, 144
Beveridge plan (U.K.), 203
BK. *See* Banana Kelly Community Improvement Association
Black, Duncan, 138
black-market social services, 59. *See also* gray-market social services
Blank, Helen, 236n, 237n, 239n, 244, 249
Blissett, M., 148
block-grant program, 52, 241–42
Blumenthal, David, 187n
blurring, 58, 60–63, 70
Borcherding, Thomas, 29
Boston Housing Partnership, 61, 224–25
Braun, Randolph, 19
Briggs, Asa, 140
Brilliant, Eleanor, 255
Brittan, Samuel, 25
Brodkin, Evelyn Z., 33, 146–47
Brooks, Harvey, 144n
Brown, Angela C., 106n
Buchanan, James M., 124
BUILD, 221
Burbridge, Lynn C., 114
bureaucracy, 144–45
Burt, Martha R., 114
Burud, Sandra L., 246
Butler, Stuart, 35
buy/provide decision, 67

Cabrillo Economic Development Corporation, 216
California Alternative Payment Program, 242
Callahan, James J., 187, 187n
capital subsidies, 111
capitalism, 36, 56
Carter Administration, 213
"categorical" constraint, 137–38

CDCs. *See* Community Development Corporations

CEA. *See* Community Equity Assistance

CETA. *See* Comprehensive Employment and Training Act

Challis, L., 166

charitable giving, 104, 104n, 123

Charlotte Gardens, 221

Chicago School economics, 27

child abuse, 194

child care, 76, 235–57, Table 9.1; employer-sponsored, 239, 240n, 242–46, 248; institutional, 167; nonprofit, 248; for profit, 245–46, 248, 250–51, 254. *See also* day care, preschool programs

child-care disregard, 239

child-care service chains, 245–46, 248, 250, 254

child policy, U.S. government, 235

Child Poverty Action Group, 165

child welfare agencies, public, 192–95

Children's Defense Fund, 240, 240n, 244, 247, 249

Children's World, 245, 245n, 251

CHN. *See* Cleveland Housing Network

choice of services/providers, 90–91, 167, 186, 188, 240–44

church, as provider of social services, 79

citizenship, 90

Civilian Conservation Corps, 111

claims against the state, 19, 42–44

Cleveland Foundation, 218

Cleveland Housing Network (CHN), 219

Cleveland Housing Partnership, 219

Cloward, Richard, 140n, 141–42, 149

Coase, Ronald, 28

Cobb, Roger W., 143, 144n

coercion, 106, 123, 131

collective action theory, 123

collective vs. proprietary ideals, 61

commercial development projects, 215, 216, 226

commercialization, 22

community action programs, 62, 197, 213

community-based organizations, 62, 101, 148n, 191, 207, 211, 215–16, 219, 223–26, 243

community development, 34–35, 182, 213–14, 215, 217, 223–24, 228–29, 231–32; organizations, 207, 215, 217, 220, 222, 228

Community Development Block Grant program, 212

Community Development Corporations (CDCs), 213–14, 216–18

Community Equity Assistance (CEA), 227

Community Reinvestment Act, 214

competition, 27, 33, 125, 166, 185

competitive bidding, 201

competitive markets, theory of, 137

Comprehensive Employment and Training Act (CETA), 111, 190–91

Conant, James, 211

Conference Board, 246

Congressional Budget Office, 239n

Conservative government (U.K.), 164–65, 168, 172–73, 175

conservativism, 44

consumer control, 110

contestability, 33

contract failure theory, 56, 129

contracting of public services, 38, 43, 52, 106–9, 134–36, 167, 175, 185–86, 192, 194, 198, 200–201, 203. *See also* subcontracting

"controlling coalitions," 124

corporate education, 67

corporate-investor-owned services, 61

corporations, 19–20, 26, 28, 213–15, 218, 220, 223

correctional facilities, 107–8

cost: analysis, 200; controls, 68; effectiveness, 112; savings, 107–8, 174, 202; of services, 107, 107n, 111, 137, 185, 197, 200–202, 250, 252–56, 267; shifting, 65, 68

council houses, 164–65

Creedy, J., 174

criterion problem, 69

cross-subsidization, 57, 66, 133

Crozier, Michael, 35

Danziger, Sheldon, 92

Davis, David G., 30

Day, P., 166

day care, 240n, 242–46, 250, 253. *See also* child care, preschool programs

day-care centers, industry-sponsored, 245

decentralization, 147

deficits, 88

deindustrialization, 185

delivery systems, 106–12, 115–17, 147–48, 202; for-profit, 106

demand, income elasticity of, 99; for services, 22–23, 103

demand subsidies, 236–45, 248–49, 254

democracy, 32, 41–42, 44

Demsetz, Harold, 28

denationalization, 37

Department of Health, Education, and Welfare, 147. See also Health, Education, and Welfare Day Care Requirements

Dependent Care Tax Credit, 237, 239, 241, Table 9.1

deregulation, 24

derived externalities, 137

Derthick, Martha, 147, 147n, 167

development projects, 215. See also housing development; community development

direct delivery of services, 98

direct grants, federal government, 57, 63

direct vs. indirect expenditure, 249

disability policy, 146

disadvantaged youth, 191

discontent, 101

discretion, bureaucratic, 146–47

discrimination, 106

distribution, 44, 61, 69, 122–24, 137n, 142, 142n, 165, 171

distribution function of government, 122–24

diversity of services, 243

Donnison, David, 34, 157, 203

Dorwart, Robert, 185

Douglas, James, 33, 125, 132, 137

Dowdle, Barney, 30

dualism, 50, 57–58, 68

Durman, Eugene, 114

Duval, E., 236n, 237n, Table 9.1

economic development, 73, 111–12, 220, 223–24, 229

economic growth, 40, 85–87, 92, Table 3.4

Economic Recovery Tax Act, 64

economies of scale, 188

economy and privatization, 100, 122–39

Edelman, Murray, 145

education, 79, 169

educational performance contracts, 108

effectiveness of social services, 158, 196

efficiency, 42, 106–15, 124–25, 136–37, 142n, 144, 149, 158, 171, 196, 252–54, 261

Egan, Mary Lou, 117n

EHAP. See Experimental Housing Allowance Program

Elder, Charles D., 143, 144n

elderly, care of, 54, 166, 187

Ellefson, Paul, 31

Elshtain, Jean Bethke, 17

Emergency Food and Shelter Program, 114

employer-based programs, 59, 61–62, 66–67

employer satisfaction, 172

employment programs, 213

employment relations, 35

empowerment, 34–35, 98–99, 105, 115–16, 144

ends of privatization, 139–42

Enterprise Foundation, 219

Enterprise Social Investment Corporation, 219

entitlement programs, 90, 182

entrepreneurship, 35–36

environmental function of government, 122

equality, 175–76

equity, 162–63, 247–49

erosion of services, 167–69

Esping-Anderson, Gosta, 145

evaluation, 163, 176, 190

"exclusive groups," 128

"exit and voice" theory, 129

Experimental Housing Allowance Program (EHAP), 109

exploitation, 129

externalities, 125–27, 137

failure theories, 124–39

Famicos Foundation, 219

family, 18–19, 78, 193, 197; as care providers, 54–55, 74, 187

family day care, 242–46

federal funds, 57, 89, 100, 191, 237n, 247–48, Table 9.1

Federal Interagency Day Care Requirements (FIDCR). See Health, Education, and Welfare Day Care Requirements

federalism, 52

fees, 65

Feinstein, Patrice Hirsh, 187

female labor force participation rates, 240, 244, 247, 256
Ferrara, Peter J., 25
FIDCR. *See* Health, Education, and Welfare Day Care Requirements
Field, Frank, 165
financial responsibility, 202–3
financing, 115–17, 187, 214, 219
fiscalization, 78
flexibility, 161–62, 202, 241
Flora, Peter, 73, 90, 140n
food services, 79
food stamps, 182
for-profit providers, 106–14, 188, 250–51; vs. nonprofits, 251, 262
Ford Foundation, 211, 213–14, 217–18
foster care, 167, 192–93
foundations, 214–15, 218, 220, 223
Foxley, Alejandro, 43
free-rider problem, 104, 123, 132, 170
Freeman, Alan, 16
Friedman, Dana, 246
fringe benefits, 66
Frug, Gerald, 20
fund-raising, 103, 105
Furniss, Norman, 140n, 142, 144
Furubotn, Eirik G., 28

Galbraith, John Kenneth, 23
Gasper, Jo Ann, 235, Table 9.1
Gassler, Robert Scott, 122
Gershuny, J. I., 76
Gilbert, Neil, 56, 65
Giving USA, 99
Glade, William, 22
Glazer, Nathan, 75, 145
goals, of social policy, 137, 158
Goodman, John C., 25
Goodman, John L., 101
Gottschalk, Peter, 92
governability, 57
government 19, 41–42, 50–51, 64–68, 130, 140; boundaries of, 140–42, 146; central, 192, 264; and industry, 265–68; minimalist, 265–68; as provider, 131, 134–36, 141, 164–65, 167–68, 188, 192; as resource of last resort, 195; responsibility of, 158, 195–98, 200, 256; role of, 15, 24, 50, 52, 56, 58–59, 67, 69, 79, 82, 102, 116, 122–24, 131, 134, 138, 143, 146, 160–61, 167, 179–84, 189, 194–97, 201, 203, 207, 262, 264–65, 268; state and local, 89; tools of, 63–68; "top-down," 51–52
government agencies, 199–200. *See also* state agencies
government funds, 35–36, 84, 86–87, 98–99, 105, 173, 188, 196, 202, 236. *See also* state and local funds
government policy, 24, 40, 66, 68–69
government programs, 60, 262
governmental control, 24–26
governmental-private relationships, 195–201
governmental redistribution, 124
governmental sector, 103; failure of, 56, 136–38; vs. nonprofit sector, 56–57; vs. private sector, 67
Gramlich, Edward M., 108
grant-in-aid system, 182
grants, government, 57, 63; private, 218
gray-market social services, 59, 61–62, 66. *See also* black-market social services
Great Society, 181, 183, 211–13
Gross National Product, 82, 85
growth, economic, 40, 85–87, 92, Table 3.4
guaranteed national income, 182
Gueron, Judith M., 190
Gurin, Arnold, 194, 200, 262

Hadenius, Axel, 88
Hadley, Jack, 110
Hahn, Andrew, 190
Hanke, Steve H., 30
Hansmann, Henry B., 56, 129–30, 136
Hardin, Garrett, 30, 131n
Harrington, Michael, 211
Hartz, Louis, 140n
Hatry, Harry, 98, 107, 114
Hawkins, Patricia Devine, 237n, Table 9.1
Head Start, 237, 239, 243, 248, Table 9.1
health care, 61, 79–80, 82–83, 160, 166, 182, 201–3, 267
Health, Education, and Welfare Day Care Requirements, 249
Heclo, Hugh, 85, 140n
Heidenheimer, Arnold J., 73, 140n
Heller, Peter, 87
Heritage Foundation, 35
Hill, T. P., 76

Hirschman, Albert O., 17–18, 36, 129,
    149n
Hispanic Housing Development Corpora-
    tion, 216, 226
Hofstadter, Richard, 101
Holmes, Stephen, 19
home health services, 188
homemaker services, 188, 199
Hood, Christopher, 50–51
Hopkins, Harry, 181
hospitals, as providers of child care, 246
household, as provider of services, 50, 74,
    76–81, 86
housing, 55, 79, 210; allowances, 109; de-
    velopment, 215–16, 219–21, 232; gov-
    ernment, 164–65; policy, 60–61; proj-
    ects, 215, 223–25, 227; rehabilitation,
    213, 221, 227; subsidies, 216; vouchers,
    110
Hulten, Charles, 100, 100n
Huntington, Samuel P., 35, 142

IBA. See Inquilinos Boricuas en Accion
IHDA. See Illinois Housing Development
    Authority
Ikenberry, John, 140n, 141
Illinois Housing Development Authority
    (IHDA), 226
IMF. See International Monetary Fund
Immergut, Ellen, 141
immigrants, in U.S., 208–9
"implicit privatization," 24
Imray, Linda, 17
in-kind assistance programs, 116
inadequacy of services, 168
incentives, 32, 63, 111–12, 131, 135, 168,
    195, 199, 245
income, 79, 241; distribution, 43, 61, 122–
    23; redistribution, 61, 69; security, 58,
    173, 176; support, 58, 168, 173, 180–
    81, 189; transfer, 172
incubator facilities, 216, 222
independence, 186–87
Individual Retirement Accounts (IRAs), 59,
    168
individualism, 140, 144
industrial development, 216
industrial location incentives, 112
industrial mix, 209
industrialization, 78, 209
industry, and government, 265–68

infant care, 245
informal sector, 26, 53–54, 59, 62, 64, 81,
    188, 197
informal vs. formal social services, 53–55,
    263
information and referral services, 246, 250,
    250n
"information impactedness," 135
innovation, 52, 185
Inquilinos Boricuas en Accion (IBA), 223–
    24
institutional services, 179, 187
insurance, 170, 180, 196
interest groups, 52
intermediate care facilities, 51, 187
internal organization, vs. contracting out,
    135–36
Internal Revenue Code, 239
internalities, 137
International Monetary Fund (IMF), 39, 50
investment credits, 266
investment strategy, 220
"invisible welfare state," 53
IRAs. See Individual Retirement Accounts

James, Estelle, 57, 60, 132–33
Job Corps, 191–92
job development, 112
job training, 190, 211, 213
Job Training Partnership Act, 190
Johnson, Arlien, 179–80, 179n
Johnson, Manuel H., 30
Johnson Administration, 181–82
joint production of services, 60
joint venturing, 226
Judge, Ken, 69, 161
Juster, F. T., 76
juvenile delinquency, 211

Kagan, Sharon L., 251
Kahn, Alfred J., 67, 236n, 245n, 247n,
    Table 9.1
Kamerman, Sheila B., 67, 236n, 245n,
    247n, Table 9.1
Karl, Barry, 140n
Karran, Terence, 88
Katznelson, Ira, 142, 149
Kay, John, 25
Kelman, Steven, 31, 100
Kennedy, Duncan, 16
Kennedy Administration, 211

Kiesler, Charles A., 185
Kinder-Care, 245, 245n
kindergarten programs, public, 244, 247
King, Anthony J., 142
Kirlin, John J., 107
Kirwan, R., 165
Klare, Karl E., 16
Klass, Gary M., 92
Klein, R., 161–62, 166
Knapp, M., 161
"knowledge" constraint, 138
Koshel, Patricia P., 108
Kramer, Ralph M., 76, 115, 140, 148n
Krashinsky, Michael, 127, 130
Krohn, Roger, 55
Kuttner, Robert, 40

labor force participation of women, 240,
    244, 247, 256
labor market, 209, 212
Ladd, Everett Carl, 100, 116
Ladd, Helen F., 89
Lampman, Robert J., 78n
Land, K. C., 76
Lebeaux, 140n
Ledebur, Larry, 112
legislation, child care, 236–40; under Great
    Society, 211–12; urban rehabilitation,
    213
LeGrand, Julian, 69
Lehrmann, Karen, 250
Lerman, Robert, 190
Levine, James A., 250n
Levinson, Phyllis M., 104, 104n, 106n
Levitan, Sar A., 145n
Levy, Frank, 100
"Lexington Village," 219
liberalism, 19, 34
liberalization, 25–27
Lindblom, Charles E., 51, 142
Linden Place Townhouses, 216
Lipsky, 70, 90, 146–47, 147n
LISC. See Local Initiatives Support Corpo-
    ration
Litwak, Eugene, 54, 77, 81
load-shedding, 52, 98, 104, 122, 256, 263
loans, for community development, 222–
    23
lobbying, 39
local amateur economy, 55–56, 66
local government, 112

Local Initiatives Support Corporation
    (LISC), 207, 214–32; Boston–LISC,
    223–25; Chicago–LISC, 225–27; Cleve-
    land–LISC, 218–20; South Bronx–LISC,
    220–23
long term care, 186–89, 196
Lothner, David, 31
low-income families, 243–44
Lowi, Theodore J., 147n
Luxembourg Income Study, 92n
Lynn, Laurence E., 116

MacArthur Foundation, 227
McCroskey, Jacqueline, 246
McGovern, George, 102
McGuire, Thomas G., 186n
"majoritarian" constraint, 138
make/buy decision, 62–63, 67
Malpass, P., 165
management, 38, 117
managerial incentive problem, 136n
mandating, 64, 170–71
marginality of private sector, 161
market, 52–53, 85, 123–31, 134; as pro-
    vider of welfare services, 76–80, 86, 90
market economies, 123, 140
market failure theory, 33, 56, 124–31, 133
market imperfections, 126–27
market sector, 73, 84; vs. state, 164
Marris, Stephen, 88
Marxism, 27
maximum feasible participation, 182, 212–
    13
Mayer, Colin, 25, 38–39
Meadowcroft, Shirley, 38–39
means-tested assistance programs, 181
mediating institutions, 34, 54, 98–99, 115–
    16, 138
Medicaid, 65, 187, 196, 204
Medicare, 187
Mensch, Betty, 16
mental health service, 184–86
merit goods, 76
Meyer, Jack A., 87, 115, 144
Michel, Richard C., 100
Mid-Bronx Desperadoes, 221–22
Middleton, Audrey, 17
militancy, 211
minorities, and urban renewal, 211
mistrust of government, 100

mixed economy, 157, 164, 176, 236, 254, 263, 265
Model Cities, 212
monetization, of welfare production, 78
monitoring, 113, 136–37, 200
motivation, 132, 158–59
Murie, A., 165
Murray, C., 158
Musgrave, Richard A., 31, 56, 122, 124
Musolf, Lloyd D., 21n

Nathan, Richard, 146, 149
National Black Child Development Institute, 243
National Health Service (NHS) (U.K.), 160, 162–63, 169
National Health Service Corps, 110
national security, public funds for, 73
nationalism, 37
Neighborhood Housing Service (NHS) Corporation, 214
neighborhoods, inner-city, 208–9
Nelson, Richard R., 130, 244
Neuhaus, Richard J., 34, 115, 130, 138, 144
New Deal, 181–82
New Federalism, 212
Newhouse, Joseph, 133
Newton, James W., 251
NHS. See National Health Service
Nielsen, Waleman A., 57
Niskanen, William A., Jr., 29, 133, 136n
"nondistribution" constraint, 129
nondominance models, 53
nonmarket failure theory, 33
nonmonetized labor, 76, 76n
nonprofit sector, 26–27, 33, 35, 50, 56–57, 59–61, 64–66, 76, 103, 105, 113–15, 130, 132–33, 136–38, 185, 191, 200, 207, 253; vs. for-profit services, 57, 251, 262; vs. government, 56–57
North River Commission, 226
Northwest Bronx Community and Clergy Coalition, 221
nursing homes, 126–28, 135, 187–88

OBRA. See Omnibus Budget Reconciliation Act
occupational welfare, 171–72
OECD. See Organization for Economic and Community Development

Offe, Claus, 140n, 144n
Office of Human Development Services, 235–36, 240n
O'Higgins, Michael, 25, 167, 171, 173–74, 262
Olson, Mancur, 102, 123, 128, 131
Omnibus Budget Reconciliation Act (OBRA), 148, 238–39, 248–49; amendments, 239
"open referrals," 194
opportunism, 135
Organization for Economic Cooperation and Development (OECD), 50, 82, 83, 97, Table 3.3, Table 3.4
organizational failure, 134–36
organizations, role of, 134, 136, 136n
Orren, Gary, 31
"overload," in government, 35, 142

Pace, Jana, 250
Pacific Consultants, 200
Palm, Sally, 31
Palmer, John, 88–89
Palo Alto Preschools, 251
Panzar, John C., 33
paragovernmental organizations, 51
Pareto optimality, 125
"partnership clinics," 185
"passing the poisoned chalice," 52
Patterson, 140n
Pauly, Mark, 133
PCC. See People's Consumer Cooperative
Pejovich, Svetozar, 28
pension schemes, contracted-out, 175
pensions, 173–76
"People's capitalism," 36
People's Consumer Cooperative (PCC), 226
Perlman, Robert, 197
Permanent Charity fund, 223
Perry, Katharine S., 245
personal social services, 78. See also public services, social services
Peters, Guy, 80, Table 3.2
Peterson, Peter G., 88
philanthropy, 33; role of, 123, 132, 132n, 255, 255n
PICs. See Private Industry Councils
pillarization, 53, 58, 61
Piven, Francis Fox, 140n, 141–42, 149
pluralism, political, 101

policing, 129, 131
politicization, 144
politics: and privatization, 21–27; of cost
    shifting, 65
postindustrial revolution, 209
poverty, 91, 92n, 182, 211; programs, 92,
    191. *See also* War on Poverty
power, 163; distribution of, 42, 142, 142n,
    165
preschool programs, 243–44, 247, 251–
    52, 255. *See also* child care, day care
President's Private Sector Task Force, 235
Pressman, Jeffrey L., 147n
PRI. *See* Program-Related Investments
pricing, of social services, 51, 200
Private Industry Councils (PICs), 190, 192,
    213
private initiatives, for urban development,
    213–14
private institutions, 180
private ownership, 27–28
private provision, role of, 99, 105, 167
private/public spheres, 141–42, 213; *see
    also* public/private distinction
private sector, 44, 80, 83, 86, 106–12, 125,
    161, 190–91, 213, Table 3.2; defined,
    22; vs. government, 67; for profit, 106–
    7; role of, 68–69, 173, 207, 264, 268
private service systems, 24, 59–63
privatization: anti-privatization case, 262–
    65; "by attrition," 24; in Britain, 164–
    76; as community development, 34–35;
    and conservatives, 44; of consumption,
    23–24; defined, 21–22, 22n, 98; de-
    mand-driven, 22–23; as economic ad-
    justment, 33; economic vs. political ap-
    proaches, 149; and employment
    relations, 35; ends of, 142; impact of,
    142, 148, 255–56; "implicit," 24; instru-
    mentalist vs. ideological view, 158–59,
    263–65; vs. national interests, 37–38;
    nature of, 98; origins of, 15; partial and
    total, 24; as policy, 43; political aspects,
    15, 139–49, 201–4; political theory of,
    35–36; political uses of, 37–42; politi-
    cally inspired, 39; of production, 23–24;
    vs. public services, 261; as reduction of
    overload, 35–37; as reordering of rights,
    42; strategic approach, 159–64; sym-
    bolic vs. mechanical view, 157
privatized delivery, 98
privatized state-owned enterprises, 38

professionalization, 128–29, 181, 193
profit-making firms, 133, 137
profit maximization, 61
profitization, 65, 133
Program-Related Investments (PRI) pro-
    grams, 217
property rights, 27–32, 42
proprietary sector, 59, 61, 65–66
protective services, 193–95
Pruitt-Igoe, 210
public: agencies, 73, 181, 201; assets, 24,
    36; effort, 82, 84; expenditure, 73, 83–
    85, 88, 92, 99–100, 124, 168, 171, 174,
    179, Table 3.3, Table 3.4; goods, 23,
    102–3, 126, 131–32; housing policy,
    210; interest, 19; organizations, 41; pro-
    vision, 44, 91
public choice theory, 27, 29–31, 39, 124,
    136n
public policy, 78, 147, 160, 210, 212, 232,
    252, 261, 269. *See also* social policy
public/private balance, 142, 162, 163–64,
    176, 184
public/private distinction, 16–17, 20, 74,
    141, 162–64
public/private social services, 50–53, 68,
    186, 213
public school–based programs, 247, 247n,
    252, 255
public sector, 22, 40, 80, 88, 100–102,
    180, 191, 265, Table 3.2
Public Service Employment Program, 111
public services, 42, 64, 181, 192, 208. *See
    also* social services
public welfare: history of, 179–84; pro-
    gram approach to, 78
"publicization," 97
Pyramidwest Development Corporation,
    226

quality control, 200
quality of social services, 43, 69, 167, 169,
    187–88, 199–200, 249–52, 254–55
quasi-proprietary model, 55

race, 209
Rasmussen, David W., 112
Rauch, Jonathan, 117
Reagan Administration, 5, 37–38, 74, 88,
    106, 143, 148, 235–40, 244–46, 249,
    255–56
Reaganomics, 88

real estate development, 216–17
recession, economic, 85–87, 99–100, 212
Redford, E., 148
Redisch, Michael, 133
redlining, 214
regulation, 51, 63, 67, 127–30, 136, 202;
  of private responsibility, 169–70
regulations, federal, for child care, 237,
  239, 246, 249–50
rehabilitation projects, 210, 223–24
reimbursement policies, 57, 63, 66–67
relative price effect, 87
religious groups, 192
relocation of economic functions, 32–34
remarketization, 167
reporting requirements, 240
resource management, 30–31
responsibility, for child care, 256; of government, 122, 158; societal, 264
retirement income, 267
revitalization projects, 215, 217, 226–28
revolving loan funds, 219–20
Ries, John C., 107
"right to buy," 165
Rimlinger, Gaston V., 140n
Ripley, Randall, 111
"risk pools," 187
risk taking, 52
Robb, Christina, 61
Robins, Philip K., 244
Rosaldo, Michelle Zimbalist, 17
Rose, Richard, 73, 76–79, 78n, 83–84,
  84n, 86–88, 90, 92n
Rose-Ackerman, Susan, 130, 132–33, 244
Ruggles, P., 167
Runge, Carlisle Ford, 31

"safety net," governmental, 195
Salamon, Lester M., 33, 35, 56–57, 64–65,
  74, 89, 105, 114, 132, 132n, 134
salary reduction plans, 239, 246
Sametz, A. W., 78
Saunders, Peter, 40
Savas, E. S., 22n, 107
Sawhill, Isabel V., 100, 100n
SBDO. See South Bronx Development Or-
  ganization
Schambra, William A., 101
Schattschneider, E. E., 143
Schlesinger, Mark, 127, 130, 185
Schmenner, Roger, 112
Schmitter, Philippe C., 49

schools, public, 108, 192, 208
Schwarz, John E., 92
SEBCO. See South East Bronx Community
  Organization
Seidman, Harold, 21n
selective incentives, 131
self-employed professionals, as providers,
  60–61, 66
self-help organizations, 62, 101, 183, 197
self-interest, 30, 56
self-policing, 128
self-provision, 138
self-selection, 129
self-sufficiency, 75, 214
Seligson, Michelle, 244n
Sennett, Richard, 18
SERPS. See State Earnings-Related Pension
  Scheme
settlement houses, 208
sickness benefits and sick pay, 170–73
Silver, Alan, 62
Simmel, Georg, 18
Simon, Herbert A., 61
single-parent families, 248
"size" constraint, 138
Skocpol, Theda, 140n, 141
slide problem, 69
small-business sector, 26; as provider of
  job training, 191
small numbers conditions, 135
Smeeding, Timothy, 92
Smith, Robert J., 30
Smith, Tom W., 88
social contract, voluntary, 230
"social equity" criteria, 142n
Social Health Maintenance Organization,
  187
social interests vs. individual interests, 140
social investment, 217–18, 229, 232
social policy, 139, 143, 145–46, 158, 163,
  211, 264. See also public policy
social security, 168, 180, 267
Social Security Act and amendments, 181,
  183, 211, 236–37, 240n. See also Title
  XX
social service agencies, 198–99
social services, 42–43, 49–70, 73, 78, 101,
  107, 113, 148, 181, 183, 193, 211; supply of, 200, 244–49. See also public services
Social Services Block Grant program, 239,
  245

social welfare: erosion of, 163; programs, 140n, 141, 189; states, 140n, 141n
Sonenblum, Sidney, 107
South Bronx Development Organization (SBDO), 221–22
South East Bronx Community Organization (SEBCO), 216, 221
Special Supplementary Food Program for Women, Infants, and Children (WIC), 110
stabilization function of government, 122
standardization of service delivery, 90
standards, 63, 113, 237, 249–50, 253
Starr, Paul, 16, 23, 25, 36, 141, 145, 202, 263, 267
state, demands on, 143; function of, 18–19, 58–59, 67, 69, 75, 174; vs. market, 90, 164; as provider of services, 79–80, 84, 92, 158. See also government
state agencies, 114, 186. See also government agencies
state and local funds, 242, 247, 253
State Earnings-Related Pension Scheme (SERPS) (U.K.), 173–75
state government, 65, 180, 193
state hospitals, 186
state-led development, 51–52
state-owned enterprises, 39–41
stimulated consumer switching, 167–69
Stone, Deborah A., 146
Streeck, Wolfgang, 49
Stretton, Hugh, 62
Struyk, Raymond J., 109n
subcontracting, 52, 57, 62–63. See also contracting of public services
subsidies, 63, 110–12, 179–80, 241, 255. See also supply subsidies
substitutability, 77
suburbia, vs. urban neighborhoods, 209
Sugden, Robert, 132
Sundquist, James, 142
Sundstrom, Gerdt, 53
Supplementary Benefit (SB) system (U.K.), 166
supply subsidies, 236, 238, 249
Sviridoff, Mitchell, 262
sweat equity, 55
syndication, 227
systemic function of government, 122

Taggart, Robert, 145n

Targeted Jobs Tax Credit (TJTC), 111
targeting, 190, 195–96
tax: benefits, 248; credits, 111, 237, 239, 242; effort, 88; exemption system, 63; incentives, 63–64, 266; relief, 168; subsidies, 79, 131, 248
tax system, as provider of funds, 239
taxation, 103, 123, 131
Taylor-Gooby, P., 162
technological advancement, 100
Terrell, Paul, 115
Thatcher Administration, 25, 170
Thibodeau, Marc, 70
third-party contracts, 134
"third-party" government, 35
Thomas, Stephen, 144n
Thompson, David, 25
Thurow, Lester, 43n
Tilton, Timothy, 140n, 142, 144
"time horizon" constraint, 138
Title XX, 183, 236, 238–39, 241–43, 247–49, 243, Table 9.1
Titmuss, Richard, 76, 157–58
TJTC. See Targeted Jobs Tax Credit
de Tocqueville, Alexis, 101
"top-down government," 51–52
Total Welfare in Society, 75–80
trade deficit, 87–88
trade unions, 171
"tragedy of the commons," 131n
training programs, 190
transferring production, 164–67
transportation, state-provided, 79
Trattner, Walter I., 97
trustworthiness theory, 129–31
Tullock, Gordon, 124

"uncontrollable" programs, 89, Table 3.5
underclass, 229
unemployment, youth, 189
unions, 43
United Kingdom, privatization in, 164–76
United States: economy, 82; government expenditure, Table 3.3; position on privatization, 41
United States Children's Bureau, 193
United Way, 114, 253, 255n
universality, vs. equity, 162–63
university sector, 169
unpaid labor, 76, 79
unpredictable events, response to, 54

Urban Development Action Grants, 112, 113
urban neighborhoods, 208–10
urban renewal, 210–11, 217

values, cultural, 139; political, 142n, 176
vendor/voucher programs, 242, 245
Vidal, Avis C., 228
voluntary sector, 33, 101, 104, 123, 132–34, 162, 192, 197; failure of, 33, 131–34
volunteer-based activities, 35, 132, 132n, 138, 194–95, 198
voter preference, 138
vouchers, 109–10, 242, 245
Vranken, Jan, 53

wage reductions, 43
wage subsidies, 111
Walker, Alan, 142n, 157–59
Wallack, Stanley S., 187, 187n
Walsh, Annmarie Hauck, 21n
War on Poverty, 52, 74, 181–83, 211–12
Warner, Amos, 179–80, 179n
Watanuki, Joji, 35
Watts Labor Community Action Committee, 217
Weale, A., 161
wealth, national, 43, 82, 84, 85
Webb, A., 158, 162, 166
Webber, Carolyn, 19
Weber, Max, 18, 139
Weidenbaum, Murray, 74
Weisbrod, Burton A., 56, 76n, 103, 114, 127, 129–30, 137–38, 186n

welfare, 73–93; production of services, 77–81; providers of services, 74; and work, 189
welfare mix, 74, 77–78, 85, 90–93, 157
welfare state, 52, 140–41, 140n, 141n, 144, 149, 207, 265
wic. See Special Supplementary Food Program for Women, Infants, and Children
Wiener, Samuel, 244
Wildavsky, Aaron, 19, 147n
Wilensky, Harold L., 75n, 140, 140n, 148n
Wilkins, Amy, 239n, 244
Williamson, Oliver, 134–36, 136n
Willig, Robert D., 33
Willis, David C., 199
Willmott, Peter, 18, 23
Willow Avenue Incubator Project, 221–22
Wilson, James Q., 145
win. See Work Incentive program
Wistow, G., 166
Wolf, Charles, Jr., 33, 125, 137, 137n
women, as care providers, 53
Women's Bureau, 245
Work Incentive (win) program, 237, Table 9.1
working mothers, 240

Yarrow, George, 34
Young, Dennis, 23, 33, 129, 244
Young, Michael, 18
youth employment and training programs, 189–92
Youth Incentive Entitlement Pilot Project, 190
"yuppies," 100n